Fate Knocked on My Door is the story of one woman's determination and courage to forge an independent life for herself, the obstacles she faces, the heartbreaking losses, and the disappointing compromises she ultimately makes. A genuine and compelling story.

~ Ellen Bass

FATE KNOCKED ON MY DOOR

By
Laila El-Sissi

Fate Knocked on My Door

Copyright 2020, Laila Radwan El-Sissi

All Rights Reserved.
No part of this document may be reproduced or transmitted in any form or by any means, electronic, mechanical, photocopying, recording, or otherwise, without prior written permission of Laila Radwan El-Sissi.

978-09903354-0-5 (paperback)
978-0-9903354-9-8 (hardback)

Cover designer: Laila El-Sissi
Editor: Janet Musick
Interior designer: Debbi Stocco

Published by: NUT

NUT

I dedicate my book to my sons Omar and Shareef. So much in *Fate Knocked on My Door* they would learn for the first time. Their love and support gave me the strength, confidence and courage to write it. To the memory of my Mom and sister Rawyia.

ACKNOWLEDGEMENTS

I would like to thank Connie Handsted for her continuous support and for, twice, taking the time to read and edit my book. In addition, I want to thank Geraldine Solon for her sincere encouragement and editing. I also want to acknowledge my friend Anis for his genuine patience, attentive ears and valid comments as I read aloud the manuscript.

At last, but not least, I want to thank all my friends around the world who have read my first book *Out from The Shadow of Men*, and asked for my next book. In particular, my childhood friends Alice, Nora, Eleonora, Esmat, Mme. Nabila, my school teacher, kawakb, Willy, Mary, Miranda, Nadia and Hala. With their sincere support, I was able to finish *Fate Knocked on My Door*.

CONTENTS

ACKNOWLEDGEMENTS vi
CHAPTER I: The Flight to Lebanon 1
CHAPTER II: Connecting with Rawyia in Beirut 7
CHAPTER III: Searching for Ghassan 17
CHAPTER IV: Meeting with Ghassan's Cousins 19
CHAPTER V: Moving in with Nagi's Family 26
CHAPTER VI: Nagi's Unexpected Approach 35
CHAPTER VII: Employer's Sexual Assault 38
CHAPTER VIII: Mr. Anwar the Neighbor 42
CHAPTER IX: Offer to Travel to Italy 47
CHAPTER X: Arriving in Rome 53
CHAPTER XI: Mr. Anwar's Marriage Proposal 65
CHAPTER XII: Back in Lebanon 73
CHAPTER XIII: In Toronto 88
CHAPTER XIV: Opportunities in Toronto 104
CHAPTER XV: Moving Out of Mostafa's Home 112
CHAPTER XVI: First Job at Eaton 115
CHAPTER XVII: Death of Rawyia's Husband 122
CHAPTER XVIII: Death of Jenny 130
CHAPTER XIX: Back to Egypt 143
CHAPTER XX: In Alexandria and Mama's Death 159
CHAPTER XXI: Amer 168
CHAPTER XXII: Coping with Mam's Death 176
CHAPTER XXIII: Falling in Love 184
CHAPTER XXIV: Amer's Personality 190

CHAPTER XXV: Car Accident 196
CHAPTER XXVI: In Paris 203
CHAPTER XXVII: Back in Canada 207
CHAPTER XXVIII: Rawyia's Struggle 211
CHAPTER XXIX: Amer's Marriage Proposal 214
CHAPTER XXX: Adham's Sexual Assault Trauma 217
CHAPTER XXXI: Visiting Amer in Egypt 220
CHAPTER XXXII: Me and Rawyia in Alexandria 224
CHAPTER XXXIII: Mixed Feelings 229
CHAPTER XXXIV: Adham's Death 233
CHAPTER XXXV: Meeting Hazem 241
CHAPTER XXXVI: Negative First Impression of Hazem 248
CHAPTER XXXVII: Dating Hazem 253
CHAPTER XXXVIII: Struggling with Emotions 256
CHAPTER XXXIX: Hazem's Marriage Proposal 262

Does one's past suddenly, and in a second, vanish?
What she lived. What she heard. What she dreamed about?
As if life got pulled out from under her feet?
Would flowers bloom in her new fate?
At what age, does one grow up?
When do we notice when we change and mature?
Every time I feared growing up,
I thought of the silkworm.
That story of the metamorphosis of the worm
Into a butterfly fascinated me
But I am curious.
Was the worm aware of her new life
As she weaved her cocoon?
Was she aware of the great beauty her cocoon held?
Where she imprisoned herself?
I think of that, and say, yes.
The silkworm believes in her cocoon.
One or tens of people we meet
It doesn't matter.
Everyone we fall in love with
Is a cocoon.
They are the people
We should trust
And count on to protect us
And keep us safe.

In spite of that, we fear
If growing old
Is a transformation to something different?
What would happen to that child
Who believed in the purity of everything?
Maybe that is the question
We should ask ourselves.
Would the butterfly forget
The silkworm?

~ Laila El-Sissi

CHAPTER I

THE FLIGHT TO LEBANON

The sky was grey before it turned black. Walls of white foam trailed me with an amplified, angry roar. I swam faster until my arms felt like sandbags. As I was on the verge of drowning, Rawyia's voice intruded on my sleep, reverberating as if from the depths of a sinkhole.

"Wake up, La!"

The engine sounded deafening, and my eyelids felt heavy. I drifted back into a deep sleep. Rawyia shook my arm. "Wake up!" she said. "We've arrived."

I remembered then. We were aboard an airplane, and we'd escaped from Egypt.

I felt disoriented. This was my first time flying. I had traveled by train from Alexandria to Cairo.

"Are we landing?" I asked.

"Yes." Rawyia squeezed my hand.

The passengers chattered and laughed. Their happiness annoyed me. Some kissed and hugged, while others stared out the windows. Families and friends awaited them, and I couldn't help my envy. Even Rawyia's husband waited for her in Lebanon.

No one waited for me on the tarmac. I longed for Mama, wishing I had stayed with her. I wondered what would have happened if I had never met Ghassan or fallen in love with him. I would perhaps have divorced and lived with Mama. I knew wish and destiny were like two wild mustangs that could not be tamed. They ran in different directions and dashed down different paths where rivers of fate and desire would not merge. To choose one was to disappoint the other. To make one happy would torment the other.

"We'll be fine," Rawyia assured. "In no time, you will forget the past—the arranged marriage and your escape on your wedding night."

"Rawyia," I said, "I can't forget Mama's cheeks bathed in tears, her lips quivering as she struggled to bid me farewell, and the despondent look on her face. I can still hear her weeping. The pain I feel shreds my heart into pieces and breathes new life into my guilt."

"I hear you, La," she said, patting me on the back. "It's a painful experience you faced. However, you have chosen a future of your own design, so forget the longing to return to Mama, at least until we settle down."

I admired Rawyia's control of her emotions. She always seemed to turn the pages of her life without regret. I knew she loved Mama, but she didn't allow that love to disturb her plans. She looked relaxed as usual, her make-up fresh, and her hair coiffed to perfection.

"Did you sleep?" I asked.

"No. Have you forgotten I've flown to Lebanon before? It's only two hours between Egypt and Lebanon, and the time here is the same as back in Alexandria. Too early for you to sleep. The afternoon is still young."

"The sound of the engine and the rocking of the plane soothed me to sleep, I guess."

I fiddled with the gold pendant Mama had given me and hoped touching it would calm me down. The sound of her voice, whispering prayers as she placed it around my neck, still echoed inside my head. It was my good luck charm.

Rawyia interrupted my reverie. "Think of the good times awaiting us in Lebanon."

I smiled. In the past, when I became emotional and tears gathered in my eyes, Rawyia would say, "Seal off those tear ducts of yours."

I expected no empathy from her. She had no patience or tolerance for emotions. I knew, though, that she was the one person, after Mama, who wanted the best for me.

"You are not the first or last to run away from home," she said.

"How do you expect me to have a good time without Mama?" I asked. "I still see her eyes shining like two bright stars in a dark sky when she wished me good night. I will always long for her shawl of love around me."

Rawyia rolled her eyes. "I love you, but I wouldn't tolerate your desperate need for Mama's love," she said.

"Rawyia, you are one year older yet, emotionally, we are a million years apart," I said. "Love will remain my foundation I will stand on going ahead in the future. I miss not just Mama, but Ghassan as well."

"Ghassan again," she snapped. "I thought you were over that puppy love."

I couldn't make her understand that what Ghassan and I had was real. I loved and expected to marry Ghassan in Lebanon. In the past, Rawyia expressed her frustration and threatened not to support me whenever I mentioned Ghassan. She had always been against him, never believing that we shared a genuine love. I couldn't explain her reluctance to discuss him, but her story somehow lacked the ring of absolute truth. Maybe she thought I would leave her to be with him when I found him.

The pilot invited passengers to look at the snow-covered mountains. Rawyia and I peered across the aisle to the right, but we couldn't see the mountains. However, the clear blue sky filled me with a desire to go back to Alexandria. I took a deep breath as my memories took over, my eyes filling with stinging tears.

"I can't wait to see your apartment," I said to change the subject.

She put her arm around my shoulders and kissed me on the cheek.

"Will your husband be waiting for us?"

"Marwan is busy," she said.

"Are you happy with him?" I asked.

"Let's not talk about Marwan. You and I are together again, and that's all that matters now. I didn't marry him for love."

Marwan was my sister's second husband. Rawyia was twenty years old, and he was sixty-nine and well off—a fact that impressed her. She wanted a comfortable life with someone easy to manipulate, and Marwan was just that.

Rawyia's life back home in Alexandria was unhappy. She had been forced to marry Gamal at the age of sixteen. In less than a year, and against our parent's wishes, she ended the marriage before she and Gamal moved into their matrimonial home. She ran away and took refuge at our Aunt Hamida's house. There she met Marwan, a family friend.

Rawyia believed no man was worthy of her love and respect. When she was a child, our stepbrother abused her. My father had trusted him to enforce virtue and protect our chastity, but that trust was misplaced.

"La, we were born free just like men," Rawyia often said.

I didn't understand what she meant because we grew up accepting the control of all men in our family. We learned as children that God ordered men to control women, and women were to obey men. Rawyia rejected that subjugation. She was a feminist before we ever heard of feminism.

Rawyia believed that, as a divorcee, she would be given full control of her life. She envisioned herself liberated and living her life as she wanted. However, she soon discovered that freedom for women in Egyptian culture was a fantasy. Instead of being independent, she became a pariah. Family and friends saw her as rebellious and incorrigible, not free and independent.

When Papa refused to take her back into the family after her divorce from Gamal, she considered getting married again. Marwan became her second husband. A liberal, he fulfilled her every expectation, and took her to live with him in Lebanon.

"I don't love him," she said again and again about Marwan. "However, I need the comfortable life he offers."

Rawyia's behavior toward men created a rift between us. Nevertheless, I admired her. She was smart, even though she failed her exams in school. She fed me words of encouragement and instilled in me the confidence I lacked to pursue my divorce from my first husband, Farook. I could not have left Egypt without her support. So I composed myself to appear happy about relocating to Lebanon, but I couldn't fool my sister.

"La, cheer up. You wanted to leave Egypt, didn't you?"

Tears welled up in my eyes.

She leaned close to my ear and whispered. "I miss Mama, too."

We hugged.

"You can count on me," she said.

"I plan to count on myself," I said defiantly.

The airplane came to a stop on the runway. The "fasten seat belt" light went off. People started to shuffle to their overhead luggage.

"This is it, La," she said. "There is no going back."

"I know, Rawyia, but I worry about Mama now that you, Hady, and I are gone from Egypt." Hady was my younger brother, who had escaped Egypt to avoid military service.

She kissed me on both eyes, her way of preventing me from crying.

"I'm scared," I confessed.

"You are a big girl, Laila. Trust me. You will forget the past once you settle down."

"I don't plan to forget the past," I snapped.

"La, look out the window. Beirut comes alive at night. No one sleeps early in Lebanon."

Rawyia's enthusiasm annoyed me. I took that moment to ask, "Would you support me to study journalism?"

Her eyes widened, then grew small and distant. She stared at me long enough to make me nervous. Growing up, I had learned that this kind of stare meant trouble.

"This is it, La," she said. "The past is over. Forget your dream of education and grow up."

Rawyia's demand sounded like lifting the lid of a boiling pot and releasing old conflicts within the rising steam. "I know, Rawyia," I said to keep her from getting angrier.

Back home in Alexandria, we argued whenever I expressed a desire to finish school. She dismissed the idea of education for herself and for me.

I decided to wait for things to calm down before I tackled the subject again. I vowed not to allow Rawyia to destroy my dreams just because she'd helped me to escape.

The pilot's voice drew our attention when he announced the weather in Beirut, and wished us all a pleasant stay in Lebanon.

"We'll be fine, La," Rawyia promised before we left the plane. "Together, we'll conquer the world." She released a faint sigh.

I grinned and kissed the pendant, thinking positive thoughts for the future. And I believed Rawyia when she said we would conquer the world.

CHAPTER II

CONNECTING WITH RAWYIA IN BEIRUT

At the airport, I savored the familiar whiff of the Mediterranean Sea. It reminded me of Mama.

Mama was an exceptional mother who loved her children and endured persistent psychological abuse from our father in utter silence just to keep our family from breaking up. When we asked her to take us and leave, she replied, "A family is like a pearl necklace. If it breaks and scatters around, it takes time and effort to restore it, even if you find all the pearls." For her many sacrifices, she owned the crown of my heart. As a young girl, I felt her affection but never thought of its depth and value, and I enjoyed the warmth of her hugs without ever thinking that removing myself from her embrace would be the cruelest alienation I would experience. She had enough love to fill the universe, but half of her children were not with her to receive it.

Rawyia held me tight in a long warm embrace. "You will love living here. I promise you."

"I never thought of the emotional impact I would have to face for my freedom," I said.

I was like a butterfly who had just liberated herself from

her cocoon's darkness with untrained, yet strong wings that fluttered free and ready to explore the world. There was nothing Rawyia could do to ease my anxiety. I was not yet twenty and had already been through marriage, divorce, taken out of school, separated from my family, and deserted by Ghassan. The thorny road to our freedom exhausted our emotions. But Rawyia appeared composed and in control of the situation.

The taxi ride to Rawyia's apartment was distracting, but pleasant. Boutiques displaying trendy fashion, along with gourmet restaurants, lined the streets. It reminded me of my parent's impression of their visit to Lebanon. They said it was the Paris of the Arab countries and raved about its beautiful beaches and mountains. We had learned in school that the first historical mention of Beirut was found in the ancient Egyptian Tell El-Amarna Letters that dated back to the 15th century BC. I couldn't wait to explore the historic cities and all the Roman ruins my parents talked about.

Even though Lebanon was not far from Egypt, the city of Beirut seemed pleasantly different. The narrow winding streets and alleys appeared clean, and the gentle breeze wafted the Lebanese aroma of spices on barbecued chicken and lamb. I sank into my seat and enjoyed the ride.

"We could go swimming tomorrow morning and then, in one hour, we could learn to ski at Mzaar Kfardebian, which the Lebanese refer to as Ouyoune Simane."

"How far are the ruins of Baalbek from Beirut?" I asked.

"Eighty-five kilometers," the driver said.

Papa mentioned the grandeur of the Roman ruins in Baalbek, where the statues of gods like Venus or Aphrodite were found. Venus was the goddess with many lovers. I looked forward to visiting her temple.

Rawyia praised Lebanese cuisine. She said it was tailor-made to expand the waistline and that appetizers, or Mezzah, came in several small dishes, plenty to feed an army.

"After the Mezza, you won't have room left for the entrees

of Meshwi or BBQ assorted meats."

Rawyia had different plans for me, but my first goal for coming to Lebanon was getting a college education and eventually lead an independent life. My second goal was to bring Mama over to live with me. I couldn't imagine not seeing her again. I didn't plan to enjoy freedom and independence without her continuous support, which infused my soul with confidence and security. My third goal was finding Ghassan, but I kept that mission to myself.

It was mid-August, and the taxi had no air conditioning. The moist air of the Mediterranean reminded me of Alexandria's humid summer that turned my hair into unmanageable tight curls. Somehow, I didn't care how my hair looked. I was excited and free of the negative criticism I heard as a young girl about my skinny figure, my olive complexion, and my curly hair.

∞

Rawyia's apartment was in a quiet neighborhood. She lived on the third floor of a high-rise, and each level had two flats. As we climbed the stairs, I heard Steve Wonder singing Superstition. I moved to the beat until Rawyia pulled at me and said, "The family is here for the summer vacation. They live in America and have two teenagers. In two weeks, they have to go back to school, and we will have the floor all to ourselves."

"How I wish I could live in any country outside the Arab world," I said.

"You never know. Your wish might come true. Did either of us think we would ever leave Egypt?"

She took me straight to my room. It overlooked the main street. It was something she thought would be different from our bedroom back in Alexandria, which faced a cement wall—part of Papa's extreme measures to shelter us from the outside world.

"La, spend as much time as you want here," she said, stepping onto the balcony and holding my hand, "no father or brother to fear. I declare you a free woman."

The balcony floor was covered with worn-out ceramic tiles and the railing was rusty, but it was paradise to me. I enjoyed the fresh air and sun as I watched people in the street—something I wasn't allowed back home.

"I love you, Rawyia." I hugged her happily.

She gave me a tour of the apartment and pointed to how she accented the modern furnishing of the foyer and salon with a Queen Ann table and a chest of drawers inlaid with golden applique. Oil paintings hung on the walls, each with a golden spotlight. I figured they were put there by Marwan, the art and antique aficionado. Rawyia never expressed interest in art.

The theme of new and old extended into my room—a vintage wooden rocking chair softened the bright orange color of the wall and carpet. Although I wasn't fond of the color orange, I appreciated Rawyia and Marwan's efforts to provide me with a cheerful ambiance.

"Are you hungry?" Rawyia asked.

"Very," I said.

"We'll start with a snack of Zaatar mini pies. They're a mixture of different herbs and spices sprinkled with olive oil—a traditional snack in Lebanon, Syria, Palestine, and Jordan." She hugged me again. I felt she'd truly missed me.

While I waited for her to prepare the fatayer, I stepped onto the balcony. I thought of Ghassan and wondered if Rawyia had told me the truth about him. I missed him. I refused to believe he had married. My heart was heavy with sadness.

I was fourteen when I met Ghassan on the beach in Alexandria. We spoke often during that summer vacation. He found me beautiful when no one before him complimented my physical appearance. My immediate family considered my olive skin and bony figure unattractive. Rawyia always got the praises, compliments, and boys' attention for her fair skin and plump figure. That day, Ghassan chose me and not Rawyia, and we strolled along the shore of San Estefano. He proved my family wrong, and that was enough to make me fall in love with him.

Ghassan was in his early twenties, and handsome. Since Rawyia had expected the attention to be for her that morning, she was surprised that Ghassan ignored her.

He had a muscular body and flaunted it in a checkered black-and-white *Helanca* swimsuit. His chest was hairy, just the way I liked, and droplets of sweat beaded his tanned body like pearls. His almond-shaped hazel eyes glistened under his thick black lashes, which made his gaze more penetrating. He favored me with a look of admiration that reached my soul and settled there unchallenged. His attention and interest changed my life. I saw myself through the flattering wink he gave me, which assured me that he liked my bony figure. Consequently, I stopped taking the fattening concoction of ghee, raw eggs, and sugar Mama had been forcing me to drink every morning on an empty stomach.

Ghassan encouraged me to finish school. I found him to be the kind of man I never thought existed—he was a liberal and believed in women's independence. Our love deepened even more after my father arranged for my betrothal to Farook, whom I didn't chose to marry. I was raised to obey my father's orders, and the betrothal was one of them. I demanded that my husband and my father break the marriage contract. But, for three years, I couldn't win my freedom, until I ran away on my wedding night and lived with my aunt for another two years before my husband agreed to give me a divorce.

Ghassan and I met in secret and talked on the phone when my parents were not home. Indeed, the divorce procedure from Farook took longer than Ghassan and I expected, but we knew all along nothing would separate us.

He studied commerce at the University of Alexandria, and still had two years to graduate. He planned to move back to Lebanon, where we would celebrate our wedding with his family. I found the joy of life through love in spite of my father's control and my betrothal to Farook. It was the kind of love that withstood deprivation with hope. Ghassan always remained on my mind and in my heart and was my one stable force in a world filled with disappointments.

When I divorced two years later, and before I left Egypt, Rawyia told me that Ghassan could not wait any longer and that he had married a Lebanese girl from his hometown. For a brief moment, life turned upside down, and the ground under my feet caved in and sucked me into an abyss. Everything around me and inside me turned black. I refused to believe her, but I had to stay in control to help myself cope with the separation from Mama. I continued this escape journey as I held onto my memories with Ghassan like the warming sensation of an invisible necklace close to my heart—something permanent and alive.

"You need to get over your puppy love, forget you ever met Ghassan, and go on with your life."

"Rawyia, I just want to ask him why he didn't keep his promise."

I hoped Rawyia would understand that I needed to do this before I could go on with my life. Instead, she threatened to send me back to Egypt. I didn't promise to forget about Ghassan.

"Where is your pride?" she burst out when she realized I was determined to look for him in Lebanon.

Rawyia treated me like a child, but I refused to let her patronize me. I had already convinced myself that there was no room for pride when one was in love and, no matter what she said, I would search for Ghassan. Somehow, I was sure he heard me when I talked to him every night before I slept and, like Rumi said:

I speak to you, not making a sound,
Sentences unavailable to ears.
We long for friends, but the healing
Of that does not come, just the longing.

Rawyia dazzled me with life in Lebanon. She was on an unrelenting effort to force me into forgetting the man I longed for and loved. I could not pretend to be happy all the time and knew I would encounter difficulties as long as Ghassan remained between us and, like Rumi said:

The deepest love is one with many challenges
He who avoids those is not a real lover
It takes great courage to do the dance of lovers.

When her attempts failed to turn me away from Ghassan, Rawyia took me to the Dolce Vita coffee shop on Al Rawsha Avenue and spent hours trying to convince me to forget him and marry one of Marwan's friends.

We strolled through the famous Hamra Street, where my eyes feasted on designer clothes displayed in the windows of boutique shops. I was happy and, to please Rawyia, I pushed Alexandria, Mama, and Ghassan out of my mind for the time being. Another day she took me to the Rock of Al Rawsha, where we ate at the famous Yeldizlar Restaurant, known for its one hundred Mezza plates. We also went to St. George Beach overlooking the Mediterranean and swam in our bikinis.

"You see, La," Rawyia said, "same sand and same Mediterranean."

We got along well until, soon after we settled in, Rawyia began to dictate what I should and should not do with my life. To my surprise, she took my father's role and believed that marriage would keep us close. She resented my aspirations and goals, and I resisted her domination. When she insisted on introducing me to potential husbands, I decided to take control of my life.

"This is my life and, from now on, I will decide how to run it," I said with an assertive tone to introduce the new me. Still, she intensified her pressure and refused to accept my decision.

When I could no longer fight Rawyia's badgering, I walked into her bedroom one early morning, sat down, charged with frustration and empowered with an assertion.

"I plan to look for a job," I said.

She pulled herself up and reached for a cigarette from a pack of Kents she had on the night table. She lit one and took a long drag. I stood up and sat on the chaise lounge away from her. I resented smoking, in spite of Rawyia's repeated attempts to get me to start. Smoke and silence contaminated the space between us. I knew my statement went against her plans for my future.

She furrowed her eyebrows, pursed her lips and, with a raspy voice said, "And how do you plan to do that? Have you forgotten you just have a high school education?"

I knew my limitations, but I believed that modest education would not prevent me from pursuing my dream of becoming a journalist. I wanted a life different from the one I left behind. I tried to choose my future and make my own decisions. I wanted my own life.

The school wasn't the only issue on which we disagreed. Marriage came up more often.

"Marriage would help you to settle down and fulfill your goals."

"Marriage is not a subject for discussion," I said, interrupting her.

Furrows, again, aged her forehead. However, this time, I challenged her with a defiant look of my own.

"I am not interested in thinking about marriage right now. I want to go to school."

"I will not be the one to finance your education," she said, raising her voice.

She was no longer the same person who helped me get a divorce. I grew determined to pursue my goals without her.

"Use men," she said. "It will be easier and faster to get to where you want to go."

Rawyia sounded bitter and vindictive. Her speeches of freedom seemed to have vanished. I had been in Lebanon for a few weeks, and the distance between us expanded. The thought of leading my life without Rawyia by my side was taking root in my head. The more she talked, the brighter a future without her was taking shape.

I had suffered to liberate myself from a culture where men oppressed women, and I was ready to go through another round of hardship to lead an independent life—a life with honesty and dignity.

This discussion with Rawyia exhausted me. I gazed in the mirror. The girl staring back was a stranger, weary and disheartened. The last few years had taken a toll on her. However, defiance and determination still shined in her eyes.

The decision to live separate from Rawyia was too early. I had to reconsider what I was demanding. I asked her to give me a few days to find a job. She agreed, but not without loading me with disturbing news about our brother Hady.

"I forgot to tell you. Hady ran away."

"Hady?" I gasped.

I had not kept up with news about my brothers. When I called Mama on the phone, she never mentioned that Hady had problems or planned to run away.

I remembered it was his turn to join the military and that he had rejected the mandatory drafting. Reda, our older brother, had served, and Hady, the middle child, was due to enlist.

The whole family treated Hady like a prince. His physical attributes were different from Reda and Samir. Like Rawyia, he was born with fair skin, light hazel eyes, wavy chestnut hair, and a tall frame. He won the attention of girls and engaged in numerous romantic adventures. "A Romeo," Mama used to call him. He followed the trendy hairstyle of the sixties, along with behavior our father rejected. Hady was self-assured and smart. It didn't surprise me to hear that he, too, had run away.

"Where is Hady now?" I asked Rawyia.

"I gave him some money and told him, 'You are on your own'."

She sounded heartless, but that was Rawyia—loving, yet lacking patience and empathy.

"Where is he, Rawyia?"

"I don't know." She shrugged her shoulders. "The last time we spoke, he was in Greece."

I could not believe Rawyia had helped Hady, our sixteen-year-old brother, who had no previous travel experience, to roam around in a different country.

"How did he get a passport?"

"It's a long story," she told me. "Just worry about your own life."

If I had known Hady planned to leave Egypt, I would have helped him and would never have let him travel by himself. I had no idea what drove him to leave Egypt. Furthermore, I worried about Mama and how she felt losing three of her children. Rawyia and I planned to never go back home and, in the process, we never thought of the blame Mama would face for helping us escape. Papa blamed her for our disobedience and our failed marriages, and I expected him to forbid her from talking to us. He had done it before when he forced Mama to end the relationship with her sister. I worried about Mama's suppressed suffering from losing us.

I despised our father for pushing us away, and I cared less for how he felt. He had different options and choices to raise us. Instead, he chose to follow the backward culture he experienced as a child. In the process, he alienated each one of us. All I wanted was his love to help me judge the men I would meet in my life—the love that would have nurtured my whole being. I felt no pity for the shame he experienced.

CHAPTER III

SEARCHING FOR GHASSAN

Rawyia's road and mine came to a fork. We were faced with making a difficult decision. I knew the choice to separate would create a rift between us. However, the time was ripe to move on without her.

From the moment Rawyia and I landed in Lebanon, I often thought of searching for Ghassan. When he lived in Alexandria, he gave me his cousin Nagi's phone number in Beirut. "You can always call Nagi if you can't reach me," he told me.

Ghassan didn't give me his parents' address or phone number. He insisted on being by my side when I met his parents. He wanted to be the one to introduce me and explain my circumstances. We had agreed to meet in Beirut once I got my divorce. But his phone calls and letters ceased before I escaped from Egypt. I had no one but Nagi to ask about Ghassan.

Two months passed before I called Nagi. A female voice answered.

It is unheard of in the Arab world to be so brazen as to announce my relationship with Ghassan to his relatives. Nagi knew about us, but I wasn't sure about his mother. However, I was desperate, and no one but Nagi would help me find Ghassan.

"Alo. Can I speak with Nagi?" I asked.

There was silence. I assumed it was a reaction to my Egyptian accent. I waited for what seemed a whole minute before I had to ask the question again.

"Who's asking?"

The warmth in her voice filled me with comfort. It was the kind of serenity I felt through Mama's voice.

"This is Laila," I said. "Laila from Egypt."

A deep sigh traveled to my ear and then a hush. I waited for her to confirm she knew about me from either Ghassan or Nagi, but her silence got louder with each passing second. I remained quiet to give her time to respond. Anxiety shook the ground under my feet.

"Nagi is not home."

I heard the sincerity in her voice and, before I could ask another question, she said, "My son is on a flight to Paris."

My heart skipped a beat. I was unable to say a word. I began to sense there was a new truth behind Ghassan's disappearance.

"He will be back tomorrow night," she continued.

Tomorrow night seemed so far away. I thought of asking her about Ghassan, but I wasn't sure he had shared our love with her.

"Laila, my dear, I am sorry about Ghassan."

With a sinking heart, sadness cascaded from the top of my head to my feet. The pain gnawed at my soul like a parasite, as quiet as a mouse, but just as voracious. Nevertheless, I needed to hear more about Ghassan.

"Are you Nagi's mother?" I asked.

"Yes," she replied.

"I would like to meet you," I said.

"You are more than welcome. Consider our home your second place in Lebanon."

She won my trust. Nothing would have stopped me from meeting her, not even Rawyia.

I suggested 7:00 in the evening the next day. She agreed.

CHAPTER IV

MEETING WITH GHASSAN'S COUSINS

Sleep teased my eyes all night. I got out of bed several times. I prepared a cup of mint tea to soothe me to rest. It didn't help. I stepped onto the balcony for fresh air and entertained myself admiring girls in trendy blazers and flared pants sauntering in the street. Most flaunted their locks in the Farrah Fawcett style. Their laughter echoed loud and muffled the sound of the pre-dawn waves crashing on the nearby shore, and the smell of tobacco mixed with the sea mist was nostalgic.

French words dominated the girls' Arabic conversations—the influence of the French colonization of Lebanon. However, I was proud of my Egyptian roots; we never conceded to speak the language of the invaders. At the same time, I envied those girls for the freedom they enjoyed. It reminded me of my controlled and fearful teenage years in Alexandria, with little or no freedom.

I grew up with many rules. No make-up, no nail polish, no friends, no chewing gum, no loud laughing, no choice of clothes to wear, no talking to boys, and no demonstration of love, even toward our father. Fear controlled every step of our childhood—fear of God's punishment, fear of my father's anger, fear of my brothers' and our cousin Amed's brutality. I was raised to fear even myself. That fear still lived inside of me, eating away my confidence like a leech. I carried those rules like links in a long chain that kept me tied to the past.

I envied Rawyia for never fearing anyone. She was daring. She challenged our father and accepted the consequences of her defiance with boldness, like the day she was caught taking a drag on a cigarette when she was fifteen years old. Papa locked her up in the pantry for a week. When he released her, she strolled out like a peacock, down the hallway to our room—her shoulders pulled back, her head erect. I still remember her cold but defiant eyes.

I tried to emulate Rawyia's strength, but I couldn't. I was shy, fearful, malleable, and quick to express emotions with tears. Going to Nagi's mother, I thought, would be the first step to clear out the baggage of the past I still carried.

At 7:00 the next evening, I rang the doorbell with hesitant fingers. My heart pounded behind my ribs. Copying Rawyia's pose, I pulled my shoulders back to pump up my courage and dressed my face with a warm smile, ready to meet Nagi's mother.

Nagi's mother had a petite frame and a dark olive complexion. Her shoulder-length black wavy hair was dense, with scattered gray streaks lining the perimeter of her prominent forehead. Her radiant eyes had stars that glittered when she smiled, reflecting affection and serenity I couldn't resist. I surrendered to her open arms like a child.

"Ahmed, my husband, is a journalist," she said. "He leaves home in the wee hours of the day."

I nodded. Nagi's mother kept a gentle grip on my wrist, guiding me to the kitchen, where she pulled out a chair facing the stove.

"Take a seat here, my dear, while I make us two cups of tea." She spoke to me as though she had always known me.

Captivated by her warmth, I sat down as instructed.

"Mariam, my daughter, left for college," she turned around and made eye contact, then faced the stove again. "She is studying to be a journalist like her father. She is as political as her papa. You will soon meet her."

She turned around, holding the hot kettle with a towel, "I know you want to know more about Nagi and his closeness to Ghassan."

My heart almost jumped out of my chest. "Yes," I said.

She fetched two glasses from the cupboard and a sugar container before she pulled out a chair and sat down. She caressed my hands with tenderness, then poured the tea into the glasses.

"How many spoons of sugar?" she asked.

"Two," I said.

She stirred in the sugar and handed me the glass. We sat in silence, each waiting for the other to talk. The joy she expressed when she greeted me somehow mellowed, but her soul reflected kindness. I sensed her struggle to open the subject of Ghassan.

"Laila, you are beautiful and still young."

I rejected her statement in silence. No one before considered me beautiful, except Ghassan. Looking at her dark complexion, I wondered if her family found her attractive. People in Egypt appreciate fair-skinned girls. Why would Lebanese people be different?

"I just want to know," I said, trying hard to stay in control of my emotions.

I sensed she knew more than she let on. There was no need to remain in suspense. "I want to find out why Ghassan didn't keep his promise to me and got married."

Nagi's mother took a few sips from her tea, then lowered her gaze to the floor.

"I am sorry," I said. "I am not trying to pressure you."

"Life goes on, my dear," she responded, "One day, you will meet a young man who will give you the love you deserve."

Nagi's mother kept her explanation short. She shook her head and sighed as if trying to release a heavy burden out of her heart. She struggled to maintain the sincerity I heard in her voice when we first met. She looked uncomfortable. I decided to wait for Nagi.

"Laila," she suddenly asked, "how about you move in here with us? We have plenty of space for another person."

Her request shocked me and made me think. What would make her feel I was alone and needed protection? I suspected she knew more about me than I was led to believe.

I hadn't mentioned my living arrangements, or my plans to be a journalist. Had she been talking to someone else before I met with her? I began to suspect that, somehow, Rawyia was involved.

"I am happy with Rawyia," I lied to appear content and appreciative of my sister's help.

"Of course you are," she said. "I knew from Ghassan you wanted to become a journalist. Who else could help you fulfill your dream better than Mariam and my husband, Fikry?"

Again, the mention of the name Rawyia did not prompt her to ask who she was. Could she have met Rawyia before? And why did Rawyia keep me from meeting Ghassan's cousins? Nevertheless, I liked the offer. It was a gift I accepted without hesitation. "Thank you," I told her.

"You could move in today," she said, smiling, "and I will not take any excuses."

I had threatened to leave Rawyia, thinking of finding a job; still, it was a difficult decision. We disagreed and argued, but I was not ready to sever the umbilical cord. She helped me all through my divorce ordeal. Without her, I would have never left Egypt. I owed her my honesty.

I left before Mariam, Nagi, and their father came home. I had a difficult mission ahead of me—facing Rawyia with my desire to move out.

At 9:00 p.m., I rang the doorbell. Rawyia opened the door,

anger shooting from her eyes. "Where have you been?" she demanded.

I ignored her inquisition and walked straight to my room. She trailed me and slammed the door shut behind her.

"I am waiting for your answer." She leaned against the door with her arms crossed.

I planned to stay calm to avoid leaving on bad terms, but her bossy tone made it difficult to maintain composure while avoiding an altercation. Part of me still felt like the little girl that needed safety under her sister's wing. The fear of separating from her and her reaction to my lateness was overwhelming. I decided to tell her about the visit, even though I struggled with assertiveness. "I went to visit Ghassan's cousins."

The look of horror on Rawyia's face frightened me. I had never seen her eyes display such anger. But she stifled her usual outbursts and spoke with a calm voice, knowing that anything else would frighten me.

"Why did you go? What she did tell you?"

"Nothing." I turned away, not liking the look in my sister's eyes.

There was something more to Rawyia's anger. There was something more about everything. There was something Rawyia knew, Nagi knew, and his mother knew, but I did not. What secret were they hiding about Ghassan? If he had married, why didn't his relatives just say so?

Rawyia had that familiar worried look. I reconsidered breaking the news of moving out, but her reaction made up my mind to take Nagi's mother up on her suggestion.

Rawyia had other plans for me. "I want you to meet Marwan's friend. We invited him to dinner," she said.

Rawyia remained the same person I grew up with—the sister that loved to control, and who expected my submission. I just wanted her to understand that I had changed, that I had goals of my own for my future.

"Rawyia! Quit trying. I don't want to meet another man,

and I won't get married."

There was a knock on the door. Rawyia ignored it for a moment, but not for long.

"Just a minute," she said.

The minute became thirty, and she kept badgering me.

"You must understand," she warned me, "I won't allow you to stay with me if you don't agree to get married."

Anger swelled up inside me. I sensed a bitter taste in my mouth, sour like bile. Memories of my betrothal came alive and empowered me to speak my mind.

"You have become as bad as our father," I accused her. "I thought you resisted and fought the oppression at home because you believed in women's rights. I guess you fooled me. You just want to control me."

The knocking on the door got louder and more persistent. Rawyia opened it and told Marwan to come in.

"My sister refuses to meet your friend," she said with frustration.

Marwan looked at me and, without uttering a word, he took Rawyia by the hand and led her out of the room.

"Let her do what she wants," he said, "not what we want."

I felt safe knowing Marwan was on my side. It surprised me that a man believed I had the right to do what I wanted with my life. I thought all men were like my father, demanding and subjugating women. I understood, then, why Rawyia married him.

I counted on Marwan to persuade her to back off and let me decide my own future. However, he was old, and Rawyia used her youth and beauty to get him to do what pleased her. I had to take my rescue on faith and believe in his show of solidarity.

An hour later, Rawyia walked back into my room, this time without Marwan. She gave me an ultimatum: either meet the man she wanted to introduce me to or leave her home.

I was stunned. I looked into Rawyia's eyes and saw an impossible future. I was pushed into independence in the three seconds it took her to mouth those words. With a modicum of thought, I chose the latter. I ignored the look of shock and disbelief frozen on her face and maintained my stance.

The next morning, with trepidation and a fist full of fear, I made the first and most difficult decision of my life. I was taught never to trust myself, so with apprehension and no idea of how I could face the world on my own, I left.

Rawyia and I parted without a goodbye. She was steadfast in her belief that I would come back, defeated and begging to be taken in. I was unsure if I could deal with life's responsibilities without her by my side, but I had to choose to either succumb to her pressure and accept another arranged marriage or face life's challenges on my own.

I thought of Nagi's mother and her suggestion to study journalism. It empowered me to take on the challenge without emotional torment. I was not sure if I still had room in my heart for more pain and suffering by going it alone because I was still grieving the separation from Mama and my siblings. Nevertheless, I left.

CHAPTER V

MOVING IN WITH NAGI'S FAMILY

It was a scorching August afternoon when I left. I collected my belongings into a small suitcase, into which I packed a handful of clothes, a photo of Mama at her niece's wedding, and a brown wool cardigan Mama asked me to keep until we met again.

I put on my favorite blue-and-red polka dot mini dress and the high-heeled shoes that gave my five-foot, five-inch frame three more inches. I ran my fingers through my hair. I had colored it blue-black for enhancement, even though the curly hair was not appreciated in Egypt or Lebanon. I focused on my eyes, intensifying their black color and sparkle. Ghassan often complimented me on their size and glow. I used eyeliner to go beyond their perimeters to make them appear more significant—a fashion in the seventies.

With my personal appearance in order, I held tight to the golden pendant Mama gave me. I wanted to feel her presence, active and alive against my skin. The separation from Rawyia was hard and took a feat of courage I wasn't sure I had. I left part of me with Rawyia. Nevertheless, I was ready to face the world alone for the first time.

Fate Knocked on My Door

∽

When I arrived at Nagi's home, I rang the bell. A girl with a joyful smile opened the door. She appeared in her late teens, with flowing golden locks draped over her shoulder like a silk shawl. She was fair in complexion with rosy cheeks and shimmering hazel eyes—eyes that added charm to her baby face. Everything about her seemed quiet and delicate until her voice exploded like fireworks. Unlike her soft-spoken mother, she was loud and vivacious.

"You must be Laila, right?"

I nodded.

"Ommy, Laila is here!" she exclaimed.

Nagi's mother had already mentioned me to the family. This vibrant young girl grabbed me by the hand and slammed the door shut with her foot. I surrendered like a child to her grip. She guided me to the kitchen, where her mother stood in front of the stove.

Nagi's mother's hair was covered with a burgundy scarf that matched her apron. She turned toward us, face beaming with a genuine welcome, anchoring me in their home without fear.

"Mariam, let go of Laila's hand," she said. Turning to me, she explained, "My daughter is happy to have found a sister."

The warmth in Nagi's mother's voice and the status she gave me lifted me from the anxiety hole I was in. Mariam continued to hold my hand despite her mother's admonition. I was happy to experience such a cheerful ambiance at their home.

"I am happy to be part of your family, Tante," I grinned.

"Laila, are you shy?" Mariam asked.

I smiled. It was not shyness I felt, but somewhat disbelief. My life was going in an unplanned direction. It was scary yet pleasant.

Mariam pointed her finger at my face, almost touching my nose. "In this house, shyness is not allowed."

She let go of my hand and walked to her mother. Picking

up a spoon, she dipped it into the pot sitting over the flame. "What are you cooking, Ommy?"

"Bamia," her mother declared with a wink. "I hope you like bamia." She ground a mixture of garlic, dried coriander, and salt in a brass mortar. When the ingredients were paste-like, she placed the mixture in a small frying pan and added two tablespoons of butter.

"I am cooking bamia the way Egyptians eat it, just for you, Laila."

I never liked the taste of okra, but I lied to please her. "Yes, of course, I love bamia with garlic paste," I told her. "Thank you."

Mariam expressed her emotion with physical touches, like most Arab people do. Every time she passed by her mother or me, she wrapped her arms around us and planted a quick kiss on our cheeks. In no time, I began to reciprocate the gesture, even though I was still a little reserved.

I was curious about how Mariam's father treated them. I wondered if he controlled them like my father did us. But I kept my curiosity to myself and enjoyed the love that surrounded me.

Soon, I was comfortable enough to participate in the cooking process. I sautéed the chicken the way our maid Om Zobeida cooked it, with a generous portion of clarified butter until golden brown. I wanted to impress them with my cooking skills.

I helped Mariam set the table for lunch. She handed me a few plates, "Five," she said, "five of us will have lunch."

It was 2:15 in the afternoon when I sensed someone standing behind me, cupping my eyes.

"Guess who's this?"

I wasn't used to such warm-hearted family closeness. I froze. When I removed his hands, I was shocked to see how much he looked like Ghassan. He shared Ghassan's olive skin and his dark brown eyes crowned with thick charcoal lashes.

The stars that danced in his eyes were just like Ghassan's. The huskiness in his voice shook me to the core. I heard Ghassan's voice. My heart sank. I glued my stare on him until I heard Nagi's mother.

"Nagi looks a lot like Ghassan," she chuckled.

I ignored her statement.

"I forgot to mention that," she continued.

"Welcome to your home," Nagi said, touching my shoulder as if to wake me up. He then walked to his mother with open arms. He hugged and kissed her for what seemed to be minutes. She would not let go of him. She planted kisses all over his face, head, and shoulders.

"Ommy, I am starving," he said, wiggling out of her embrace.

I followed Nagi, anticipating Ghassan's name to jump out of his mouth. He avoided eye contact with me. I debated whether to keep my anguish hidden or to be bold and honest. I decided to wait for Nagi to approach the subject.

Nagi's lengthy frame and the nobility of his airline uniform impressed me. His likeness to Ghassan turned my day upside down. I could see and hear no one but him. My feet were glued to the floor, but my eyes followed him with admiration. I watched his every move as he shuttled between the kitchen and dining room, carrying serving dishes like an experienced waiter. He acknowledged my attention with a wink. But Ghassan still owned my heart.

Mariam, her mother, and Nagi behaved like bees in a bee colony, each performing their roles with a smile. The apartment radiated with love. When they finished serving the food, Mariam took me by the hand and followed her mother and Nagi to the balcony.

"Baba will be here in a minute," she said with the excitement of a child.

Just then, Nagi announced spotting his father's car in the distance. They all rushed inside. I stayed. I wanted to get a glimpse of the man so loved by his family.

Neither my siblings nor I were ever excited to see our father come home. We dreaded mealtimes because of him. Mama was the one who owned our hearts. She had enough love to cover for our father's detachment.

The scene in the dining room shocked me. Mariam, her mother, and Nagi fought over who would get the first hug from their father. He reached for his petite wife and wrapped his arms around her waist. She offered her lips, and they kissed. The sight of genuine love took me by surprise. I wished my parents had behaved with such affection. This family must be unique, I thought. The father released his wife and took both Nagi and Mariam into one big embrace.

I felt like I was watching a movie. Then the husband acknowledged my presence with a smile. The open and harmonious love in this family allowed me to overcome the fear of uncertainty I carried when Rawyia and I separated. I wanted to stay with them forever.

"Laila, meet my husband, Fikry," Nagi's mother said.

I extended my hand. Fikry took me in his arms. "Ahlein bi, Laila," he said (Welcome, Laila). "Where is Majnoon Laila?" He laughed.

I smiled. I knew the folk story he referenced. It was about a man who loved a girl named Laila, but her parents stood against their marriage. The man in the fable lost his mind and wandered the streets, sad for losing his beloved Laila. Hence the name Majnoon Laila (the one who lost his mind because he lost his dear Laila.)

I wanted to tell him that, in my case, I was the Majnoona—the one who had lost her beloved Ghassan and came to Lebanon looking for him. The mention of the fable empowered me to ask about Ghassan. But, as I was about to speak, Nagi's mother gave her husband a scornful look, sharp enough to silence everyone. I put my intention on hold to wait for a more appropriate time.

During lunch, Mariam and her father engaged in a heated discussion about the election in Lebanon. To my surprise, they shouted at each other. I had no idea what was behind the instability of the country. Each had an opposite opinion and supported different parties among the nine parties fighting for power: Maronite Christians, Sunni Muslims, Shiite Muslims, Greek Orthodox, Druze, Greek Catholics, Armenian Orthodox, Protestants, and Armenian Catholics. I had no prior knowledge or interest in Lebanon's complicated political situation. Nagi and his mother appeared uninterested.

Fikry ended the dispute by placing a kiss on his wife's hand—a "thank you" gesture for the meal. The affection between them got me thinking about the relationship between my parents and how dispassionate it was. Papa never kissed Mama or thanked her for cooking, or anything else for that matter. I felt sorry for Mama and grew more resentful of my father. He never appreciated or valued her love and devotion to him and to us. On that day, I made a solemn oath to free Mama from the cruelty of my father.

The heated discussion came to an end when Mariam's mother stood up and excused herself. Fikry followed her, and together they disappeared into their bedroom. Mariam, Nagi, and I cleaned up after lunch, washed the dishes, and left the kitchen spotless. It looked like this was the way a family was supposed to function. I admired their cooperation. The respect and openness between Mariam and her father impressed me the most.

If I had not seen verses from the Quran hung on the walls everywhere in their apartment, I would have thought they were not following the teaching of Islam. Were they practicing a different faith than the one I was taught and the one our father enforced on us? Why didn't Mariam's father force her into marriage? And why did he let her go to college? Did the Islam they practiced allow girls to mingle with boys? I wondered if our parents taught us a different religion—the kind that promoted the oppression of women.

I forced myself to maintain a happy face and followed

Mariam to her room. Nagi excused himself to take a nap.

"My father and I take politics seriously," Mariam said.

I nodded, figuring two journalists wouldn't talk about gardening or cooking. I wanted to tell her how lucky she was to have a father like hers. But Mariam continued talking about politics. It frustrated her that no one valued her point of view. I expressed solidarity, even though I didn't understand and wasn't interested in Lebanese political disputes.

"I agree with you, Mariam."

She must have realized the subject bored me. "We will share this bed," she said. "It's big enough for both of us, don't you agree?"

I smiled as she opened one side of the wall unit. A closet extended from one end of the wall to the other and reached the ceiling.

"This side will be yours. Let me know if you need more space."

She offered the use of her clothes if I needed them. We were both a small size. I had brought with me two dresses, two skirts, a wool sweater, and a blouse. I welcomed the offer when she promised to wear my small collection in exchange.

Later that night, Mariam and Nagi invited me to join them for a night at a discotheque downtown.

I put on one of Mariam's red strapless dresses. She wore the black version of it. We looked like sisters, except she was fair in complexion and I was brunette. I hesitated going out in such a revealing dress, but Mariam assured me her parents would not mind or criticize our choice.

I had never felt as proud of my figure as I did that evening. I used to wrap a scarf around my bust to evade Papa's disapproving look.

I looked at myself in the mirror and forgot about the past. I winked. The girl wearing the red halter dress smiled.

I heard a whistle and saw Nagi's reflection in the mirror. He was as tall as Ghassan. I covered my bare skin with both arms, but he removed them. "No need to feel shy," he said. "It's normal to dress this way in Lebanon."

When Nagi's mom and dad woke from their afternoon nap, they complimented the way I looked. I was delighted and appreciative of their liberal attitude toward women.

∽

We danced and drank orange juice until midnight at the Cave de Roi. Mariam danced with Nagi's friends, and I danced with Nagi all night. I tried to open the subject of Ghassan, but the music was too loud for a serious conversation.

The uplifting ambiance and safe interaction between boys and girls in the disco got me thinking about what my father told me. "If a boy and a girl meet up without the presence of parents, the devil will invade their privacy and entice them to engage in sex." None of us kissed nor had sex that evening. Had my father lied, or was he quoting from a different holy book? He deprived my sister and me of a college education, fearing we would engage in sex with boys at the university.

At last, life offered me the stability I was looking for. But something was missing and kept me from enjoying what I had. I missed Mama and my sister.

I could not call Mama, and Rawyia refused to answer my phone calls. Calls to Egypt were expensive, and I was not working, so I wrote Mama several letters, but never got a reply. I suspected my messages ended up in Papa's drawers. He kept the key to our mailbox.

On several occasions, I ambushed Nagi to extract an explanation about Ghassan's marriage, but my efforts failed. He always found an excuse to avoid the subject.

Nagi flattered me with compliments. The attention pleased my ego, and the resemblance between him and Ghassan made it easy to accept them. I began to miss him when he went to work or socialized with his friends, and I looked forward for his return. But I kept those sentiments to myself. In the Arab world, divorced and runaway young women lose their place in society. They become pariahs with the Scarlet Letter pinned on their chest, just like Hester Prynne. I suppressed my emotions when Nagi was home to maintain the respect and trust I gained and treasured.

CHAPTER VI

NAGI'S UNEXPECTED APPROACH

For three months, I lived with Nagi's family, enjoying a safe and loving atmosphere. I could not have wished for a more stable environment. I stopped having the dream where I was back in Alexandria, locked up in a dark cell with black iron bars. That lock-up had no windows, and no one heard my screams. A tiny speck of light appeared in the ceiling and disappeared the moment I stopped screaming.

Summer in Lebanon and Alexandria was typical of all Mediterranean cities—hot and humid. Lebanese, as well as Alexandrians, don't have air conditioning at home. They flock to the seashore to get relief from the scorching sun. Even when the sun retires, the heat lingers.

Lebanese keep their windows open during the summer nights, and no member of the family retires before grabbing an icy bottle of water and placing it next to their bed.

One of those summer nights, I forgot to follow the routine. It was 2:00 a.m., and I woke up thirsty. As I opened the refrigerator door, someone behind me pushed it shut.

I turned to find Nagi, dressed in his airline uniform, grinning from ear-to-ear. His breath was so close to my face; I froze as perspiration bathed my body. I stood there with my back to the fridge as he rested his arms on the refrigerator door. The scent of his Aramis and the lustful look in his eyes hypnotized me. My knees buckled. Then, he released one arm, and with his finger collected beads of sweat from my forehead and licked it. I shivered with pleasure.

For a moment, my past and present vanished except for that one moment, which I enjoyed without guilt. However, I thought of the consequences—the trust, and respect I stood to lose from the family that treated me like a daughter. I couldn't betray the sanctity of the home they opened for me. I sobered up before losing my resistance and jeopardizing the respect I cherished. I bent down, ducked under his arms, and ran to my bed, shaking.

I never talked to anyone about what happened. Nagi behaved as usual, and we never mentioned that hot summer night. We continued to go out dancing as if nothing had happened. But there was a difference in Nagi's behavior. He acted as though I belonged to him and him alone.

"No going out and dancing in my absence," he ordered.

I enjoyed the individual attention, but it scared me. I remembered Rawyia's warnings, "Sex is all men want from girls."

After what happened between Nagi and me, I no longer felt comfortable living with them and needed to find a place of my own. So, I asked Nagi's mother if she could ask her husband to find me a job.

One month later, in September, my dream came true when Fikry told me he had registered me at the university. "You will attend college this semester," he told me.

I could not contain my excitement. I hugged Fikry and showered Tante with kisses.

"But I have no money," I said with sudden realization.

Tante grabbed my hand and stepped onto the balcony. "Don't worry about money now. Fikry will find you a part-time job."

"Thank you, Tante," I said, hugging her.

The dream I thought would take years to come true came faster than I'd hoped. I called Rawyia. I wanted her to hear the good news and acknowledge my accomplishments.

"Rawyia, I have news," I told her.

"So, you came to your senses, at last," she said.

"No, but I am going to college."

There was silence. Then, a deep sigh. "What do you want from me?"

"Your love and support," I said.

"Who's paying for this education?" she demanded. "Don't count on me."

Rawyia's answer was depressing but not surprising. I knew how she felt about education, but I hoped she would be happy for me.

"You will always have my love, and that's all," she said.

That was all I wanted from Rawyia.

CHAPTER VII

EMPLOYER'S SEXUAL ASSAULT

The first year of college went smoothly. I excelled in every subject, a fact that made Nagi's family proud of me. I became closer to everyone in the family. But Mariam and I became inseparable. She helped me acquaint myself with the university routine and the Arabic language.

I searched the college bulletin every day looking for a part-time job. I found an ad for a position at an attorney's office during summer vacation. Against the family's wishes, I applied for the job. They wanted me to focus on my studies, even though they promised to help me find part-time work. I knew I could manage both.

I went for the interview with my hands shaking and insecurity surging. I had no prior experience for a legal position. But I applied anyway.

Mr. Tony, the attorney, spoke French and expressed his pleasure that I spoke French as well. He figured that I was Egyptian from my accent.

"Did you learn French in Egypt," he asked.

"Yes," I said.

He noticed I was wringing my hands. He stood up and

walked around his desk and sat facing me. He then took my hands in his and looked me in the eyes.

"I will train you," he said, squeezing my hands. "Don't worry."

Mr. Tony stood almost twice my height. His eyes had a penetrating stare that stripped away my confidence. He appeared as old as my father. Grey shoots speckled his dense black hair and, when he smiled, wrinkles at the corner of his eyes deepened, and his brows furrowed when he spoke.

I kept my gaze on his hairy arms and waited for him to release my hands.

"I will do my best to follow instructions," I said.

He stood up, still holding onto my right hand, and guided me to the front desk outside his office.

"This is your office," he said. "I expect you here three days a week after your summer classes."

We didn't discuss salary, the number of hours I would work, or any other requirements of the position. Nonetheless, I couldn't be happier.

Thank you, Mr. Tony," I said. "I will make sure you never regret hiring me."

Life was kind to me at this time. I used my modest salary to contribute to the Nagis' household, buying groceries and presents for each member.

I also called Mama often to tell her about the progress I was making in my life. In spite of my good news, she cried every time I called. I hoped reports of my progress and contentment would keep her from crying, but it didn't. I even lied about Rawyia's behavior so she wouldn't worry. "Rawyia is helping me," I told her.

I promised Mama that, once I settled down in my own place, I would send for her to come and live with me.

I felt joy at college and satisfaction at work, until that afternoon in Mr. Tony's office.

It was a July summer day when heat and humidity were

intense in Beirut, and Mr. Tony asked me to take half of the next day off.

"Go spend the morning at the beach," he said. "I am taking the day off, but please come back in the afternoon."

Mariam, her mother, and I spent all morning at the beach sunbathing and swimming. At two o'clock in the afternoon, I excused myself and headed for work. I found no need to go home and change my clothes since Mr. Tony would not be coming to the office.

It was steaming hot that afternoon. I walked into the office wearing a yellow-and-white polka dot braless mini sundress.

Two hours passed before Mr. Tony appeared at the door. I was surprised and uncomfortable. I covered my chest with the file I was working on.

"I stopped by to check if you needed me," he said, proceeding into his office.

I froze in my seat and hoped he would not call me into his room. I collected all the legal documents I had been working on and filed them in their designated folders. Then I used the speaker on my desk and informed him that I would leave for the afternoon.

"Please, come in and shut the door behind you," he said.

I knocked, opened the door, and stood there. Mr. Tony walked toward me, took my hand, and sat down on his chair. I held a few inches away from him. His heavy breathing was loud. His cigar-contaminated breath pierced through my dress and settled on my skin. I took a few steps back. He leaped like a hungry tiger, grabbed my wrists, and pulled me closer. I freed myself from his grip and ran to the door. He followed me. Using his large frame, he managed to pin both of my arms to the wall above my head and proceeded to fondle my breasts. He hovered his salivating lips close to my mouth. I rolled my lips inside my mouth and pressed hard. I wiggled my reed-like frame and freed myself, but he grabbed me again by the waist. I begged him with tears to stop. To my surprise, he let go of me.

"Please go," he said.

I opened the door and ran out, chased by his voice, repeating, "I am sorry."

I walked home, my eyes swimming in tears as I remembered Rawyia's warning, "All Arab men want nothing from a girl but sex."

I cried all the way back. Somehow, after the long cry, I grew stronger with determination to keep going. I refused to let what happened keep me from achieving my goals. It was not my first disappointment, and I knew it would not be the last.

My red puffy eyes betrayed me when I got back home. I explained what happened. Tante was not surprised; she had expected such an incident. She told me that Arab men don't have respect for divorced women, and that Arab societies condemn young divorced women. They consider them weak prey for sexual assault. Furthermore, women have no rights in the court of law.

"From now on, no more working for you," she said. "Focus on college."

But I needed to work. I could not accept living without my financial contribution.

"I must find another job," I said.

Tante heard the determination in my voice and promised to help. The whole family showered me with love and attention, but no one knew what happened except Tante. I trusted her.

Months passed, and still Ghassan's whereabouts had not popped up in discussions. Rawyia still refused to see me, and I lost the income that helped me call Mama. I had nothing left but college.

The second year at the university could not have started any sooner. Attending classes was my happiest time in Lebanon. I promised myself not to let anyone or anything derail me from studying. I took a one-way trip to my goal and left behind the unrelenting cruelties of the past.

CHAPTER VIII

MR. ANWAR THE NEIGHBOR

Mr. Anwar, an old man in his seventies, occupied the apartment next door to Nagi's family. Every Friday he came over and played backgammon with Fikry. He ate dinner with us whenever Nagi's mother cooked his favorite dish—Kibbeh. I asked Mariam if Mr. Anwar was a relative.

"Uncle Anwar is a friend. We have known him and his two late wives for ten years, "she said.

The warmth they displayed toward Mr. Anwar made me trust him. He became the uncle I never had. Papa had no brothers.

Mr. Anwar gave me the same loving attention I received from Nagi's family. He never missed a morning to greet me before I left for college. He waited in front of his apartment with a cup of Arabic coffee in his hand.

"Good morning, sunshine," he said.

"Good morning, Uncle."

"Call me Anwar," he insisted.

I never did.

I learned from Tante that he had been married twice. Both

his wives had died. His four daughters were married and lived in different cities.

"How did his wives die?" I asked Tante.

"Complications of cancer," she said.

"Both had cancer?"

"Yes," she replied.

I made time to chat and listen to his life story whenever I had free time.

"My first wife died with cancer," he said. "She was thirty years old."

Furrows revealed sadness, which he camouflaged with a constant smile when he visited Nagi's family.

Nothing I could say would have made a difference to his sorrow.

"How about your second wife?" I asked.

"She was much younger than my first wife, May."

I was curious to know how much younger, and how long he mourned his first wife.

"How young was she?"

"Noora was twenty-seven when we married."

By now, I was confused. How old was he when he married May and Noora? I stared at him, perplexed.

"She also died from cancer, right?" I asked him.

"Yes," he replied, "breast cancer."

I said nothing waiting for him to tell me more. But he maintained a silence I could not ignore.

"When did Noora die?"

"A year ago," he told me. He sighed.

I turned my gaze away to avoid looking at the grooves carving his forehead, giving his face a sharp look.

"How long did your marriage to Noora last before she passed away?" I wondered.

"Four years," he responded.

He continued to spill out bits and pieces every time we met on my way to college.

Mr. Anwar had a sense of humor we all enjoyed. His jokes made Mariam and her dad stop their political arguments and listen to his stories. He entertained us with folk stories, especially the one of Majnoon Laila. He recounted the fable often.

Mr. Anwar would sometimes refer to himself as Majnoon Laila, and we would laugh. He was a grandpa figure and we enjoyed his presence.

One day, when the elevator of the apartment building stopped working, I climbed the stairs. Mr. Anwar was waiting for me.

"I recognized your footsteps," he said. "No one but you would run up to the fourth floor in high heels."

Mr. Anwar's attention was comforting. I looked forward to our brief chats outside our apartments. He became the father figure I wished for when growing up.

He listened and remembered everything I told him about my life, and always said the right thing to win my trust.

"I made sure my children got an education before they married," he said, "and I gave them the right to choose whom to marry." He assured me that my father loved me and that culture was to blame for the strict upbringing.

"Your father wanted to secure your future with a mature man who would take care of you," he explained when I told him about my marriage and divorce.

"Farook was thirty-nine years old," I explained, expecting him to react in shock.

Mr. Anwar grinned. "You are divorced now. Think of tomorrow. Age doesn't mean anything," he said.

His statement about age took away layers from the warmth I shared with him. However, when he offered to help with my Arabic literature, I accepted. Arabic is a complicated subject. Mr. Anwar mentioned that he had a master's degree in Physics but had been retired for the past five years. He now spent his time reading. His collection of books included the Quran, Hadith Al-Bukhari, and Abbas Mahmud El Aqqad,

Naguib Mahfouz, Anis Mansour, Moliere, and Victor Hugo. The varieties impressed me. I valued his opinion and advice. But not when he dismissed the importance of age compatibility between married couples.

Mr. Anwar and I met on Fridays in his apartment so he could help me with my studies. Within a few weeks, he became my confidante and the male figure I trusted without reservations.

"You must always look at the positive side of what happened to you," he counseled.

"I can't find anything positive in leaving school at fourteen and being forced into marriage to an old man at fifteen," I retorted. I was still angry with my father, but I allowed Mr. Anwar to open the subject every time we met.

"Your father did not know any better. He raised you the way he believed to be the best. He himself was a victim of his own upbringing," he reiterated.

I nodded. I knew, deep in my heart, that my father loved me, but failed to make me feel his love. All I saw, as a young girl, were the extreme measures he took to preserve my virginity. In the process, he sheltered me from the outside and robbed me of self-exploration, self-reliance and, most of all, self-confidence.

Mr. Anwar helped me sort out my feelings and focus on the opportunities waiting for me to explore. His advice made me feel like a person with a virgin soul, emerging from a dark cocoon, ready to face a bright future.

I asked for his advice about the conflict between Rawyia and me. He supported my independence and urged me to continue a life separate from her. "Marriage," he said, "could hinder your goals unless you find a man who will help you would help fulfill your dreams."

I believed Mr. Anwar. He provided the confidence I needed to keep going without making me feel pressured or indebted to him. However, my heart was still pumped with Ghassan's blood. The last time we were together in Alexandria, we poked each other's fingers and, in a rite of devotion, vowed to remain faithful to each other until death do us part. I couldn't consider the idea of his being married, as Rawyia told me.

I waited two months before I approached the subject of Ghassan with Mr. Anwar.

"I still love him," I said. "Ghassan promised to marry me once I got the divorce."

I didn't see the same enthusiasm Mr. Anwar had shown while discussing all the other issues of my life. "That boy," he snapped, "doesn't deserve your love."

He surprised me when he called Ghassan a boy. I didn't expect that reaction. But I believed Mr. Anwar wanted the best for me. I refrained from discussing Ghassan with him any further.

CHAPTER IX

OFFER TO TRAVEL TO ITALY

Halfway through my second year in college, Mr. Anwar caught me unprepared. "I have a big surprise for you," he said. "It will change your future."

I couldn't imagine anything that could stop me from pursuing my goals in Lebanon. I had everything in Beirut—a family that loved me and education.

"I don't need surprises," I said. "I am happy."

"You will be happier in Italy," he said.

"Italy?" I screamed.

Excitement lifted me off the ground. I wanted to fly. I had big dreams, but not as big as going to Europe. "But I don't speak Italian."

He started laughing and couldn't stop. For a moment, I thought he was joking and couldn't believe how gullible I was.

"So, you are not serious?" I asked.

He continued laughing, then took a deep breath. "I never forgot hearing you talk about your desire to travel to Europe," he said.

I remembered expressing a wish to visit Europe, but I never expected to fulfill that dream. I mentioned France because I had fantasized about living in France all through my childhood.

"Italy is not far from France," he said.

"When?" I asked.

"Any day you are ready," he replied.

"What about college?" I wanted to know.

"There are colleges in Italy."

I was confused. My thoughts jumped from one possibility to the other.

Mr. Anwar kept a wry grin on his face and had an empty stare. I couldn't read his thoughts.

"Do you mean a move to Italy for good?" I asked.

He nodded with triumph. His grin turned to a smile of pleasure. He approached and said, tilting his head to one side, "Don't I deserve a hug?"

"For what? You haven't told me yet how and why I would go to Italy."

Amidst the uncertainty, happiness bubbled deep inside me. The idea to travel outside the African continent was a dream I could not refuse.

For a moment, I forgot about education, Nagi's family, my search for Ghassan and, like a grateful daughter, I hugged Mr. Anwar.

"So, is that a yes?" he whispered. "You want to go to Italy?"

"Yes," I said, and stayed in his arms until he let go.

"How about a cup of tea before I explain," he said.

I got to know that Mr. Anwar was a patient man, but not on that day when I dropped by his apartment for a brief chat about my college lectures as I had done often. He spoke of his brother, who resided in Italy with his teenage daughter. "I don't hide anything from Gamal," he said. "I shared your story with him."

I was flattered to know that my life story was interesting to both of them. He whistled, while preparing tea, the tune of the French song, "La Femme de mon ami," by Enrico Macias.

I lost track of time. The grandfather clock in the den struck

10:00 p.m. and I was supposed to be back at Nagi's by 9:00 p.m. I ignored that and followed Mr. Anwar to the kitchen. I said nothing. He, too, was quiet. I glued my eyes on his mouth and waited to hear more about my trip to Italy.

He offered me four Manaeesh with Zaatar and olive oil. He knew this was my favorite snack. I could never resist the aroma of the spices that always permeated in his apartment, but not on that day. I took no notice. All I wanted was to know more about my new life in Italy. Besides, Nagi's mother was waiting for me to eat dinner.

"Here," he said, "I baked Manaeesh this morning, just for you."

I excused myself and thanked him for the treat. I thought, before I got all excited, I should discuss his offer with Nagi's family.

"I have to go. Tante is waiting for me."

Tante and Fikry had stayed up. Nagi was on duty, and Mariam had already retired for the night.

"So, what kept you so late at Anwar's? Was it your college work or listening to his life story?" Fikry asked.

"He talked about Gamal, who lives in Italy," I said. "Mr. Anwar asked if I would travel to Italy and work for his brother."

"Yes," Fikry said, "I met Gamal when he visited Anwar. He is a gentleman."

Uncle Fikry said little about Gamal. But he shook his head and looked at Tante, astonished.

"I expected Anwar to talk to me first," Fikry said. "What kind of work did he offer you?"

"I don't know yet," I confessed.

"You don't speak Italian," Nagi's mother said, pointing out the obvious.

There was silence in the room. I sensed from the displeased look on Fikry's face and Nagi's mother's concerned tone that Anwar's proposal was surprising, if not disturbing. I excused myself.

I was exhausted yet sleep eluded me. I prepared a warm glass of milk, drank it, and went straight to bed.

∞

In the morning, I attended my classes. I was tired, but eager to see Mr. Anwar later that afternoon. I had questions and concerns about the move to Italy and his brother Gamal's job offer.

On that day, Mr. Anwar broke the habit of waiting for me at the stairway and stayed inside his apartment, leaving the front door ajar. I was surprised, but ignored the change, giving him the benefit of the doubt since it was the first time.

When I walked in, I found him in his den, wearing his reading glasses with a book in his hands.

"Please take a seat," he said. "I will be with you in a second."

Mr. Anwar always looked me in the eye when he spoke. Not this time. He chuckled. I sat down on the chair opposite his desk, quiet but impatient.

"So, you agreed to travel to Italy?" he asked.

The air flowing to my lungs gathered into a solid lump at the back of my throat. I swallowed a few times.

"My brother, Gamal, needs an assistant," he continued.

His statement pleased me. The travel to Italy had a boosting effect on my ego. I wanted to prove to Rawyia and my father that I had succeeded on my own, even if it cost me further alienation from everyone dear to me. Europe was far away—a different continent.

I was ready for a change after my long internal struggles, unpleasant experiences with Arab men, and my lack of financial independence. I had two more years of college before I would graduate, but I chose to embrace the opportunity of living in Europe to explore the world outside Egypt and Lebanon. It was a dream I never thought would come true.

Mr. Anwar was like a fairy striking my life with a magic wand. Once more, fate knocked on my door and offered me bigger dreams.

Nagi's family respected my decision and wished me luck. "Our home will always be open for you," Tante said. "You can come back anytime."

I was relieved. I needed to know I had Nagi's place available in case I failed in Italy.

Mr. Anwar purchased a one-way plane ticket to Italy. I accepted it, but only after he agreed to let me reimburse him when I got paid from my job in Italy.

"But what if I don't like it there?" I said.

Although I was excited at the prospect of what life would be like in Italy, I wasn't ready to sever all connections with my roots. A one-way ticket would hinder my return in case I faced difficulties coping with my new life. What if Mr. Anwar's brother found me unfit for the job? What if his family rejected me? I preferred a round-trip ticket, but I could not be choosy. I was not the one paying the airfare.

"A one-way ticket," Mr. Anwar said, "will force you to stay patient and think twice before making a hasty decision."

Mr. Anwar had a point. I convinced myself it was for the best.

"Don't neglect your education," Fikry said.

I promised Nagi's family that I would pursue my studies as soon as I settled down.

Mariam and Nagi wished me luck and, with teary eyes, we embraced and said goodbye. Tante handed me a miniature copy of the Quran. "Put it in your purse," she said. "It will keep you safe."

I contacted Rawyia and informed her about the move to Italy.

"Although I like the idea," she said, "I am not sure you have enough courage to be so far away and on your own."

Rawyia's statement challenged me. I vowed to prove to her wrong.

"When are you leaving?" she asked.

"Tomorrow at 6:00 a.m."

I hoped I could see her before leaving, but she wished me luck and hung up.

※

At the Airport, I heard Rawyia's voice loud behind me.

"La," she yelled.

I saw a tear hanging at the edge of her glasses, and her eyes were red and glistening. All the love we shared and our childhood memories pulled us into a long embrace. Our hearts spoke the words we could not verbalize. Rawyia would not let go, but I released myself from her arms. I left without looking back. That was all I needed to calm down.

I would not tell Mama about the move until I settled down. I knew she would suffer if she knew I was moving to Italy alone.

CHAPTER X

ARRIVING IN ROME

Mama's words still echoed loud inside my head. "Accept your fate." she said. "It's your destiny."
When I was fifteen, I challenged that destiny and liberated myself from the arranged marriage. Or did I? Had Mama been right? Had fate been in control of my life all along? Was the life waiting for me in Italy another destiny that cemented Mama's words?

At the Fiumicino Airport in Rome, Mr. Anwar's niece Nora welcomed me. Brunette, she had a thick chestnut mane gathered upon her crown with an elastic band. Shielded behind a pair of prescription glasses, two small emerald pupils swam in a pool of white mass, void of any warmth. Her lips were closed in straight line. She wore blue jeans with a plain white tee shirt and flat white sneakers. She stood, arms crossed over her chest, her legs apart.

"Laila?" she asked.

I assumed Mr. Anwar had described me when he spoke to Gamal.

"Yes," I replied.

"I am Nora."

I extended my hand. She ignored it. "Follow me," she said.

My excitement overshadowed her bossy behavior. Infused with euphoric happiness, I floated behind her like a hummingbird searching for a hidden sweet side in her personality to approach. But she kept her distance.

The Italian language got my attention. It sounded like musical notes. I was enchanted, even though I couldn't understand it. The Latin roots of the French language, together with the hand gestures of the Italian people, helped me decipher some words.

The aroma of baking bread wafting from vendors at the airport made me hungry. But Nora kept up a racing stride, so I had to settle for the nostrils' satisfaction. I barely noticed the leather boots displayed at the airport boutiques, but I promised to buy myself a pair with my first paycheck.

It was Sunday morning in April. Easter fresh air flirted with our hair. The Mediterranean blue sky was patterned with white puffs, and the pleasant warm weather felt like a mother's embrace. I fell in love with Rome.

We rode in Nora's gray Renault. She kept up her silent treatment until I couldn't take it anymore.

"How was your day?" I said.

"My father," she said, "wants me to take you to the Coliseum."

I was uncomfortable, but I stayed mute, as she was cold and unwelcoming.

"You don't have to," I said.

She drove to the destination, ignoring my reply, and stopped facing a humungous stone structure set in a vast circle. I remembered seeing this ancient building in my history books.

She parked the car not too far from the structure and asked me to follow her. I did. But, by then, I was confused by the cold reception. I hoped the rest of her family would be more welcoming.

We toured the ancient Roman amphitheater with her as my tourist guide. She explained in perfect French the history and purpose of the theater-like structure. She then took me to underground cells where the hungry lions were once kept and told me to roam on my own. She did not like to visit that place. It reminded her of the many Christians who were eaten alive by those lions. I didn't know what made her think I would enjoy visiting this place where Christians were mauled by hungry animals. I walked around quickly and returned to find her sitting on one of the scattered broken stones around the Coliseum.

"Are you tired?" she asked.

It seemed that she was now making an effort to appear warm. She even smiled. I grinned, thanking her for taking me to this historic structure.

The flight from Lebanon had taken less than four hours. I had plenty of energy left for more sightseeing, but her reserved behavior kept me from enjoying or focusing on the beautiful scenery while we drove. Still, I went along with her plans for the day and ignored her silent treatment.

"We will go see Papa," she said. I relaxed, thinking I would at last meet her father Gamal, Mr. Anwar's brother. But then she glimpsed at my face. "You have a cappello?"

I shook my head. I had no idea why I would need a hat to meet her papa.

"*Nessun problema*," she said.

I stayed mute until she parked her Renault in a huge parking lot not far from the most beautiful dome I had ever seen. The streets to the parking lot were jam-packed with small cars and pedestrians like ants headed in one direction in absolute silence.

We joined the procession until we came face to face with a magnificent dome adorned at its summit with a cross. I figured this was a church. It looked a hundred times bigger than any churches I had seen in Egypt. Instantly, spirituality took over, and serenity filled my soul.

Mama used to visit St. Fatima Church in Alexandria to light a candle. She often took Rawyia and me with her. We never questioned why she would go to a church and not a mosque. Mama loved Mary, Jesus's mother, and she called her Mariam. She whispered the name Mariam when she lit the candle. It was then that I learned Mariam was revered in Islam. Mama told us that Mariam would be the first woman to enter paradise.

The sun welcomed the masses' devotion with warmth and the air, crisp and gentle, played with the scarves covering old women's heads. Hundreds of people of all ages and genders faced the church and stood with their hands in prayer position. Sad and loud cries echoed and filled the space around me like a choir. They all had their eyes fixed on the dome of St. Peter's Church. A chill ran down my spine. I looked at Nora, and she, too, gazed directed at the dome. I remained quiet but anxious to see what the masses expected to see.

A few minutes that seemed like hours passed before the crowd around me engaged in a screaming frenzy. I saw hands reaching in supplication at the dome. I looked up and saw a figure in white clothes, looking over from a small window and waving his hand to the crowd. Then, like a spell had fallen on the crowd, they all went down on their knees, praying with overwhelming emotions.

I stood, although people around me asked me to kneel. I couldn't. Mama had told us to never kneel to anyone but God Almighty, and this man was not God.

I felt proud of myself for refusing to kneel and for being the one person standing in the hundreds around me. I crossed my arms and looked straight at the man standing in white clothes. I couldn't see his face as I stood very far, but I felt his eyes aiming straight at me. I remained in my position until the Pope gave his sermon and blessed the crowd with the hand cross sign before disappearing inside.

Infused with spirituality, we drove back home in utter silence until we reached a small villa. I knew my behavior at the church at St. Peter's Basilica jeopardized the slim chance of friendship I gained earlier.

I followed Nora into the main entrance. A tall slim African man took my suitcase and disappeared at the end of a long corridor. Then a gray-haired woman with a snow-white apron around her waist appeared through a revolving wooden door to my right. Her thick eyebrows, still maintaining the integrity of their original golden color, were anchored over a pair of sky-blue eyes that reflected warmth and kindness. Her delighted expression brightened her freckled face and deepened the wrinkles around her eyes in a soft and warm appearance.

"Ciao Caro, Nora," she said.

Nora walked straight through the long corridor and disappeared into a room on the right, ignoring the blue-eyed woman's greeting. I relaxed and felt less troubled about Nora's aloof behavior.

"*Lo sono* manager Genevieve," she said.

"Salut, Genevieve," I said, "je m'applle Laila."

She nodded and headed toward the alley.

"Alors, on parle en francais," she said.

She guided me to a room across from Nora's space and asked me to freshen up before joining Mr. Gamal and Nora for a meal. There was no mention of Nora's mother. I figured she must be somewhere and would come back.

"Merci, Genevieve," I said.

She left the room, shutting the door behind her. I sat on the white wood bed. I looked around, admiring the ivory theme of the room. The sheer snowy drapes allowed the flowery, well-manicured panorama and the bright sun outside to soothe my anxiety. The scattered white metal frames of yellow tulips hanging on the wall, and the leather chair that matched the pale ivory wall paint reflected a tranquil atmosphere I needed.

Still, tears gathered in my eyes. I imagined the warmth in the room I shared with Rawyia in Alexandria. I longed for her love. I wished my sister was with me.

I don't remember how long I sat on the bed, reminiscing about the closeness Rawyia and I shared growing up. The yearning for the family I had run away from was burning inside of me, I sobbed until Genevieve called me to have lunch.

I wiped my tears and walked out to the dining room. Genevieve respected the sadness written all over my face and refrained from asking me if I had refreshed myself from my journey. Mr. Gamal, who had been waiting for me sitting in a chair with arms, stood up and extended his hand to greet me.

"*Ahlan wa Sahlan,*" he said in Arabic.

He was stocky and of medium height compared to his brother, who stood above five feet, eight inches. He appeared much younger than Mr. Anwar. Except for a slight baldness, he held onto a substantial number of light brown hairs free of gray. His round, chubby baby cheeks and child-like laughter eased the tension I had felt since I landed in Rome. He gestured me to take the chair next to him. When I sat down, he patted me on the head.

When Nora walked into the room, the delight on Mr. Gamal's face subsided. She took a seat on an armchair facing her father.

Mushroom soup was served, followed by spaghetti with fresh tomatoes and Pellegrini water. I couldn't resist the aroma of the spaghetti sauce, and hunger helped me ignore my gloomy surroundings. I started to eat.

Except for the sound of spoons hitting the soup bowls and the chirrup of a passerine standing on the tree branch facing the dining room window, the room was shrouded in silence.

I thought about asking if Nora's mother would join us. But the lack of warmth between Nora and her father prevented me. Instead, I immersed myself in assumptions about the cold vibes between them.

When Gamal finished drinking his soup, he broke my chain of assumptions. "Mariam," he said, looking at Nora, "passed away five months ago."

Nora stood up, threw her spoon on the table, and walked out of the room. I assumed Mariam was Nora's mother. The statement shocked me. I wanted to know more about Nora's angry reaction. I attempted to follow her, but Gamal continued, "Nora is having a hard time with the loss of her mother."

I nodded but moved to follow her.

"Join me in the den for an espresso," Gamal insisted.

"Maybe she needs someone to talk to," I suggested.

"Have you learned to type?" he interrupted.

His suddenly aloof attitude was disturbing. But I remembered why I had come to Italy—work and study.

I had done some typing at the attorney's office in Lebanon, but not enough to qualify me as a typist. Besides, it was all in French. However, I knew I would have no problem figuring it out, no matter what language Gamal required.

"I did some typing at my previous job," I said.

He smiled.

"I want you to call me Gamal."

I nodded with a grin.

"Always be ready on short notice to join me wherever I go." The sudden change of tone in his voice scared me. He had become authoritative. I took a sip of the espresso Genevieve served and waited for more instructions. He handed me a notebook and a pen.

"Be ready at 8:00 a.m. to have breakfast with me, and always have this notebook handy to record my orders. I want you to ask if you don't understand anything."

Cold air filled the room and turned my anxiety into a shiver. He closed the window. But, still, I shuddered.

"Spring weather in Rome turns cold in the evening," he said. "Did you bring a coat?"

"No," I stammered.

"Tomorrow, go shopping with Nora and buy yourself one."

"I don't have money," I snapped. "Besides, I don't feel the need for a coat yet. I will buy one when I get paid."

The way Mr. Gamal demanded what I should do with my life was frightening and all too familiar. He smothered me with his imposing approach.

To cut his patronizing attitude short, I wished him a good evening and retired to my room. I showered and went to bed.

The next morning at 7:00 a.m., I walked into the dining room, holding the notebook and pen ready to assume my duties. I was still agitated by Gamal's overbearing approach and unsettled from Nora's cold reception. The tension between her and Gamal still shrouded the room with an eerie atmosphere.

Genevieve served espresso without sugar. I was used to having sugar with my Arabic coffee back home in Alexandria and in Lebanon. When she brought in the *fette biscottate*, I asked her if I could have sugar.

"You prefer café latte?" she asked.

Relieved, I replied, "Yes, please."

A few minutes passed before Gamal walked in, dressed in a white shirt and dark blue pants. A deep magenta silk tie hung untied around his neck. A refreshing fragrance filled the room. His beard looked shaved, and his face lit with an inviting smile. I relaxed.

"Buongiorno, Laila."

"Bonjour," I replied.

He acknowledged me with a nod, and a sense of comfort filled me.

"Can you help tie my cravatta?" he asked.

Cravate is French for a tie, so I assumed cravatta was Italian for "tie." Eager to please him, I began my first attempt ever to tie his tie. I failed. He faced the mirror hanging over the antique cabinet and, in slow motion, made a perfect knot.

"Tomorrow morning," he said, "will be your turn." He chuckled.

Gamal's warm approach gave me a sense of tranquility at times, and a sense of uncertainty at other times. However, at this moment, my fear subsided, and I began to feel hopeful again. There was so much I wanted to know and so much I wanted to do.

The next morning was my second attempt with the necktie; I succeeded. I became an expert and looked forward to this brief informal encounter every morning.

Gamal asked Nora to take me shopping for clothes suitable for work. "Nora, take Laila shopping today. A two-piece outfit would be appropriate," he said, "a blazer, a skirt, and pants instead of the mini-dress to wear at the embassy."

"I want to buy my own clothes," I asserted.

"You can pay me back from your salary," he said.

I rode with Nora in her Renault. She was speeding like all the other drivers on the road and remained quiet.

"You don't have to take me shopping," I said.

She ignored me.

I didn't know how to deal with her. I attributed her behavior to the loss of her mother. I wanted to help but was careful not to cross her boundaries. I decided to give her time to open up.

She took me to a store and picked up a long camel-colored wool coat.

"This will keep you warm," she stressed.

I liked her choice, but I wanted to appear assertive. I picked up a long black wool coat. Even though black was not a color I liked, I tried to impress on her that I had opinions of my own.

She then drove to a shoe store, still in annoying silence. I picked up a pair of black leather boots similar to the ones I saw displayed in a boutique at the airport. I wondered how many paychecks it would take to pay for the coat and boots.

The girl at the cashier stated the charges in thousands. I panicked.

"Nora, please return the boots," I said. "I don't think I could afford to pay back four hundred thousand liras."

"Italian currency is in liras, and the conversion to the dollar is in thousands," she mocked. "Don't worry; the amount is not that much."

Relieved, I agreed to continue shopping for a pair of brown pants and a wool beige sweater, both chosen by Nora. I went along with her choices to win her friendship. I succeeded. She invited me for coffee and pastry at a local bakery. She loosened up a little, but was still stingy with her emotions.

"I miss Mama," she confessed.

Her sudden trust startled me, but I composed myself and expressed sorrow with a frown. I wanted her to let out all the sad emotions she had bottled up since her mother passed away.

"She was my friend," she choked.

I didn't understand what she meant by 'my friend.'

"How about your father?" I asked.

"He is not my friend," she said, almost lashing out.

I sympathized with her show of anger. Her closeness to her mother struck a chord with me. I was grateful Mama was still alive.

"Would you like to leave?" I suggested to get her out of her sad mood.

"No!"

We stayed at the bakery talking and reminiscing about her mother. When she paid the receipt, she smiled.

"You and I could be friends."

"Of course," I said.

A warm and amicable relationship developed between us. We became inseparable and, except for the time I spent with her father, we listened to music together and went shopping and sightseeing. I tutored her in the Arabic language, and she introduced me to the Italian language.

Gamal soon put me on a strict work schedule. He assigned numerous documents to type—enough to keep me busy every morning. I learned from the letterheads that Mr. Gamal worked in the embassy.

In the beginning, Nora helped me. She did most of the typing, and we would then go out walking downtown and return home for lunch before her father came back. Gradually, and when I became comfortable typing, she would just sit in the room with a book and wait for me to finish.

Nora had just completed four years of college and had a desire to receive her master's degree. Since she was without school obligations, she shopped often for herself and for me, whether I wanted to or not, and she always refused to let me pay for my clothes.

I did not discuss my salary with her, but the checks exceeded my expectations. I was able to save most of my earnings for my education and to support Mama when she came to live with me in the near future.

Gamal blessed the closeness I developed with Nora and eased my assignments to allow us to spend more time together. His daughter's happiness was his priority.

Gamal was also sensitive toward my family situation and allowed me to contact my mother using the home phone whenever I pleased. I called her once every two weeks.

"Something doesn't sound right," Mama warned. "Gamal is a widower, and you are young."

I dismissed Mama's suspicion about Gamal's ulterior motives. He treated me like a daughter. But I could not get Mama to see him the way I did.

Five months passed, during which I learned enough of the Italian language to qualify for a course in a community college. I had saved enough of my salary for the dream I was keeping alive.

"I would like to register for a course in college," I said, trying to appeal to Gamal's gentle side.

The kind look I was used to seeing in his eyes turned cold. I saw a different man—the man Mama warned me about.

"You are not ready yet," he snapped.

Not sure how to respond or how much I would lose if I

questioned his reasons, I swallowed my disappointment and excused myself. I didn't need to hear any more to understand he had no intention of allowing me to pursue an education.

Instead, I used my saved money for a return ticket to Lebanon, keeping my return plan to myself. I contemplated moving out and starting a life on my own in Rome, but the thought of living alone scared me. I had no choice but to go back to Lebanon, to the family that encouraged me to continue my education.

CHAPTER XI

MR. ANWAR'S MARRIAGE PROPOSAL

One evening, Mr. Anwar materialized at Gamal's house. Gamal and Nora were not surprised. Even Genevieve and Zein, the African worker, knew about his arrival. I, however, was surprised.

"Your room has been prepared, Mr. Anwar," Genevieve said.

"The bath is ready, as you requested," said Zein.

Even though I was astounded to see him, for a brief moment, I wondered why he hadn't mentioned his visit to Italy. I received him with open arms and a warm hug. The surprise was pleasing.

Mr. Anwar and I spent a lot of time together. Gamal bought Anwar and me movie and theater tickets. Most weekdays, Gamal and Nora didn't come home for lunch. Anwar took the chance and baked my favorite Lebanese snacks. He also showered me with expensive pieces of jewelry he had brought from Lebanon. I sensed a web of special attention weaving around my everyday life. It was comforting.

"You can have few days off," Gamal said.

I wasn't clear as to why he gave me days off.

"I want to work," I said.

"Spend time with my brother. He needs your company to overcome his loneliness."

His request confused me. Why did he choose me to entertain his brother? Why give me days off while I got paid for pampering his brother? Nevertheless, I accepted.

The time I lived at Nagi's family, Anwar had been a good listener. I had trusted him and valued his opinion. But I wanted to focus on my goals and dreams and not on spending time with him doing nothing but having fun. The few days off that Gamal had granted me turned into weeks during which he pushed me to get closer to his brother.

"I want to go to college," I admitted to Anwar.

"Anything you want, you will get," he said.

Soon after, I noticed changes in the way they all treated me. Genevieve called me signorina and not Laila. Nora became aloof. The warmth that had developed between us changed into coldness and avoidance. On the other hand, I enjoyed Gamal and Anwar's excessive attention. I felt like a daughter who was lucky and blessed with their love. They provided me with a new trendy and stylish wardrobe. They also moved me to a room in the family quarter next to Anwar's bedroom. It was like I was promoted in the household from a secretary to a family member. Nothing in the way they treated me raised a flag or was worrisome.

One evening, when I was alone in my room, Nora asked me, "Do you know how old Anwar is?"

"Sixty-seven," I said. "He told me when we met in Beirut."

Nora could not understand how much I wanted a father figure, and that Anwar was the person I relied on to guide me through the turbulent time I had encountered since I left Egypt. I could talk to him about anything. He provided wise advice that supported my aspiration for education.

On college registration day, Anwar came with me. He asked if we could go for a coffee first. I agreed. I noticed his hands were shaking, and he seemed disoriented. He drove without paying attention to the road and passed by the coffee shop. He also ran a red light. When I alerted him, he apologized. I attributed his lack of concentration to his old age.

We ordered two espressos; then, he lit a Kent cigarette. His hands were still shaking. I waited for him to start the conversation as he had always done, but he remained quiet and spaced-out.

"Hey," I teased. "Where are you?"

He ignored the question and focused on extinguishing his cigarette. He then lit another one, inhaled deep, and released the smoke upward. By then, I knew something serious occupied his mind and that he needed to talk. So I waited.

"I have a proposal," he mumbled. "I want you to think before you reply."

"How much time are you giving me?" I giggled.

"A week," he said.

"A week is too long. How about now?"

"No," he said. "You need time to think over this proposal."

Like an impatient little girl anxious for a surprise, I begged him to reveal the proposal that would change my life all over again.

I crossed my arms, rested them on the table, and leaned forward, ready for him to speak.

He hesitated and directed his gaze away from me. He reached for the Kent pack again as he held a cigarette hanging between his fingers.

"You know," he said. "I would do anything for you."

I nodded with a smile. By then, I began to feel uneasy. There was something unusual and different about the way he spoke. He stuttered to find the right words and avoided eye contact. I noticed his legs were shaking and hoped he would calm down and start talking. When the waiter stopped by our table to ask if we needed anything, we both ignored him, even though my stomach growled, begging for food.

Spring was over. I saw through the glass window snow flurries cascading like stars. Everyone in the room expressed joy for what appeared to be the first snow of the year. It was the first time I had seen snow-white florets that showered from the sky. I excused myself and walked outside. I didn't realize I was the only one in the street, amazed by the snow. When I went back inside, Anwar was calmer and ready to talk.

"I want you to be my wife," he whispered, searching my eyes for a reaction.

I was taken aback by his daring proposal. My lips parted, but my voice died. The room spun. My body swam in perspiration, and my mind wandered back to the moment I turned fifteen and my father announced, "You and your sister will be married next week." Rawyia's voice tolled in my head. "Men want nothing from a divorced girl but sex."

I could see Anwar's mouth moving, but I couldn't hear his voice. I watched him through eyes floating in tears. I searched for the fatherly love he had showered me with and the kindness and trust I had come to rely on. Instead, his gaze was void of the kindness he had exhibited since he arrived. His eyes spewed perversion. The furrows on his face that I once admired turned into gutters harboring wickedness. He no longer looked distinguished with scattered gray hair as he appeared when I first met him. It became clear to me that I had been set up by him, his brother, and Nora. Each one of them played a role in the charade. All the care and help they offered had an expensive price—my future and my freedom. I refrained from asking him why he had not revealed his intention in Lebanon. I realized I had been trapped and that I had to think before reacting to his proposal.

"You don't have to answer now," he said, noting my hesitation.

My heart raced. Shaken and confused, I maintained a calm demeanor. I gave him no sign of acceptance or disapproval. Still, the experience of a sixty-seven-year-old man gave him the advantage over the mind of a twenty-one-year-old. He read disappointment and displeasure on my face.

I had to think since I had no place to go to in a new country with a language I had not yet learned to perfection. I remembered Mama's advice. "Your future life is the reflection of your own choices." My mother was right. Something was peculiar about Anwar and his motives, and my future would not include him.

"As my wife," he interjected, "you will have the education you aspire to and a home where you would be its queen."

Tears rolled down my cheeks. I remembered Mama's words when I was fifteen as she tried to convince me to marry Farook, a man forty years my senior. "He will treat you like a queen," she said.

"I don't want to be a queen," I answered. "I want to be a student." But I could not give Anwar that same answer.

The more Anwar spoke, the deeper my rejection and loathing grew. The night rolled in, announcing time to leave. We had been sitting since 2:00 in the afternoon, and now the clock struck 7:00 p.m. With coffee swimming in my stomach and a dry mouth, I asked Anwar if we could leave.

"Let's have dinner somewhere," he said.

I had no desire to spend another minute with him. I had decided to return to Lebanon and wasn't sure how Anwar and Gamal would react to my decision.

"No, thank you," I said. "Please take me back to your brother's home."

Like a cyclone, Anwar's proposal destroyed the foundation of my hopes, dreams, and goals. During the ride home, I thought of Mama and Rawyia and felt sick from the bitter taste of defeat. Going back meant failure. I wanted Mama to be proud of me, and I hated to hear Rawyia gloat about how right she had been all along. Even though I needed emotional support, I chose not to tell Rawyia or Mama until I got back to Lebanon.

That evening, I camped in my room. I couldn't resume the

regular routine with Gamal and Anwar. They would soon learn of my decision. I was not sure of their reaction, and that terrified me.

Nora walked into my room, uninvited. "I see," she said, "my uncle proposed."

I nodded, widening my eyes. She got closer and whispered in my ears. "I hope you turned him down."

Her words lifted my spirit. I found an ally to trust and reveal my plans, so I hugged her.

"Don't worry, Laila. You can count on me. You are not the first one that my uncle promised a job and brought here."

I was upset with Nora for not warning me. "I could have saved him the trip if I knew about his intention," I said.

"Pappy treats my uncle as a father."

The age difference between Anwar and his brother was visible. Anwar was much older than Gamal.

"My grandparents were killed in a car accident when Pappy was three years old, and my uncle was twenty. He undertook the father role."

"But he has married twice already," I said.

Nora ignored my statement and continued. "Pappy is indebted to his brother. My uncle waited until Pappy finished college before he married."

"But I ran away from home because I was forced into a marriage I didn't want," I said.

"Don't worry, Laila. Pappy doesn't approve of his brother's behavior."

With Nora's support and knowing that Gamal was dismayed with his brother's many attempts for marriage, I got the courage to turn Anwar's proposal down without hesitation.

The next morning, Genevieve knocked at my door. I invited her in. She had a bouquet of a dozen red roses. I knew they came from Anwar. No one had sent me roses before.

"Please take the roses to a different room," I said

She complied with a smile.

I knew that if I accepted Anwar's proposal, I would have fulfilled my dream for a college education. But I was not ready to exchange my freedom, even for a college education.

After that experience, I developed a more profound suspicion of men's intentions. I imagined every man in my life had an ulterior motive. I believed there was a hidden reason for the way each one expressed his love. I had no doubt that Papa loved me, but the way he demonstrated his love was selfish and unrelenting to the rigid rules he imposed on us. Reda, my older brother, and Ahmed, my cousin, were raised and trained to feel superior to us. Our father blessed their abuse and control.

Farook, the man I was forced to marry, also had a share in the way I perceived men, especially older men. He dismissed my request for a divorce and instead obtained a court order to force me to accept the marriage. Ghassan, the man I loved and believed, the one man who could restore my trust in men, cemented my disappointment in men when he left me and married another girl. Even Nagi didn't behave any different to help me hold onto the good impression I had developed about Lebanese men.

Growing up, Mama said I was born with a heart full of love and compassion. I believed her. I cherished that character trait in myself—a quality Rawyia fought hard to change. She urged me to use my head and not my heart to survive. I could not, and, in spite of my many disappointments, my heart was full of passion, ready to erupt for the right man, but not for Anwar.

"Please stay," Gamal said. "I will ask my brother to leave."

I lost trust in men's promises. Gamal could have been honest, but I could not take the chance. The only people I trusted were Nagi's mother and Fikry. I felt safe with them.

"I prefer to go back to Lebanon," I said.

Anwar avoided all contact with me during my last three last days in Italy before he flew back home. I welcomed his behavior with a deep sigh of relief.

My friendship with Nora deepened. Gamal respected my

desire to leave, but he asked if I could keep his daughter company for another two or three months.

"Every day I spend in Italy would make it hard to leave," I said.

I wanted to get back to college in Lebanon and not waste any more time.

I felt stronger and proud of myself for turning down the offer. I thought of what Mama told me about fate and destiny. She always believed no one had control over fate or destiny. I thought she couldn't be right. I convinced myself that the decision to leave was mine and that I was the one steering my future.

CHAPTER XII

BACK IN LEBANON

I planned to contact Rawyia for moral support upon landing in Beirut. I had missed her. I was let down and embarrassed at my first failed attempt at independence without her help. I hoped she would understand and refrain from saying "I told you so."

I longed for Mama's love as well, but I postponed a phone call until I settled down. I wanted to keep the pattern I started since I left, to just call her when I had good news to share. It tore me apart to hear her voice cracking and fading away, every time we spoke on the phone. She controlled her emotions to spare me worry and to keep me focused on my future.

"Alo, Rawyia, I am back," I said, holding on to the golden pendant Mama gave me to make sure it was still there around my neck. I wanted to feel Mama's presence alive against my skin for support.

First, there was a painful silence, then the gloating sound in her voice smothered all the hope I had left. "So, you are back. I hope you're ready to accept your sister's advice."

I had no doubt Rawyia wanted to help me. But I rejected her solutions. Marriage was not the way out. She chose a loveless marriage for herself for financial comfort. I couldn't spend the rest of my life in a marriage built on lies and deceit.

I had planned to go back to Nagi's family but was embarrassed. I wished Rawyia would ask me to come live with her. I just wanted a place where I would gather my thoughts and start fresh.

"My home is open for you; you know the condition," she told me.

Rawyia's unrelenting pressure could not have been more empowering. The more she pushed the marriage solution, the stronger I grew. I wasn't sure what I would do next, but I was determined to follow my dreams and stay free. "No one, not even you, Rawyia, could force me to abandon my goals," I told her.

Desolate but resilient, I took refuge at the Nagis'. They received me with open arms. None of them questioned my coming back, and life continued like it had not been interrupted.

I missed most of my second year of college. I spent the rest of the summer studying to catch up. Nothing occupied my mind except the final and Mama. I wanted to have an education and a secure job to help secure a comfortable life for her and me when we reunited.

I resumed the routine of my life with a pretend happy smile while loneliness drained my spirit and left me depressed. I longed for Mama and Rawyia, and I could no longer continue living on Fikry's financial support. I withdrew from social family gatherings. Nagi's family respected my need for space.

When I settled down, I called Mama and informed her about my return to Lebanon. She prayed for me without asking why.

"You can always come back home," she said.

She promised to help me continue my education. But I was not sure she could keep her promise. Life in Lebanon, with all the hard times I faced, offered me the freedom I would not have in Egypt.

The brief time I spent in Italy opened my eyes to a different world—a civilized society where girls and women were not forced to marry to follow an archaic culture. I left Italy dreaming of living there, but I knew that dream would not come true unless I had a college degree.

Living with Nagi's family went smoothly. Ghassan seemed to have vanished off the face of the earth. I assumed he left the country with his wife. It was time to let go of waiting and reminiscing; keeping his memory alive was distracting.

Mariam graduated and started a new job with her father as a journalist. I saw less of her, but she made sure to spend time with me whenever she had a chance. I developed a deep fondness for Nagi's mother and connected Mama with her. They became close friends. Mama felt comfortable with my living arrangements until, one day, she mentioned my father's cousin Mostafa, who resided in Canada.

When my grandparents passed away, my father lived with his maternal uncle, Mostafa. He had married a European woman, left Egypt, and settled in Canada.

"Mostafa," Mama started, "is in Alexandria visiting."

Growing up, Mostafa was Papa's favorite cousin, and he had not visited Egypt since he left fifteen years ago.

"Your father," she said, "is in Syria".

I paid little attention to Mama's dilemma. Next time we talked, she mentioned that Mostafa had gone back to Canada and that he had felt disappointed at not seeing my father.

"Mostafa," she said, "talked to me about how much he owed your father for helping him in school when they were young and living together."

Mama could have talked all her life about what my father had done in his life, and it would not interest me a bit. Since I left Egypt, I had no desire to know anything about him.

"Would you like Mostafa's address in Canada?"

"What for?" I said.

"I talked to him about what happened with you and Rawyia,

and he blamed your father."

Mostafa was the only one outside our family to have blamed my father. Mama's statement attracted my attention and made me want to know more about that cousin whom I never met nor heard of growing up.

"Yes, Mama, send me his address, please."

I was busy trying to put my life together, and the telephone conversation with Mama revolved around the progress I made in my life. She never talked about herself nor my siblings. I brushed off the sadness in her voice, and her loss of hope of ever seeing me again, which she tried to convey in so many different words.

"May God keep me alive until I see you," she murmured.

Her voice cracked every time she expressed her wish. My heart ached with longing. Everything I did revolved around her coming to live with me. But she always had those ominous words that she would not see me again. Unlike her, I was hopeful and optimistic about our future together.

"Mama, you will see me, and soon," I said.

My own struggle kept me from thinking of Mama's suffering. All three of her children were wandering alone around the world. Every time I called her, she offered to send me money. I turned her down.

"Don't worry, Mama. Rawyia is taking good care of me," I said to comfort her.

"I know, dear, Rawyia calls me every day."

My sister and I shared concern about the hard time Mama was going through since we left home but we always found solace in believing that Mama would one day soon join us.

"How about Hady?" Mama asked choking.

"He is fine," I lied. I worried about Hady's whereabouts. Rawyia informed me that he called her, and that he was working odd jobs as he traveled around Europe. I wondered what kind of job he was doing. Hady was a teenager, inexperienced, and had been a spoiled child. But I knew my brother to be independent, proud and determined. If he wanted something, he would go after it, no matter how difficult it was. He would not ask for anyone's help.

Hady ran away from Egypt to avoid being drafted into the army. Our father could have helped him skip the duty with a signature. Instead, he denied our brother the parental consent that would have kept him in school and out of the military. It was his way to punish Hady for having a girlfriend. I understood why my brother severed the umbilical cord that connected him with everyone in Egypt. I promised myself I would search for him once I settled down.

It took Mama three weeks to get Mostafa's address in Canada. Papa had the address, but I knew Mama couldn't get it from him. He would have been suspicious and would have refused if he had known that she wanted the address for me. When my sister and I left Egypt, Papa made Mama swear to never contact us. But she did.

I kept the address for months. I thought of Canada as a backup in case things didn't work well in Lebanon. I had never met Mostafa. I thought of writing to him, but I feared he would tell Papa. Mama said Mostafa loved our father and respected him, but she also mentioned that Mostafa blamed Papa for forcing us into marriage. I had faith in his support.

Nagi's family offered me the college opportunity, security, and safe shelter until Fikry lost his job. I knew the time had come to move on. I was ready for that day.

Nagi's mother asked me to stay. I refused and decided to move on. She respected my decision and assured me their home would remain open if I ever came back. I had no one but my Uncle Mostafa, and I reached out for his help.

"Dear Uncle Mostafa,

I hope my letter will find you and your family in good health. I am not sure if we ever met before. I am Laila, your cousin Kamel's middle daughter. Mama informed me that she has spoken to you about my marriage and divorce.

I learned from her that you chose a European woman for a wife and that you have two daughters. I am sure they enjoy a liberal life in Canada.

Since I left home four years ago, I've been searching for a better life. All doors slammed shut in my face. You and your family are my last hope. If you could help me move to Canada, I would be indebted to you for the rest of my life. I am not sure how I would travel, but I count on you to find me a way. Please let me know if you could help."

I wrote another letter to Mostafa. In that letter, I explained in detail what had happened to Rawyia, Hady, and me, and how Rawyia had been pushing me to marry someone again just to stay safe. I mentioned the kindness of the family that embraced me, and that I found it hard to burden them now that Fikry had lost his job. I mailed the letter with trepidation and hoped he would offer some kind of assistance.

I was lost, vulnerable, and insecure as I entertained all alternative possibilities, but none seemed feasible without financial freedom. Moving in with Rawyia was one solution, which I refused to consider. I thought of asking Mama to send me money until I got a job, but Papa controlled the household finances, and Mama could not send help without his knowledge.

Nagi's mother insisted on keeping me at their home until I got a response from Mostafa. I agreed. Although I appreciated their help, the once-solid ground under my feet turned mushy.

I checked the mailbox every day and befriended the postman. I learned the meaning of patience during my divorce ordeal. But, this time, the waiting was painful. The independence I dreamed of depended on Mostafa's reply. Either destiny was still not done with my future, or she would give up on me. The thought of going back to live with Rawyia under her conditions tormented me.

Depression crept in, and I lost weight. Mariam and her mother provided extra care and love, but nothing helped. I feared the uncertainty of tomorrow.

Fate Knocked on My Door

It had been six weeks since I mailed the letter to Mostafa. The waiting was over one afternoon when the mailman knocked on our door.

"I have a letter for Mademoiselle Laila," he said.

His voice was loud, and it reached me in my room. I came out running. He hid the letter behind his back.

"I need my reward first," he said.

He handed me a receipt to sign. Mariam went inside to get money.

He handed me a thick white envelope. Glancing at the sender, it read Mostafa and the word Canada at the bottom of the sender's address. I thanked the postman and ran to my room, stamping kisses on the envelope.

Fear of disappointment kept me from opening the envelope to read what Mostafa had sent me. Mariam walked into the room and snatched the envelope from my hand.

"If you don't open it, I will."

She ran out of the room, waving the letter. "Catch me if you can!"

Nagi's mother walked out of the kitchen, laughing. "Give Laila the letter."

I was apprehensive and not ready for a disappointment. I left them in the living room and walked to the kitchen. I uncovered the steaming pot on the stove and tasted the rice. I was hungry; nevertheless, my appetite needed a happy trigger to activate it.

Footsteps trailed behind me. I stayed still. Mariam wrapped her arms around my waist with the letter in one hand. "Here, open it now!" she demanded.

"No, you open it," I said.

Mariam picked up a butter knife from the drawer and proceeded to the bedroom. I followed. A letter, papers that looked like forms, and a long thin rectangular booklet with the word Air Canada printed on it materialized from the envelop.

Mariam screamed, jumping up and down. I froze.

"Good news?" I asked.

I assumed Mostafa had sent me something good, but I stayed calm with a heart ready to jump out of my chest. Then I collapsed on my bed.

"You're going to Canada!" Mariam said. She threw the contents of the letter on my bed, then took me in her arms. She showered my face with kisses. "Get up!" she ordered.

I stood up. She took my hands and forced me to twirl.

I wasn't sure whether to join her in the joyous laughter or wait to see what my uncle sent me. I thought it was a blurry dream, the kind of dream where one couldn't remember the details, or if they were good or bad. When Mariam at last calmed down, apprehension turned into fear—fear of the unknown.

I released myself from Mariam's grip and picked up the ticket. I could not understand English very well, but I knew what an airplane ticket looked like. I didn't need to read the content of the letter to realize the booklet was an airplane ticket, and what that ticket would do for me and for my future.

I thought of Mama. I wanted to let her know that she was right, and that destiny was not done yet with my future. I could not move. My body shook like it had been struck by a tremor.

"Calm down, my dear," Mariam's mother said, and handed me the folded papers to read.

"It's an open ticket to Canada," Mariam said.

I did not know what an open ticket meant, but I figured from Mariam's joyous reaction that it was something good.

"With this ticket," Mariam said, "you can travel to Canada any time, and come back here anytime you wish. It's valid for one whole year."

Though I still couldn't understand what she meant, I felt happy to know I could come back. I paced the room, then froze. I couldn't handle the elation running through my veins like numbing medicine, paralyzing my thinking. The thought of leaving the Arab world never crossed my mind, but now it was a reality I had to learn to accept. Mariam's mother placed the bundle of papers in my hand.

I opened the handwritten one.

"Dear daughter," Mustafa wrote.

My body stopped shaking. The ground under my feet stabilized. I regained the confidence I thought I had lost, and my surroundings seemed to share my joy. Birds flying outside the room tweeted louder, and the aroma of the Lebanese spices that had always permeated the apartment became intense. I didn't need to read any further. I had a ticket, and Mostafa considered me a daughter. Destiny could not have offered me more. I felt blessed.

Mostafa's offer fulfilled the dream that I once considered a mirage. I asked Mariam and her mother to pinch me. I needed to know I was awake and not sleeping. My heart raced, but this time, it ran with joy. I had cocooned myself inside a shell of uncertainty and loss. But the words in Mostafa's letter came like the dew shower that falls on a closed bud; they opened a new and promising future. I could not turn it down.

Then I opened the other papers. They were documents that I couldn't quite decipher. On top were printed the words Immigration and Naturalization. I handed them to Mariam. I knew what the word immigration meant but couldn't make the connection.

"How lucky you are!" she exclaimed.

"I know," I said, not knowing what she meant.

"They are immigration documents!"

I wasn't sure of what immigration was all about, or how it would affect my future. However, Mariam's reaction and the happy smile on her mother's face gave me a sense of peace. This immigration must be good.

When Mariam explained that the papers were applications to apply for admittance into Canada, the room spun. The mixture of joy and ambivalence was more than I could handle.

"Can I have a moment to myself please."

Mariam and her mother kissed me on the forehead and walked out.

The next morning, Mariam helped me fill out the application. Except for my passport, I did not take any personal documents when I left Egypt. I asked Mama to mail copies of my birth, marriage, and divorce certificates. Canadian immigration also requested a letter of recommendation from my employer.

Mr. Tony was the main employer I worked for after I left Egypt. The thought of seeing him again made me sick to my stomach. I had spent three months working in his office before I quit when he sexually assaulted me.

I called the Canadian Embassy and asked if they would waive the letter.

"Without the letter, we would not process your application," the girl in the embassy said, hanging up before I could state the reason for my request.

I put the application aside for one week, trying to find a way to avoid facing Mr. Tony again. Mariam and her father called his office several times to ask for a meeting. His secretary turned them down with different excuses.

"Ask the secretary to send Laila a letter of recommendation," Mariam said to her mother.

The next morning, the secretary called and informed us that Mr. Tony asked me to meet him in his office alone.

"Why alone?" Mariam's father asked.

The secretary hung up without answering the question.

I contemplated dismissing the immigration opportunity until I called Rawyia and shared my thoughts.

"That would be the biggest mistake of your life," she said. "What are you afraid of? A man? You are stronger than any man. Face him with pride and learn from your experience. The kind of man that attorney is will not be the first or the last you will meet. You have chosen to lead an independent life so don't allow this despicable creature to stop you."

Rawyia's support surprised me. She had been distant and

even pushed me to marry for security reasons. I wanted nothing more than to leave Lebanon with her blessings.

"Thank you, Rawyia. I have always counted on you for advice, and you have not disappointed me."

"Immigrating to Canada is the opportunity I wish I had before I married Marwan. In Canada, all you need is a job to support yourself while going to college. You will never lead an independent life in Lebanon or any Arab country."

We laughed. Rawyia made my inevitable transition sound rosy, and I believed her.

"I promise to invite you over once I settle down," I said.

"Think of yourself, La," she said.

The next morning, I set up an appointment with Mr. Tony. When I entered his office and saw him sitting behind his desk, all my enthusiasm turned into disgust. I turned around to leave.

"Please stay," he said. "I am sorry for the pain I have caused you."

I didn't feel sorry for him and I did not forgive him. I thought of Rawyia's words before I turned around and looked him in the eye.

"Have you prepared the recommendation letter?" I asked.

He fetched it from his drawer and proceeded toward me. I took a few steps back. He stopped, then placed the letter on his desk. I took it and walked out.

I accepted the idea of immigrating. However, the thought of being so far away from Mama was painful. I knew she suffered as well, yet she demonstrated strength for my sake.

"I am happy," Mama said. "However, the farther you go, the less hope I have to see you again."

I listened to Mama weep, and I thought of going back to Egypt to spare her the heartache. "I could come back if you want me to," I told her.

"You have no future here," she said, her voice cracking.

"I promise to come back for you, Mama."

I meant my promise. In fact, finding a job was important to help me bring Mama to live with me.

Mama counted on me to help her get out of Egypt, although she never expressed in words her desire to leave home. Canada became the country where all my dreams would come true.

Rawyia praised the move to Canada. "Now I feel at peace, knowing you will be living in a country far away from here."

I realized then why Rawyia was hard on me. She knew that, as a Muslim, divorced, and a young Arab girl, I could not survive on my own in a country that perceives girls as an inferior species to boys. She worried about me, and I discovered she was right all along.

Rawyia asked me to move in with her while I prepared for the trip to Canada.

We spent three weeks shopping for things I would need in Canada. In her desire to shower me with clothes, shoes, purses, makeup, and toothpaste, she forgot that, in Canada, I could find everything. She filled me with advice that I heard before about not trusting men.

"Don't worry about Mama," she assured me. "I will take care of her."

Rawyia promised to follow me to Canada and bring Mama with her.

Every day that we spent together, my heart was shredded a hundred times over. I felt weak and unable to show strength. Rawyia knew what I was going through but, like she had always done, she stayed strong, pumping me up with courage and confidence. She did an excellent job of hiding her sadness. She carried herself with the majesty of someone sure of her authority.

"You are my favorite," she said. "I will always look after you, no matter how far you go."

Memories floated in the distant horizon, reminding me of the time Rawyia and I were young girls living in Alexandria. We grew up in a family of six children, an aunt, a cousin, and five maids. Rawyia performed the role of the older sister with perfection. We laughed, cried, and played together. We went to the same school and shared a bedroom. We fell asleep in each other's arms soothed by our breathing sounds.

"Please forgive me for pushing you to get married," Rawyia said.

Tears of gratitude welled up in my eyes. I hugged her. I never doubted Rawyia's love. I was used to her emotional control in times of pressure.

"I am glad you approve," I said.

"As a matter of fact," she replied, "going to Canada would be much better than staying here. I wish I had waited."

"Would you divorce Marwan if you had an opportunity to travel?"

"Yes, I would," she said.

We laughed and hugged. No matter how much we disagreed, love brought us back together.

"You were the one that stood by me when everyone in the family considered me immoral and rebellious," Rawyia said, stamping kisses all over my face.

For a moment, we were again the two happy young girls plotting a new adventure.

"Moving to Canada," she said, "will be perfect for you to pursue your studies and work at the same time."

"Yes, and without a husband," I said.

"Don't fall in love before you reach your goals," she cautioned me.

I smiled at how Rawyia kept on giving me advice on the last night we spent together.

We couldn't sleep, so we moved onto the balcony. The full moon lit up Rawyia's eyes enough to expose her trapped tears. We ran out of words. Our souls and hearts communicated until the fresh air of September chased us inside. We fell asleep in each other's arms, just like we did as young girls back in Alexandria.

The next day, we stopped by Mariam's home. Fikry, Mariam, Nagi, and their mother were home.

"I will visit you in Canada," Nagi said.

Nagi's father asked me to follow him to the dining room. He retrieved from his pocket a folded packet of Canadian dollars secured with a red rubber band.

"This is a thousand dollars," he said, handing it to me. "You will need it."

I knew he wanted me to feel comfortable accepting his generous offer. A thousand Canadian dollars was a lot of money, though, and Nagi's family was not wealthy.

"I cannot accept it. Thank you for offering," I said.

I turned around to leave the room. He grabbed me by the hand and insisted.

"I will accept one hundred dollars or nothing," I said.

He handed me two one-hundred-dollar bills.

"Thank you," I told him, grateful for his offering.

The goodbye was painful, especially the farewell of Nagi's mother. She cried as if Mariam was the one leaving. She couldn't let go of me until Fikry separated us. As I expected, they expressed their commitment to helping me if things didn't work out in Canada.

"Our home will always be open to you," Mariam's parents said.

Out of curiosity, I asked Mariam to let me know if she heard from Ghassan. I still hoped Rawyia had lied about Ghassan's marriage, and that one day he would show up looking for me.

"Look after yourself," she whispered.

At the airport, I caved in to my emotions and cried hard in Rawyia's arms. She, too, couldn't control herself. We both feared the long distance would separate us, and I could see the concern in her eyes. Until that moment, I didn't realize how much I was going to miss Rawyia.

I knew we would reunite again someday soon. With that hope, I let go of Rawyia's embrace and faded away from her sight, going through the security gate, waving goodbye and blowing her kisses.

CHAPTER XIII

IN TORONTO

During the flight to Toronto, like a silent spectator, I pondered over the years that had gone by. I tried to stop stressing over things I had no control over to allow the other self inside me to emerge—one who was calmer, wiser, and more secure. But the separation from the people I loved was challenging. I was seventeen when I had last seen Mama on my wedding night. In a few months, I would turn twenty-one and would be thousands of miles away from her. It broke my heart to think how stressful this was for her. However, the encouragement she provided, along with her sacrifices, would be cherished forever.

Mostafa resided in the province of Ontario—the English-speaking part of Canada. His house was in the suburbs of Toronto. I wasn't sure if he and his family spoke Arabic. Mostafa had lived most of his life away from Egypt. I read in Mostafa's letter that he had two teenage daughters. I counted on them to teach me English.

Fikry showed me on the map the vast land Canada occupied. He also mentioned that, in parts of Canada, like Montreal and Quebec City, people spoke French. I thought if I could not learn English, I could always move to one of those two cities. In a rare moment, I thanked Papa for putting me in French schools, and I thought he might have been a good father after all. However, that empathy faded away once I remembered he was the reason I left Egypt.

The long flight to Canada gave me plenty of time to reminisce about the life I left behind. No matter how much I tried to detach myself, I still struggled with different exhausting thoughts—longing, uncertainty, excitement, regret, and triumph. I imagined Mama and Rawyia watching me, and I raised my can of ginger ale and said softly," Cheers." Not long after, I fell asleep for the rest of the flight.

The first pleasant experience with Canadians occurred at the airport when I stopped by the immigration officer's desk. He asked about my status, and I replied, "Alien."

He responded with a smile, "Welcome! You won't be 'alien' in Canada after today."

His reception gave me hope and tranquility. I believed then and there that Canada was the country where I would spend the rest of my life.

Mostafa and his wife would be waiting for me at the airport. I had no idea what he looked like, but he had no problem recognizing me. "Laila!" he hollered. "I couldn't miss you. You look like your father."

I had been told that I resembled my father. I heard Mama and my aunt praise Papa for his good looks. I didn't see him as handsome. As a young girl, I focused on his mean demeanor and not his physical attributes. Anyway, I smiled, even though I didn't appreciate the compliment.

Mostafa wrote in his letter that he owned an athletic club in Toronto. When I met him, I questioned his claim. He was stocky and overweight around his middle. The blond, blue-eyed woman that stood next to him was built like a man—considerably taller than Mostafa, with broad shoulders, layered with fat as well. She appeared reserved and stingy with enthusiasm.

"Melissa, my wife," Mostafa introduced us.

I approached her for a hug like the traditional way we greeted back home when we meet someone for the first time. She pulled back and settled for a handshake. Mostafa wrapped both hands around mine—a cultural gesture to signal a warm welcome.

I was taken aback by Melissa's cold welcome. When she eyed me from head to toe with displeasure, my heart pounded hard. I was baffled and nervous. What had I done to annoy her?

"You should have worn jeans," Melissa said, looking at the black mini-dress I wore.

Embarrassed and surprised at her comment, I turned my gaze to Mostafa, searching for his reaction. He looked amused, giving me a sense of his disapproval of her statement. I grinned.

Melissa spoke perfect Arabic, and that made me happy. Mostafa must have taught her. The joy of hearing her speak my language helped me overcome her mean comment.

I had worn a mini-skirt and medium-heel white shoes. Weather in September was still hot and humid in Toronto. The air was clean, and the sun blazed in the indigo sky. There was enough warmth in the atmosphere to melt the cold demeanor of Melissa. I had to stay positive and convince myself that Mostafa loved me. After all, he was my father's cousin, and they were raised together in the same household after Papa lost his parents when he was five years old. Mostafa walked ahead of us to the parking lot without saying a single word.

He came back in a station wagon. The body had brown wood, and the gate opened sideways. I noticed a "Country Squire" sign on the frame. The station wagon was more significant in size than any car in Lebanon or Egypt.

The silence during the car ride made me nervous and uncomfortable. I thought maybe my choice of clothes triggered Melissa's dismay. I sank deep in my seat and remained quiet.

"The girls," Melissa said, "Nora and Naira are still in school. After school, they have piano lessons."

"Great." I said, "I can't wait to meet them." Because she spoke in perfect Arabic, I replied in Arabic.

"I will go pick them up," she said. "Mostafa is going back to work."

"It's okay," I said. "Don't worry about me."

"We are not," she snapped. "You will get used to the routine."

The rigidity in her voice gave me the chills. For a moment, I questioned the move I made. Nevertheless, I convinced myself that there was much to gain from living in Canada, and the freedom to choose my future gave me the strength to stay positive.

For a brief moment, Mostafa caught my eyes through the rearview mirror. I read assurance in the way he looked at me. His eyes shined with a warm smile to comfort me. I smiled and threw my shoulders back. I turned my gaze to the street, admiring with fascination the vast space, clean roads, and the quiet ride so different from Lebanon, Egypt, and even Italy. Back there, the sound of car horns blowing was deafening. Lebanese people impressed me at how they followed driving rules, until I saw the Canadians' respect for traffic lights. I fell in love with the country. Streets were vast compared to the narrow and ancient roads in Egypt, Lebanon, and Italy. Roads were constructed many decades ago before Canada was established as a country. It struck me how the streets were empty except for cars. There were no pedestrians or vendors on the street, like in the Middle East and Italy. A massive building as big as the pyramids appeared; it had glass windows and no balconies. But why would they need terraces? There was nothing there to entertain them.

It took Mostafa one-and-a-half hours to drive through different freeways before we reached their home: a three-story house nestled in a well-manicured cul de sac. Maple trees lined the sidewalk on both sides. The streets were flat, unlike back home where potholes were the norm and broken sidewalks were left without maintenance.

Mostafa's neighborhood seemed deserted except for a young blond girl who strolled with a white poodle on a leash. She smiled when our eyes met, even before we got out of the car. The summer sun bathed us with a moist breeze, but the heat failed to melt the icy attitudes of Melissa and Mostafa. The rigidity between them reminded me of the chronic tension between my parents. I wished they had the love and warmth that connected Nagi's parents and wondered if I could survive in this stoic environment. I figured, since Mostafa grew up with my father, he would not behave any better than my father. I counted on Nora and Naira to compensate for their mother's aloof welcome.

I stood in the foyer, holding my small suitcase. I glimpsed at myself in a mirror hanging on the wall. Humidity dampened my hair and turned it into what looked like a ball of tangled wires. I ran my fingers through the tight curls and then shook my head with displeasure. I had always hated how my hair looked during the summer months in Alexandria. But, over time, I learned to accept everything about me, even my curly hair. This would be the least of my worries after moving to live in Canada. I looked again in the mirror, threw my shoulders back, and smiled. A current of empowerment ran through my veins, which I needed to stay on a positive track going forward in this new country.

Nora and Naira had left a trail of clothes all over the family room. I figured from the size of the tee shirts and shoes that they must belong to the girls. Half-empty glasses of milk still sat on a table in the kitchen, and one charred square of bread on a plate still emitted a stuffy smell in the house. Open glass jars of red and orange jams sat on the counter, and two full glasses of orange juice were untouched.

I pulled out a chair and looked out the window. The setting sun painted the sky a dozen shades of magenta, punctuated by gray clouds. I remembered the sun in Alexandria when it kissed the Mediterranean goodnight and melted away over the horizon. Mama waited for that moment before she announced it was time to leave the beach and head home. Looking outside the window, all I saw was Mama standing by the stove, her beautiful smile lighting up her face, making her very special falafel that she prided herself on as being the most delicious.

Papa, who refused to acquire the taste of fried food, made an exception for Mama's fried falafel. The round balls were the size of meatballs. She mixed dry fava beans, green onions, leeks, parsley, coriander, yellow onions, salt, cumin, and a dash of cayenne pepper. She soaked the dry fava beans overnight. In the morning, she put all the ingredients in the manual grinding machine until she got the right consistency of paste. She preferred it a little coarse. She poured oil into a deep pot and let it reach a high temperature. She then formed the mixture into a ball and, one by one, she coated each of them with sesame and dropped them into the hot oil. When they turned golden and crisp outside, she placed them into a colander to drain out excess fat. They were green and moist inside, and their aroma was irresistible.

"What makes your falafel so special?" I asked.

She raised her hands close to my face, wiggled her fingers, and smiled. "The secret is in those fingers," she said.

I swallowed, sensing the aroma tickling my taste buds. Painful loneliness and longing for Mama settled deep in my heart and shook me to the core. I shivered and struggled to keep tears from flowing down my cheeks.

I walked back to the foyer and collected what the girls had left behind on the carpeted floor. I wanted to win Melissa's acceptance from the first day.

Before she left to pick up her daughters from school and take them to their piano lesson, she pointed out a room on the second floor as the one I would occupy. I had to convince myself that this was the way people in Canada communicated. The absence of emotions hit me hard. Melissa had not shown any consideration of how I felt coming to a new country and a new home. I hoped she would have received me with open arms.

Mostafa had already left in the Audi. I tried to cope with disappointment, but could not. I longed for Mama and Rawyia. I needed their emotional support, love, and affection.

I straightened the family room and cleaned the kitchen before I took my suitcase and went upstairs to my room.

It was all white and sterile like a doctor's reception area. Windows were closed, trapping the odor of soap and shampoo mixed with the cinnamon in the zucchini muffins. I chuckled. Back home, we never used zucchini for the baking.

A white wood bed was tucked in one corner facing the closet. A small square mirror hung on the wall, reflecting the mature maple tree in the neighbor's backyard. The sky-blue shag carpet broke the cold theme of the room. But it was the white dial-up phone on the square white night table that filled my soul with warmth. It would connect me with Mama and Rawyia. It became the roommate I needed in my lonesome space. I waited for Mostafa to return so I could ask him if I could use it to call Mama and Rawyia.

I arranged my clothes in the closet and took a shower. It was already dark outside. The crickets began a loud chorus I was not used to. I covered my ears with a pillow and fell asleep.

The next morning, I woke up to the sound of whispers. The sunlight had already penetrated through the sheer drapes and illuminated the room. I opened my eyes and noticed the door ajar and two pairs of happy eyes staring at me. I sat up and smiled. They pushed the door wide open, jumped in bed and showered me with hugs and kisses. In broken Arabic, they introduced themselves.

I knew from Mama that Nora was one year older than Naira and was the outspoken one. They could be mistaken for twins. They reminded me of the closeness I shared with Rawyia. Naira and Nora were gifted with long golden thick hair, fair but sun-saturated complexions, almond-shaped and large sky-blue eyes—a witness to their Scandinavian ancestry. But the long black lashes originated from their father's side. Mostafa had written in his letter that Nora and Naira were in junior high, so I figured from the dark blue uniforms they had on that they attended a private school. They gave me no chance to ask questions, brush my teeth, or dress up. They grabbed me by the hands to join them for breakfast.

Nora and Naira took a turn serving me a glass of milk, another filled with orange juice. Melissa, who had been in the kitchen preparing breakfast, greeted me with a cold "good morning" without eye contact. The girls each planted a quick kiss on Melissa's cheek. She did not reciprocate. I gathered the girls had inherited the warmth from our side of the family.

Melissa offered me something brown and shaped like a mushroom. "Would you like to try a zucchini muffin?" I never liked zucchini and had never tried a muffin, but I liked the aroma of this homemade Canadian treat. I served myself. She then asked if I wanted to try a Macintosh apple. "It's tangy and crisp," she said. In no time, I acquired a taste for this kind of apple. The ones we had back home were red and golden, which I found tasteless.

Mostafa joined us and, like Melissa, he was stingy with words during breakfast. Anxiety crept inside me and I wondered if their disconnection was caused by my presence or if they had been distant before I became part of their family. I felt grateful for Naira and Nora's warmth and happy demeanor. I counted on them to break the icy, sterile ambiance in the house.

The routine that Melissa had mentioned when she picked me up from the airport began when they all left the house after breakfast and came back late in the day.

I spent my days cleaning and watching Sesame Street on TV. Melissa advised me to watch it if I wanted to learn English. But I needed to practice speaking English with someone.

It was seven in the evening when they all came back home.

Melissa looked surprised, but it was the girls who hugged and kissed me.

"Thank you for cleaning the mess we left behind," they said.

"You don't have to clean. We have a housekeeper that comes twice a week," Melissa told me.

Nora, Naira, and Melissa asked me to speak Arabic with them. The chance of learning their language became almost impossible. I had to find a way. I knew that, with my French education, English would be easy to learn. Melissa and Mostafa had no time to drive me to and from the community school close by their neighborhood, but more than walking distance. There was no bus route close by. I needed someone to drive me.

With each passing day at Mostafa's home, boredom and loneliness filled me with depression. I explored possibilities of work. I searched in the *Toronto Sun*, but all the jobs listed were tailored for English-speaking people. I thought of going back to Lebanon. I spoke to Rawyia on the phone. She discouraged me from returning home and urged me to be patient.

"Don't ever think of coming back," she said. "Stay where you are!"

Many times, I cried, but Rawyia kept the pressure on. "You will thank me one day," she said.

Mama asked me to return to Alexandria. She could never hold back her tears when we spoke on the phone. She had lost Rawyia, Hady, and me, and she wanted nothing more than to have us back at home.

"I worry," Mama said, "that I will die before I see you."

Torn between Rawyia's advice and Mama's suffering, I fell apart, lost weight, and stayed in my room most of the time when Mostafa's family were home.

"What's wrong?" Mostafa asked. "Has anyone done something to upset you?"

"No, I just miss Mama," I said

"I understand." he said, "Life could be boring here if you don't find something to keep you busy."

"I want to find a job," I told him.

"First, learn the language, and I will help you find something," he said and kissed me on the forehead. "You just turned twenty-one last April?"

"Yes," I replied with a smile.

"Would you like to go with Melissa and me to a party?" he asked.

I nodded. I wanted so much to go out and meet other people.

To cheer me up, Mostafa and Melissa took me to one of the parties they attended. Naira and Nora stayed home. It pleased me to be treated like an adult.

I put on my black mini-dress. I revived my sad face with light makeup and used Nora's hot iron to smooth my curls.

I learned from Mostafa that the party would be at one of his associates' homes. "They are all Canadians," he said. "Of course, not counting you and me." He laughed.

From the outside, Mr. Edward's home looked larger than Mostafa's home. I noticed many Mercedes parked in the long driveway and on the street leading to the house. I figured they were wealthy people, and I worried if I would fit in.

When we arrived, I saw people entering the house, but they were all as old as Mostafa and Melissa, even older. Once inside, I realized I was the youngest guest. Lost, I took refuge in a dark corner of the living room, leaning against the wall and crossing my arms over my chest instinctively. I wandered with my eyes, admiring the art hanging on the walls and the classic style of furniture that reminded me of home in Alexandria.

A woman with a white apron holding an oval platter with hors d'oeuvres invited me to try some. I could smell the melting cheese aroma stuffed inside the round pastry puffs. I picked up the white napkin she offered and took one. Then I turned my gaze to the faces of men and women dancing and to the ones drinking. None of them had a dark complexion like Mostafa and me. I felt thirsty and hungry for more appetizers but felt shy, so I remained standing in my corner until a tall and not-so-old man stopped and stood next to me.

"Would you like a drink?" he said.

I nodded.

I had not paid attention to his facial details, but his light brown eyes that sat deep under his golden eyebrows struck my shyness like an arrow zooming at a target with success. I shook.

The tall man came back, holding two crystal glasses half-filled with golden liquid and ice. He handed me one drink and then touched his to mine.

"Cheers," he said.

He introduced himself as Michael, and I replied, "Laila."

I recognized the smell of alcohol when I took a sip from my glass. I knew it was whiskey. I had seen Rawyia drink with her husband, and I had become familiar with the smell. I never acquired the taste for drinking alcohol, in spite of repeated attempts by Rawyia. After the first sip, I placed my glass on the closest table, and I felt Michael's eyes follow me.

"Would you like a coke or apple juice instead?" he asked.

"Yes, please," I replied.

Before Michael returned with the drink, Melissa appeared and asked that we leave. I followed her, not knowing why we had to end the evening before it even started.

In the car, Mostafa drove and Melissa started speaking in a language I was not familiar with. She sounded angry, and Mostafa kept nodding as if in agreement with whatever she complained about.

I sat in the back seat and wondered if I had done something wrong, but remained silent all through the ride back home.

Mostafa and Melissa disappeared into their bedroom, and I could hear them shouting. I went to my room, closed the door, and forced myself to sleep.

In the morning, Mostafa and Melissa's argument continued loud, still in the language I could not understand. I heard my name mentioned and figured the dispute must have been about me. The anxiety and fear I experienced when I grew up listening to my parents argue returned. Fear turned my hopes and dreams upside down. A gut premonition warned me about gloomy days developing, and that staying at my uncle's house would soon come to an end. I prepared myself for the worst.

I stayed in my room until everyone left, and the house sounded quiet. I walked around the house, consumed with insecurity, loneliness and loss. I needed Rawyia and Mama's love and encouragement to continue my life in Canada.

I called Rawyia first. She had been the one that filled me with confidence and painted a rosy picture of our lives away from home.

"Alo," I said. "It's me, Laila."

"I know," she said. "What's wrong, La?"

Rawyia knew from my voice that something was wrong. She would not have asked me what was wrong unless she sensed something unusual and the timing of the call. Morning in Canada is late night in Lebanon.

"I want to come back," I said.

"You will stay where you are!" she ordered.

Rawyia's voice came through the telephone line like bullets aimed at each thought I had in my head about going back. I took a deep breath and fought a strong urge to cry.

"Let me tell you," she snapped, "my husband is very sick, and I am pregnant."

Rawyia's news about her pregnancy filled my heart with happiness. But sadness tinted the joy upon hearing about her husband's sickness. She sounded concerned and disturbed.

"La," she said with a mellow voice, "promise me to never give up."

"I promise," I said.

"Write me the reason for wanting to come back," she said.

I honored the promise I made to Rawyia and searched for ways to keep myself occupied and connected with the outside world.

Melissa kept a notebook on the kitchen counter. I tore out

a blank sheet and sat on the bench adjacent to the bay window.

The pen hung between my fingers, and the blank paper stared at me. I froze. I had been two weeks in Canada and hadn't explored what the country offered immigrants.

I put the pen down and pumped up myself with courage. I knew that living at my uncle's house would be a detriment to achieving goals. I had to make friends. The person outside Mostafa's family was Michael, and I had not taken his phone number.

It had been three weeks since my arrival in Canada. After the party where I met Michael, Mostafa and Melissa never took me anywhere. Even the weekends were for Naira and Nora's activities.

One day I asked them to find me a position at Mostafa's health club.

"We are not hiring now," Melissa replied.

"Even without pay?" I asked.

She raised her eyes brows in astonishment. I figured she didn't like me getting close to my uncle.

"Melissa is a jealous woman," Mama reminded me during one of our phone conversations.

"She can't be jealous of me," I insisted.

"Well, I know she won't be," Mama said, "but, just in case, don't be surprised."

I dismissed Mama's warning. Melissa met Mostafa in Sweden. They fell in love during one of his swimming tournaments and got married.

∽

I can't remember how long I thought of ways to connect with the outside world. I stared at the thick telephone book that sat on the kitchen table.

Then Rawyia's voice jumped inside my head. It was like she communicated with me on a spiritual level. "Don't resist the changes that come your way. They could be the best things that happen to you. Let go of the past, and don't let it suck you in like a whirlpool. You will get stuck there forever." Her words energized me.

I picked up the telephone book and flipped its pages. Then an idea flickered in my mind, like a candlelight in a dark tunnel. I shut my eyes and took a deep breath. I placed my pointer on a random spot. That phone number became the target for a solitary game, which I named "My quest for friendship." I had not thought of what I would say if someone answered but, out of despair, I played the game. I picked up the receiver and dialed.

"Alo," I said. "My name is Laila, and I am Egyptian."

There was a disappointing silence. But, just before I put the receiver down, a soft female voice reached my ears. "Yes?" she said.

I waited to hear more, but we both expected the other to engage in a dialogue.

"My English is not good," I said.

I got no reply. I figured there was no need to continue.

"What language do you speak?" she asked.

"French," I replied. My heartbeat fluttered with joy. I couldn't believe the female voice was engaging in conversation with me. I looked up to the ceiling and thanked God in silence.

"D'accord," she said, "Je parles le Francais."

Her command of the French language was an invitation to keep me going. Curiosity connected us. But something else warmed my heart. The tone of her voice and the chuckle she failed to suppress when I introduced myself as Egyptian pleased me.

"I am new in the country," I said in French. "I picked your number from the phone book." I paused for a few seconds and continued with excitement. "I am searching for friends. If you have doubt about my honesty, please hang up."

She replied with loud laughter that puzzled me, and yet I

felt comfortable enough to keep the line open.

"I was born in Egypt," she said in broken Arabic.

I screamed with joy, "Impossible!"

"My name," she said in Arabic, "is Tania."

I pinched my cheeks. I wanted to make sure I wasn't dreaming. Excitement exhausted me and, like a runner who reached the finale in a race, I pulled a chair out and collapsed.

Every breath I took got louder and louder. I couldn't find the proper words to express my joy. I wanted to hear more of what Tania had to say about her life in Egypt. I was confident that I had found a friend in Canada, and I believed that fate had again played a role in my life.

The warmth in Tania's voice filled me with hope I had not felt since I landed in Canada.

I was now shaping my destiny. Mama had told me that God ordered people to make an effort to pursue their goals, and HE will help. This is what I had done, and God stood by me.

"I left Egypt," Tania said, "right after the revolution of Gamal Abdel Nasser."

It was the first part of the seventies when Tania and I connected, and the 1952 military coup in Egypt had forced many to leave. Many foreigners left Egypt for fear of discrimination—Greeks, Italians, and Jews fled the country after the military coup and the ousting of King Farooq. Since I had never been good at math, I couldn't make the quick calculation to figure her age.

"What nationality are you?" I asked.

"Italian," she said, "born in Alexandria, and live in Canada."

We both laughed. It felt like we knew each other.

Mostafa's house had central air conditioning, but the excitement kept me warm. Perspiration oozed from my forehead and ran down my back. I had many questions but couldn't decide which one to start with. A constant smile was glued on my face as if Tania was sitting with me in the kitchen.

"I was born in Alexandria," I said. "I lived in Rouchdy."

Tania laughed out loud, and she couldn't stop. I knew, after the laughter, I would hear another surprising coincidence.

"We lived in Rouchdy as well."

We each stayed silent. We had to absorb what we both heard and confirm to ourselves that it was a reality and not a dream. I began to doubt every word Tania said. Such a coincidence doesn't exist in real life.

"Tell me I am not dreaming," I said.

"I am in shock," Tania said.

Then we both spoke at the same time as if our minds had connected, and our souls engaged on a deeper level.

"We have to meet," we agreed.

⁌∾

Rouchdy is a small city, and half of its residents came from upper-class families. The other half was from European background Italians, Greeks, and Jews, and their children attended French, English, or German schools. Before I asked Tania about which school she attended, I took a deep breath to slow down the heartbeats racing inside my chest.

"I graduated from the Lycée," she said, as if she had read my mind.

We awakened our dormant roots with the memories that we both had experienced on the beaches of Alexandria, and we brought them back to life with laughter. Finding Tania gave me peace and awakened the security I had enjoyed under the wings of Mama and Rawyia.

Tania and I exchanged telephone numbers and addresses before she excused herself and rushed to pick up her son from school. I walked to my room, collapsed on my bed, and stared at the medallion above. I couldn't believe what had just happened. It was like a dream, and I didn't want to wake up.

CHAPTER XIV

OPPORTUNITIES IN TORONTO

A few days passed, during which I received a letter from Rawyia. She informed me that Hady, our brother, had married a Swiss girl and that they had settled in Zurich. She sent me his address and phone number. Hady was just twenty; how could he marry so young? He didn't finish his education yet. I blamed my father for pushing him out of his country and out of school.

I called Rawyia.

"Now that Hady has settled down, I am relieved," Rawyia said, releasing a deep sigh.

"What do you mean, settled down?" I snapped.

"It's the way for him to settle down," she interjected.

"Marriage?" I screamed. "He is too young. How could he support himself and his wife?"

"Oh, don't worry," she said. "Marriage is the quickest way to settle down."

Arguing this subject with Rawyia would not have gotten me anywhere. I cut the telephone call short.

Hady's news disturbed me. I knew my brother could not have fallen in love with that Swiss girl. He had a girlfriend in

Alexandria whom he had been in love with for three years. However, Rawyia had no time nor the desire to babysit anyone. Her husband was dying, and he might not even see his unborn child.

A few days later, Rawyia called.

"If Marwan dies, I would have to go back to Alexandria," she said.

For Rawyia, going back to Alexandria would be like reliving the hell she had run away from.

"Don't worry, La. Marwan provided plenty of financial security for me and my unborn child. I won't need help from Papa."

"I worry about you going back to Alexandria," I said.

"I will be fine. You just take care of yourself." She sounded confident.

Rawyia's husband was dying, and she would have to return to the same people she had run away from. She would not just face the family, but also the whole society that condemns women with a child and no husband. The idea of going back to Alexandria, which I contemplated in moments of desperation, faded upon hearing of Rawyia's setback hardship.

My sister was bold. She had proven time after time that she was able to face the world to accomplish her goals. My life in Canada needed my full attention, and counting on Rawyia's help had to end.

In the morning, when Mostafa and his family left for their routine activities, I cleaned the breakfast mess they left behind in the kitchen, then brewed a fresh cup of coffee.

I pulled out a chair, sat down, and wondered where fate was taking me. Bemoaning fate doesn't change anything. Yet I couldn't help but wish that I had finished college before I left Alexandria. There were times I wanted to rebel against having been born a girl. When you are born a girl in any Arab country, you're damned.

The grandfather clock that hung on the wall in the corridor seemed to have taken longer than usual to strike ten. Tania and I had promised to call each other at that time. I cupped the mug of coffee to warm up my cold hands. The autumn sky began raining the cold mist of fall. I stood by the bay window, fascinated by the crimson-and-gold shade of maple leaves on the trees in the neighborhood. Mostafa mentioned that these were Canada's national trees. Back home in Egypt, sycamore and mulberry trees never turned red or gold. They were evergreen. My heart rejoiced at the changes.

Tania and I conversed both in French and Arabic.

"Tania, please," I said, "talk to me in English."

"First, let's reminisce about our life in Alexandria," she said.

Tania insisted on speaking broken Arabic with me. "I never thought of how much I missed Egypt until you called me," she said with a sigh.

"You know what Egyptians say," I said with a chuckle. "He who drinks from the Nile will always go back."

"Yes, Laila, it's my dream."

"Not mine," I stated emphatically.

I got to know a lot about Tania and her husband, Michael, who spoke both English and Hungarian, but not French or Arabic.

I learned that Tania's husband, Michael, owned a hairdresser salon in downtown Toronto and that she had devoted her life to raising her five-year-old son, Tony. She promised to find me a job through her husband's clients.

She invited me over. I asked Melissa to take me to the bus station, which was a good twenty minute walk. I needed time to adjust to the chill of October that hit Toronto with snow flurries. I had seen snow in Italy. However, the weather was not as cold as it is in Toronto. Melissa and the girls wore boots, hats, and fur-padded jackets.

The wool coat I brought with me was too light for walking in the freezing weather. Nonetheless, I was happy to take a walk to get used to the freezing wind before Tania offered to pick me up and drive me to her home.

Melissa offered me one of her jackets. It was too big. Naira and Nora's jackets were too small. Mostafa promised to take me shopping one day for winter clothes. He also mentioned that his brother Fahmy and his family lived close to downtown. I never met Fahmy or his family when they lived in Alexandria. I looked forward to meeting them.

At Tania's apartment, Tony could not stay still. The angel that plunged into a deep sleep during the car ride turned into a bumblebee buzzing around and spreading joy all over the family room. Michael wrestled with Tony while Tania prepared dinner for her son and for us. The aroma of garlic and olive oil took me back to Alexandria.

I joined Tania in the kitchen to help, but she asked me not to since the kitchen was too small for two people. I peeked into the steaming pot.

"I knew from the aroma you were cooking pasta," I said in French.

"Yes, of course, Laila," she replied in Arabic with a smile. "I learned how to make pasta in Alexandria."

"Did you speak English when you lived in Alexandria?" I asked.

"Of course not," she replied, smiling.

"How long did it take you to learn English?"

"Don't worry," she said. "You'll learn it in no time. From now on, I will speak with you in English."

We laughed and hugged.

"Once Tony eats his dinner," she said, "he will settle down, and we can talk."

Michael asked me if I felt comfortable speaking English.

"I could learn," I said in English. "I'm a fast learner."

He smiled. "Good English," he said, continuing to wrestle with Tony.

"I think we could find a job for Laila," he said. "What do you think, Tony?"

For a moment, I thought I was living a dream,

When Tony had his dinner and fell asleep, Tania gave me her undivided attention. She explained how Michael met different people through his profession, and that one of his regular clients was the general manager of Eaton, the largest department store in Toronto at that time.

"I promise to talk to Mrs. Edward about you and your situation. She might offer you a job."

I wanted to walk up to Michael and hug him, but I refrained from expressing emotions with an embrace, for which we Egyptians are known.

"Thank you, Michael," I said, and pointed above. "Someone up there is looking after me."

The bond that connected Tania and me deepened that evening, and I felt hopeful for the first time since I landed in Canada.

Upon returning home, I wrote Rawyia a letter about my new friends and the potential job. I had no doubt in my mind that Michael would help me.

I promised Rawyia to visit Hady on my first vacation and to help her immigrate to Canada with her son.

Events could not have moved faster. Within a week, I got a call from Michael. "Mrs. Edward wants to meet with you."

I scratched my head. There was no time to enrich my English vocabulary.

"You will be fine," Tania said. "Mrs. Edward knows about your limited command of the language."

I wanted Michael or Tania to come with me for support, but they advised against it.

The meeting was set for the following Monday morning at 9:00. Mostafa offered to drive me to Eaton's department store on his way to work. "This could be your best opportunity to learn English," he said.

I nodded, but my hands trembled. Any position in a department store required English. I wished my uncle lived in Montreal or Quebec City.

"You will do fine, Laila," Mostafa reassured me, patting me on the head.

I wanted to trust myself and believe this interview would be my gateway to independence.

Early Monday morning, Mostafa drove me to Eaton. I pulled back my shoulders and forced a smile before I waved goodbye. Then I walked inside the Eaton store. I took the escalator, holding on to the golden charm around my neck. It was engraved with verses from the Quran, and Mama assured me that God's words would protect me. I rubbed it harder.

Mrs. Edward's office was on the fifth floor. I proceeded with trepidation to the rosewood door, took a deep breath, and knocked.

"Enter, please!"

I faced a small-framed woman wrapped in a light blue two-piece suit, and around her neck, a red silk foulard that gave her freckled complexion a radiance overwhelming the shy wrinkles around her eyes.

Ambient classical music and soft lighting in the room grounded me with comfort. I stood a few feet across from her desk with heartbeats that refused to slow down. The room reflected the lady's genuine warmth. Fresh red roses were behind her chair on the rosewood commode, yellow roses on her desk, and the soft grey walls were covered with a watercolor painting of different flowers. The sweet fragrance of her perfume, mixed with the scent of roses, reminded me of Mama. My heart opened up. I stood silent to let the joy of the moment settle all over me. And, then, with the confident tone of a woman with enormous power, she spoke. "Sit down, please. I need a salesgirl in the candy department."

My heartbeats settled down and drummed a tune of joy. I smiled. I couldn't believe Mrs. Edward dismissed the issue of the language.

"We will train you to handle the cashier machine," she told me.

Cold sweat slithered along my spine like worms. Counting money, and math in general, had never been an easy subject, even in school.

"You won't have trouble learning, right?" she asked, looking me straight in the eyes.

I gave her a confident smile and a nod.

"You will have three long months of training," she said.

She asked me to start the next day, and I agreed.

Melissa and the girls were waiting for me.

"I have a job," I said.

Nora and Naira hugged and kissed me. Surprisingly, Melissa congratulated me. "But how will you manage transportation?" she asked.

I hadn't thought about transportation or the distance I had to travel to work. The Mostafa family lived in the suburb of Toronto, and Eaton was downtown, a good two-hour drive back and forth.

"You need to find yourself a place close by your new job," Melissa blurted.

"No!" exclaimed Nora and Naira in one voice. "Laila can take public transportation."

I heard the sincerity in their voices. However, during moments of quiet introspection while living with them, I sensed Melissa's rejection and distant demeanor. She wanted me out of the house, and she couldn't hide it.

Mama had warned me about Melissa's jealousy, but I had shrugged it off. She had no reason to feel insecure. Mostafa's father was Papa's maternal uncle. We learned back home that Mostafa and his brothers were like our uncles.

"I am sorry," Mostafa said. Mostafa worried that my father would be disappointed. He loved and respected Papa.

"No need to feel sorry," I said. "You both helped me beyond my expectations and opened doors for me. I am indebted to you and your family forever."

Moving closer to the store would be convenient since I had

no car. I needed a place close to public transportation. Mostafa suggested that I move in with his brother Fahmy until I found a place of my own. I thought it would be a good idea, and Mostafa told me he would arrange it.

I doubted the moves I had taken, but I had no control over events that shaped my future. Like a free bird, my wings flew me to new territories where I had to adapt and surrender once more to destiny.

Without Rawyia and Mama beside me, I trained myself to face life's challenges alone. However, I needed emotional support, which I received in the letters we exchanged often. Their words helped me combat fear and insecurity. Mama's notes filled my heart and soul with love. Rawyia's words were the backbone that supported me whenever challenges became hard to face—like moving out of Mostafa's home.

"Don't ever look back!" Rawyia wrote. "The road is wide open ahead of you. You just have to follow it without fear."

Sometimes I got angry reading Rawyia's letters. They were devoid of emotion. I heard her patronizing voice in every word, even though they were meant to encourage me. She knew how fragile and insecure I had been as a child, and that I was still the same emotional, frightened little girl. But when I re-read her letters, I developed trust and respect for what she had been doing for me. She wanted nothing but to see me healthy and succeeding on my own.

Rawyia avoided writing about her husband's sickness, and I became entangled with everyday challenges. I stopped asking her about Marwan. I looked forward for her encouraging letters, and for Mama's loving words. They became my trusted companions in Canada.

CHAPTER XV

MOVING OUT OF MOSTAFA'S HOME

Unable to support myself, moving in with Mostafa's brother Fahmy and his family sounded ideal. The emotional stress of separation and the longing for Mama in my diaspora were also still raw, but the new living arrangement was comforting. Farida, Fahmy's wife, acted like my surrogate mother, and I received her advice with an open heart. I needed her care.

"Before you make a change in your future, put your brain in gear. You are smart and courageous," she stressed.

No one had ever told me that before. When I was a young girl, Papa raised me to trust only him. Even Rawyia preached independence and self-reliance but didn't allow me to make my own decisions. So, even with Farida's encouragement, here I was at twenty-one, scared and doubting myself.

Fahmy had just immigrated to town. He was six feet tall, with an inflated belly, and thighs layered with fat. When he walked, he leaned on each leg like a duck. He carried a white handkerchief at all times to pat dry the beaded sweat on his forehead and neck. His breathing sounded like the last breath of a dying person—shallow and breaking. His lips developed an attachment to cigarettes, like babies to their pacifiers. The time I saw him without a lit cigarette hanging from his lips was when he slumped on a chair in the family room after a long night of driving his taxis.

Farida was petite with a full frame. She enjoyed cooking. Every day she prepared a different Egyptian dish—Moussaka, pasta with béchamel sauce—but *Mouloukhia* was my favorite. She made it with okra leaves, using lamb or chicken soup with garlic and coriander paste. She also baked Hawawshi every day. Hawawshi is a dough filled with ground meat and spices that's very popular in Egypt. I learned the art of cooking Egyptian dishes from Farida.

Farida didn't speak English and stayed home to raise Nawal and Nassim, both high school students. They didn't speak English, either. We communicated in Arabic, and that became a hindrance to learning English. However, Farida was happy to have found a companion. Life in Canada shocked her. She missed the interaction with neighbors and family: the noisy streets and the vendors that delivered vegetables and flatbread in bamboo baskets, which she lowered with a rope from the balcony; radios that blasted into the early morning hours with love and longing songs; the joy of gossiping, which Egyptians can't control even when reminded of the Prophet's warning, "Gossip is like eating the flesh of dead person." It is one of the major sins after blasphemy and ending a life. But Farida entertained herself with me, gossiping about family members.

Fahmy's family lived in a three-bedroom apartment in a high rise in downtown Toronto. Each occupied one bedroom. The kitchen and family room were combined into one large area where they ate their meals and entertained. There was no place for me to sleep except on the brown sleeper sofa they used to watch TV. It was stained, but I pretended not to notice. I sat on it and said, "This is my bed."

Farida had a different arrangement already planned. "Fahmy works all night," she said. "I don't like to sleep alone."

I believed her because I didn't like sleeping alone either. I have always shared a bed with Rawyia. It suited me to share her bed.

Their apartment was in walking distance from Eaton. But Fahmy insisted on driving me to work. During the short ride, he told me stories about the years my father and his three sisters lived with them as orphans.

"Your father's grandmother abused them," he said.

"I know; my aunt told me."

Even though I rejected Papa for what he did to us, I didn't like to be reminded of the suffering he endured as a child. Part of me still loved him and appreciated the comfortable life he provided.

"He persevered," I said.

It saddened me that Papa never spoke to us about his childhood. He always spoke with pride about his professional achievements, which he used to justify his self-proclaimed divine authority.

Papa lost both his parents when he turned five. That's when love disappeared from his life. He never received it nor learned how to give it. The more I learned about his childhood, the less angry I became and the more I pitied him.

Fahmy encouraged me to forgive my father. I wrote Papa a letter expressing love and understanding. He never replied. He remained proud. It was hard for him to forget that we ran away, and it was painful for me to forgive him for forcing me into an arranged marriage.

CHAPTER XVI

FIRST JOB AT EATON

The first day at Eaton could not have been more memorable. Mrs. Edward put me in charge of the candy counter. I handled the sales part with the little English I had learned, but I failed at the cash register.

I relied on my smile to win customers' patience and trust. They complimented me on my smile, so I used it to cover up for my incompetency. Customers pointed to the candy they preferred, and peeked at the piece of paper I had hidden under the counter to help me with English words. Closing time at the end of the day was stressful. The total on the register never matched the cash collected. Either I counted wrong, or I just gave back extra change to customers. Whatever the reason was, I replaced the missing money from my own pocket to avoid embarrassment with the manager.

With time, I handled the cash without personal financial losses. The joy with working grew, especially with the bouquet of roses I received every week from an anonymous client. To this day, I never knew who my admirer was. Life was good, and the time to pursue my education was ripe. Taking English courses was a priority. I searched for a community college close by and found one.

A few weeks passed. On a serene late autumn evening lit by a full moon, Fahmy took the night off. We gathered around the table for Hawawshi and drank tea.

"I plan to register for an English course," I announced.

There was silence, with a surprising look on Farida's face and frown on Fahmy's.

"It's an evening course," I added. "I would keep my job. It will help me advance and earn more."

Still, there was no response. Many things came flooding back—memories of the look on Papa's face when I revealed my desire to take the high school exam. How he locked me up in the pantry to deny me an education. No one helped me, not even Mama. After that day, I didn't need help, and no one could lock me up again.

"I've made up my mind and will register for the winter semester," I said, amazing myself by the determination in my voice.

I shared my progress with Mama and Rawyia. Hady also received regular letters; I explained how much money I was saving for visiting him. He wrote that he also had found a job in the corporate office of Jelmoli, a department store in Zurich. His command of the French language helped him find that position. He explained in detail how embarrassed he felt working in an all-women office. I laughed when he told me how the winter rain messed up his hair. He had curly locks like mine, and we both wanted to have straight hair that didn't curl up with the rain. "By the time I reached the office," he wrote, "my hair looked like sheep fur."

Nevertheless, Hady enjoyed his life in Europe. I couldn't wait to meet his Swiss wife.

"Analiese is six years older than me and very skinny. You know I never liked skinny girls. However, she takes care of me."

Hady was nineteen at the time he settled in Zurich. I remembered Nareeman, the girl he had been in love with since he was fourteen years old. Hady promised to marry her once he graduated from college.

When he described Analiese as skinny and taller than he was, I knew he could not have fallen in love with her. He was not fond of bony girls. Arab men, in general, prefer women's bodies well-padded with meat, and Hady was no different. Nareeman was plump and stood five inches shorter than Hady—a height that gave him a sense of power. He was five foot eleven, and tall and muscular. I was shocked to hear about his marriage until I called him.

"What drove you to marry so young?" I asked.

"I had no other choice," he said.

I was curious as to how and where they met. The last I heard from Rawyia, Hady was in Greece. He never traveled to Switzerland. "Where did you meet her?"

"I met Analiese in Greece," he said with a sigh. "She liked me and promised to help. I didn't believe she would until I arrived at the Swiss border in a decrepit Fiat I earned in exchange for washing dishes at a restaurant. I fixed it and drove it to Switzerland."

Hady was spoiled as a child, and to hear that he worked in a restaurant to survive was upsetting. I sensed there was more about his journey from Greece to Switzerland. I chose to wait until he felt comfortable to share it with me.

"I had no papers or passport," he stressed to justify his choice. "I called Analiese, and she came to the border. She tried her best to help me. She even proposed marriage to keep the border police from sending me back."

I waited in silence to let him collect himself and to keep him from sensing in my voice how sad I was.

"I had no choice but to ask for asylum." The confession took me by surprise. I was not sure what it meant, and what the legal repercussions of such action would be. Hady was not involved in politics. How did he convince the border police?

"Did they accept your asylum request?" I asked him.

"Yes," he said, "I told them I had to run away from Egypt because I refused to join the army."

"They believed you?"

"Yes, they did, and I will explain when I see you."

In his letters, Hady said that he had stayed faithful to Analiese in spite of temptations he faced at work.

"The women I work with spoil me," he wrote. "I am the only guy in the office and the youngest."

Hady's news about work empowered me to try harder to establish a future for myself in Canada. To settle down and earn money meant I could travel to see him, and get Mama to leave Egypt and come settle down with me in Canada.

∞

At Fahmy's house, I could not practice English. They all spoke Arabic, and Farida continued badgering me with religious lessons all aimed at women's positions and their roles in men's lives. She thought a husband would be better than work and school.

"God ordered women to obey men," she said. "Besides, you will end up marrying a man who would for sure ask you to stay home and raise your kids."

I couldn't win an argument with her. She was submissive and obedient to her husband. She quoted verses from the Quran, which I couldn't challenge. I had heard the same verses at home from Papa and still couldn't be convinced that God wanted women to live as second class people. Arguing about religious beliefs would get me in trouble, so I chose to move out. I told Uncle Fahmy that I needed to be surrounded by people who spoke English to help me learn the language fast. I promised to visit often, and I kept my promise.

Mrs. Edward found me a room to rent in one of her friends' homes. The lady, Mrs. Thompson, was an English teacher married to an attorney and had a six-month-old baby. I couldn't be any happier. It was like a dream come true.

Mrs. Thompson offered to give me English lessons and a part-time position. In return, I looked after their baby when they went out together.

At last, life smiled and favored me with good luck. I began to trust the decisions I made and felt comfortable living my life alone and far away from Egypt. I relished the taste of freedom and appreciated the western culture that provided opportunities I could not have had if I had remained in Egypt.

Between my work at Eaton and the English lessons with Mrs. Thompson, I felt comfortable enough to register at the local community center for an accounting course. I thought, with numbers, I would have less reading and writing of the new language. I also wanted to learn a skill that would help me get a better-paying job. At Eaton, I earned the minimum wage. I had to race with time to fulfill the promise to bring Mama and Rawyia to Canada.

Halfway through the accounting course, I dropped out. I never liked math. It was a struggle to follow through with the English lessons, accounting homework, and my job at Eaton. I moved out of Mrs. Thompson's home and rented a room at the YMCA. I shared an apartment with Jenny, who was twenty-seven and unemployed.

Two weeks passed before Jenny walked into my room one evening, her eyes red and half-closed, her hair oily and stringy. She had a stoic expression on her face. I wasn't sure if it was a smile or a pretend smile. I had smelled an unpleasant odor in the apartment but couldn't figure out where it came from. Jenny always had the door to her room closed. We never talked except the day she introduced herself when I moved in.

When she walked into my room, she was holding a cigarette between her fingers and an ashtray in her left hand. I noticed the way she inhaled. It was like sucking in the breath to her existence. I waited for her until she finished, admiring the smoke circles she released from her mouth. The odor was strong. She sat on the wooden chair behind my desk.

"Would you like to try it?" she asked me.

"Try what?" I replied.

"Marijuana."

I was never introduced to nor heard the word before. "I don't smoke."

"This is harmless," she said. "Come with me."

I followed her to her room. The odor was so pungent I felt sick to my stomach. She opened the window. It had a better view of the Maple Leaf Garden, where the national hockey team played and trained. She picked up a small pot with long green leaves and pointed to the pack of cigarette papers scattered on her bed.

"This is what goes into the cigarettes I roll up myself."

I didn't understand what she meant. I stayed standing at the window.

Sitting cross-legged in the middle of her bed, she picked up a small plastic bag containing dried-up leaves and rolled herself a cigarette. "It helps me cope with my parent's rejection," she explained.

She inhaled and talked with a rhythmic rocking of her torso, and her left hand shook. I noticed tears gathering in her eyes. I sat facing her on the bed.

"I am Dutch. My parents live in Amsterdam. They told me to never come back."

I listened to her for hours. Somehow her life story touched me. Her parents kicked her out at fifteen. She hitchhiked across Europe. At nineteen, she came to Canada on a tourist visa and then applied for immigration.

"Are you in contact with your parents?" I asked.

"No," she answered.

"How do you manage your finances?"

"Welfare and a boyfriend. I give him sex and, in exchange, I get a regular supply of dope and enough to buy food."

Every night, we spent time talking. With time, she respected my desire to not have her smoke in my room or the living room. I convinced her to look for a job and not sell herself.

It didn't take long before I saw drastic changes in her life. She found a job as a salesgirl in a local store. She made an effort to diminish her marijuana addiction and stopped seeing her boyfriend. We talked about our different cultures and religion. She expressed the desire to learn more about Islam. I gave her some books I read about the Prophet Mohammed's life. It was my way of keeping her occupied and enjoying the attention I gave her. I convinced her to go visit her parents to let them see the changes she made for herself. To my surprise, she agreed. We promised to travel together. I would visit Hady in Switzerland, and she would visit her parents in Holland. We would then meet in Zurich and fly back to Canada together.

CHAPTER XVII

DEATH OF RAWYIA'S HUSBAND

"La! It's me, Rawyia."

It had been six months since I last talked to Rawyia. She used to call me every other week in the middle of the night. I was busy with work, and she with her sick husband. The tone of her voice sounded sinister.

"Rawyia, what happened?"

There was silence followed by snivels. I sat up. I couldn't remember the last time I heard my sister cry. No matter how many problems she faced, she never shed tears. She taught me to control my emotions. She was the strong one. But now she sounded broken.

"Rawyia, don't cry, please," I begged her.

"La, Marwan is gone," she cried. Rawyia had mentioned that Marwan was gravely ill, and she was pregnant.

The statement shattered my mind. I wasn't sure what to say. It was the first time Rawyia reached out to me for comfort. The distance between us made it impossible. I fought a strong urge to cry.

"When did it happen, and where are you, now?" I asked her gently.

"We buried him yesterday."

Muslims bury the dead right after death. The farewell is done the same day in the evening. Mourners gather at the deceased's home, drink sugarless Arabic coffee, and take turns reading verses from the Quran until they finish reading the whole book. I worried about Rawyia. She was alone and pregnant.

"When are you due?"

"In three weeks," she said.

Marwan's family didn't approve of their marriage. The thirty years' age difference worried them. I can't remember how long we were silent, listening to each other's breathing. Our minds communicated. We were one year apart, but our souls connected like identical twins.

"In a few hours, I will embark the ship headed to Alexandria."

"But you're pregnant." I was shocked at her announcement.

"I want to be with Mama," she murmured.

"Apply for immigration to Canada and come live with me."

"No," she said. "I wrote to Abdel Kader. He is waiting for me. Take care of yourself, La." She hung up.

She had met Abdel Kader following her divorce from Gamal. It was an instant attraction. He was married and had a child. According to Sharia, he was allowed four wives. He offered Rawyia marriage. She demanded he divorce his wife, and he refused. The relationship ended, and she moved on.

Rawyia confessed she had serious passionate sentiments for Abdel Kader. However, their interlude only lasted a few months, and she didn't allow her emotions to keep her in Egypt. She married Marwan because he offered a life in a different country. Rawyia never spoke with affection when she mentioned Marwan. She said that all she wanted from a man was a child. Marwan granted her wish. I wasn't sure if Rawyia was ready to accept Abdel Kader's offer and become his second wife.

I chased sleep for the rest of the night. I thought of different ways to help Rawyia. I wanted her and her baby to be with me.

No one back home would receive her with open arms except for Mama. And Mama would not be enough. Papa would be the one she needed to accept her and her child back in the family. Exhausted, I fell asleep.

In the morning, I went to work, mentally drained and physically tired. I didn't share my concerns with Farida and Fahmy or with anyone for that matter. I tried to ignore it, but I couldn't. Instead, I developed a sense of responsibility toward Rawyia. I couldn't imagine myself living in Canada with a promising future while she faced the patriarchal society we ran away from. She was a wanton in the eyes of Egyptians. Rawyia was alone, and she needed me.

Four weeks passed before Rawyia called me from Alexandria.

"Alo, La."

I heard a baby crying in the background. Rawyia sounded tired, but I was excited to listen to her voice.

"Is that your baby crying?" I asked.

"Yes, La. It's a boy, and I named him Adham. I delivered him on the boat." Rawyia sniffled and then continued. "You know, La, Adham was born to a life without a father and without a country."

I heard a baby suckle, mixed with snivel. Rawyia seemed defeated. I searched for words to pacify her, but I couldn't find any. I sensed despondency in her voice. I was sure she wanted a family, stability, and a secure future for her child. She was alone. Tears welled in my eyes.

"Oh, Rawyia, I want to see him." I was excited to see this new addition to our family.

"I will mail you his photo," she said.

"Where are you staying?"

"At home," she said. "But I am leaving soon."

I was perplexed. I didn't expect her to return home but leaving so soon meant trouble. Papa must have asked her to leave. I worried about her and Adham. She never asked for help. She remained proud and defiant through her ordeal.

"Rawyia, I want you to start your immigration process. I am a Canadian citizen, and I could sponsor you."

Rawyia took a deep breath. "I cannot talk anymore right now. I will call you soon."

I waited for months for her phone call. However, it never came. I was detached from my family in Alexandria except for a few letters from Hala, my younger sister. She sent Rawyia's address.

"Mama misses you and your brother," Hala wrote in every letter.

༄

It was spring when I received a cassette in the mail from Mama. I had asked her to send me a recording of her voice. I lay down on my bed, both hands under my head and crossed my legs.

"Louli, my dearest daughter."

Utter silence followed her words. My breathing raced, and my heart constricted. Sadness cascaded through me and enveloped my body in a wave of sweat and chills. Tears streamed from the corner of my eyes onto the pillow. I sat up to check if something caused the sound to be mute. Then I heard Mama sobbing. She couldn't control herself. I never heard her cry so loud. Her pain and suffering shredded my heart to pieces. I never imagined my absence would put her in such agony. She never complained before. I wanted her to stop and start talking. Instead, I broke down and sobbed with her. I turned off the recording and turned it back on. She wept more before she, too, turned the tape off and then came back on.

"Forgive me for losing it," she said, "I just miss you and don't want to die before I can hug you."

Her recording session was interrupted by bursts of sobbing. Guilt tormented me. I tried to convince myself that it was Papa who should feel guilty. But I couldn't. I was the one that caused

Mama's grief. She knew I planned to run away after the divorce. Still, she helped me, knowing well that she might never see me again. I was selfish and would never forgive myself.

"Your brother Hady and your father got me vitamins, but the ones you sent me were the best." She wept more. "I felt strong and healthy every time I took them. The loose black tea you sent me is the best. I drink it all the time."

I smiled at her loving approval of the things I sent her but, the more I listened, the worse I felt. I couldn't continue living so far from her. The distress of longing was more than I could tolerate.

She continued. "Farook and I crossed paths downtown. He was happy to see me. He said he still loved you and showed me your photo. He had it in his wallet. I told him to forget you. He was sad."

I didn't know why Mama would mention the man I divorced. He was the reason behind our separation. Mama didn't blame Farook. She believed Papa was the one who messed up my life. Nevertheless, I was annoyed to hear her mention Farook.

Her voice continued. "I miss you, and I miss Hady. I have sent him a recording as well. Stay connected with him. You are now not his sister but a mother to him as well. I want to tell you that I am preparing for my passport. Your father doesn't know yet. Soon, my dear Louli, I will take you in my arms. Don't be surprised when you see me. Stress has ravaged my body. I have lost a lot of weight and developed diabetes. Don't ever go to bed sad or crying. Learn to let go and always keep your face lit with a smile. I pray for you and Hady. May God keep me alive until I see you both."

There was silence, then more sobbing. It was the last thing.

I turned the tape on again and listened to Mama's voice several times before I fell asleep.

Mama's words prompted me to rearrange my priorities. Attending college for a degree could wait. I focused on work to earn enough money for her visit. I wanted to provide the best accommodation and take her everywhere in Canada and, most important, to save for a trip to Switzerland. I wanted her to see me successful. I entertained the thought of taking a second job to buy a small used car.

I would add Mama to my OHIP (Ontario Health Insurance Provider) health service and take her for a complete check-up. I planned to rent an affordable small studio to share with her. I longed to sleep in her arms, hear her breathing, and smell her skin. I planned to let her taste the flavor of freedom away from Papa's control. She would be the queen of my heart and my world.

It was the end of 1973 when Mama sent me another letter explaining the immigration process would take a year or more. That gave me enough time to prepare for her visit.

A few months later, Hady contacted me. "Alo, Laila, it's me, Hady."

He sounded down. It was almost Christmas time. Back home, we celebrated Muslim holidays. I figured he must be lonely at this time of the year.

"How are you? I miss you," I replied.

"Can you take off from work and come to Switzerland?" The pleading tone in his voice reached me like a cry for help I couldn't ignore.

"How soon do you need me?"

"Soon." He sounded disconsolate. Hady was homesick. So, despite all my responsibilities, he became a priority. I went to Mr. Roy, my manager at work, to ask for time off.

Mr. Roy was not just my manager, but a father figure to me and the other three girls who worked in the company. He was in his mid-fifties, married with no children. He taught me with patience the file system and corrected my English with a genuine desire to build my confidence. His kindness helped me open up and share my story with him. After the first three months, he increased my salary, and that helped me move out of my uncle's home.

"Good morning, Mr. Roy." The bran muffin and dark coffee he brought from the coffee shop down the street were still untouched.

"Good morning, Laila. What brings you to my office?"

"I am sorry, Mr. Roy," I said with embarrassment for interrupting his breakfast. "I will come back."

He offered me half the muffin. I took it; I couldn't resist the aroma of cinnamon. "Hady, my brother, asked me to visit him," I continued. "He sounded sad."

"Your brother is in Switzerland?"

I nodded.

"When would you like to go?" he asked.

I couldn't believe what I heard. I hadn't been working there for long. Joyce and Lina, my coworkers, told me I needed to work for one year before I could get a paid vacation. His response brought tears to my eyes. I wanted to hug him.

"In one week," I said.

"If you need anything, let me know."

"Thank you, Mr. Roy."

Reuniting with a member of my family felt like going home. I couldn't be any happier to at last meet with my brother. I wanted to make up for all the things he missed from home. I planned to cook all the dishes Mama cooked for us. I remembered he liked *Mouloukhia*, but wasn't sure if I would find the okra leaves in Zurich. I couldn't wait to hear the details of his journey to Switzerland. In the evening, I called him.

"Hady, I am coming to see you."

"When?" he asked.

"Don't know yet, but soon. I will let you know when I reserve the flight."

"Do you need money for the ticket?" he asked.

"Don't worry; I have enough to pay for it," I said.

Even though he was two years my junior, he acted like a responsible and caring brother. He offered me financial help when he just started working. I wanted to be the big sister who looked after him. He always refused my help. He behaved with maturity beyond his age.

"Do you need anything from Canada?"

"No," he said, "I just want to see you."

CHAPTER XVIII

DEATH OF JENNY

It was September 1974. I had saved enough money for my trip. I bought a travel book to familiarize myself with the country. I learned the culture was diverse. Swiss people spoke three languages—French in Geneva and Lausanne, German in Zurich, Bern, Lucerne, Basel and Winterthur, and Italian in Lugano and Locarno. It had one of the highest mountain ranges in Europe—the Alps—with seventeen peaks, some above 4,000m elevation. To have a chance to visit a country like Switzerland was a dream come true.

Hady spoke very little of his wife. He mentioned that she was an accountant, kind, and loved him to death. I figured with both salaries, they managed the lifestyle in Zurich, the most expensive city in Europe.

Hady and I grew up, each in our own world. He chased girls and fell in love many times over while Rawyia and I were kept in isolation from the rest of the family. Our room was next to our parents' bedroom. We enjoyed our privacy. However, we resented the freedom our parents gave our brothers. Our father believed our isolation would preserve our chastity.

I had mixed emotions about the visit. Nevertheless, I was

happy. I looked forward to the brother-and-sister relationship. I wanted to hear all about his escape from Egypt and travel around Europe. Rawyia spoke little about his adventures before he reached Zurich.

It was noon when Swiss Air landed in Zurich. The airport was small compared to the Toronto and Cairo Airports, with not much to see except for travelers rushing to their destinations. Ladies in hats, fur coats, and suede boots caught my attention. I figured winter had already invaded the city.

I picked up my suitcase and proceeded to the exit. Hady waited for me, dressed in a navy-blue trench coat, white shirt, and jeans. He was clean-shaven. Gray shoots peppered his once-chestnut hair. When our eyes met, his smile exposed well-preserved, pearly teeth that Mama attributed to Papa's good genes.

For the first time, I saw a birthmark on his upper lip that I had never noticed before. His hazel eyes still shined in spite of the hard life he experienced. We shared the curled-up lashes inherited from my paternal aunt.

We embraced; he patted me on the back, and I did the same. He took the suitcase and held my hand, and then wrapped his arm around my shoulder. He was two years younger than me but acted like he was my guardian—maybe because he was raised in a culture that gave men that responsibility. I was sure he did that because he loved me, and our culture had taught him to protect his sisters. When we reached the street, he put down the luggage and hailed a taxi. Not a single word was exchanged. I sensed the heavy load of pain he carried. He no longer walked like a peacock to win a girl's admiration, nor flashed his muscular physique as he did in Alexandria.

The sun struggled to push its way through the thick, cloudless gray sky, the air so cold I shivered. It was much colder than in Toronto. Streets were narrow but bustled with small cars—Fiat, Renault, Lamborghini, and Firebird.

We were both quiet. I thought of what happened to both of

us—how we ended up on different continents, how young we both were, how unsure of our future. I was sure, from the way he gazed into empty space, he also sifted through the same events that brought us together. We maintained the silence and gave each other time to absorb what happened. Hady held my hand all the time, keeping his gaze outside the window on his left. I had my sight unfocused as my mind traveled through the painful past that brought us together.

"How are you, Laila?" he asked.

"I am fine, and you?"

He shook his head and smiled.

We behaved like strangers. It was at that moment I felt the impact of what my father had done. He not just sheltered Rawyia and me from men outside the family, but from my brothers as well. We never learned to connect like brothers and sisters. We rejected their superiority and the privileges Papa gave them just because they were born boys. We never learned to love our brothers.

"I cannot believe we are here alone," I said.

He again shook his head in disbelief. "I can't believe I am here, either, and already married."

I wasn't sure how to react. I waited to learn why he married, and why he ran away from Egypt. He was still a teenager.

He carried my suitcase to his studio. There was a kitchen counter, a stove, a sink, and a mini fridge. The place was small and dark. A love seat and a table were squeezed in one corner, with a long narrow window on one wall.

Hady reached for a brass handle on the wooden frame against the wall and pulled it down. It opened into a bed.

"Don't worry. You, me, and Analiese will manage."

"Does she work late?" I asked.

"Yes, and you will meet her tonight. Let me take you on a tour around the city."

We walked to the tram station, where he purchased two tickets from an automatic machine on the tarmac. I would have loved to walk. The streets were crowded with boutiques, and outdoor cafés, and people dressed fashionably. It was a scene seldom seen in the streets of Canada, where a car is a must to reach any destination.

Bahnhofstrasse, the famous street in downtown Zurich, was picturesque. The ground was covered with marble stones. It was the most visited road in Europe. The cold breeze didn't keep people indoors.

"Bahnhofstrasse is the most expensive street in the world," Hady said.

For a brief moment, I wished I could live in Switzerland with him. I had missed him as much as I missed Mama and yearned for the family warmth. Mama would have loved to be with us in this beautiful place.

Hady held my hand and explained that Bahnhofstrasse connects Lake Zurich with the Main Railway Station. We walked for miles and talked for hours along the banana-shaped Lake Zurich. Hady spoke a little about his emotional escape and the long, arduous train ride around Europe. It was painful to hear. Our tears mixed with the first September drizzles and bathed our faces. We didn't feel the chill. We sat on a bench and tried to make sense of the circumstances that brought us together in Zurich.

"You know the movie *Midnight Express*?" he said.

"No."

"I came very close to a confrontation with the Turkish police as I rode the train, just like what happened to a young man in the movie. Except in my case, it was no passport and not drug possession."

He choked and struggled to hold his tears. I took him in my arms until he calmed down. The rain shared our tearful moment and poured hard. We were soaked.

"I had lost my passport and heard so much about Turkish police brutality that I jumped out of the train."

He sobbed as he talked. It was hard to hear him talk as he

struggled with the memory. We walked back to his apartment in utter silence.

The road to my freedom was as painful as what Hady had endured before he reached Switzerland. He never complained or asked for anyone's help. He had a lot to tell me about his days in Europe without a passport. Nevertheless, I decided to let him choose the time to talk.

Before we climbed up the stairs to his apartment, he stopped.

"I met my wife in Greece. We decided to get married. I entered Switzerland and asked for political asylum, and they granted me the status."

He knew I was curious about how he ended up in Switzerland without a passport. Now I was even more interested to know about the asylum issue.

☙

The aroma of chicken and rosemary that Analiese had prepared permeated the studio and awakened my appetite. She hugged Hady first and then me. She handed him a large towel. They disappeared into the bathroom for a few minutes, and Hady came out dressed in his pajamas.

"Laila, it's your turn," Analiese said. "Please, feel free to put on some dry clothes."

Analiese pulled down a table from the wall and draped it with a yellow cloth. She served chicken and salad. It was delicious.

"Tomorrow, I will take you down to the old city of Zurich," she said.

I nodded with a smile. I was not in the mood for sightseeing. I was concerned about Hady and eager to know more about what happened on the train and his claim to asylum. I concluded he wouldn't be able to go back to Egypt, and would never see anyone from the family, even if he wanted to see

Mama in Canada. I saw a sadness in his eyes. He camouflaged it with a stoic smile.

Mama would fall apart if she knew. Hady avoided any mention of Mama. It was like he resigned himself to the possibility of losing the chance to see her again. But I wasn't ready to give up. I promised myself to do whatever it took to get him to see Mama. I would get her to fly on Swiss Air with a stop-over in Zurich.

The mission to get Mama to come live with me in Canada became a priority. The task was almost impossible to achieve. Papa would not allow her to travel and, by law, she had to get her husband's approval before she applied for a visa.

The next day, Analiese took me to a hole in the wall in the old town. The night club was big enough for fifteen people, but there were more than fifty crowded shoulders while many more sat on tables just to listen to the jazz player. It was the first time I heard live jazz.

The African musician played Duke Ellington, but it was Hello Dolly by Louis Armstrong that electrified the room. That evening, I acquired an appreciation for jazz and white wine.

Analiese ordered two glasses of white wine. I hesitated at first. Alcohol was forbidden during the month of Ramadan in particular. I was supposed to fast as well, but I wasn't. My parents didn't enforce the five pillars of Islam: the declaration that there is no God but Allah and that Mohammed is the Prophet, and pray five times a day, fast the month of Ramadan from dawn to sunset, perform the Haj to Mecca, and give alms to the poor. We were taught the five pillars but, except for my parents, none of us practiced.

Hady and I enjoyed each other's company and counted our blessings rather than talked about our misfortunes. He tried to convince me that he was happy and lucky to live in one of the most beautiful cities in the world. Zurich had the lakes, the Alps, and famous winter ski resorts like *Flumserberg* and *Sattel-HoschstuckII*, and banks like Credit Suisse where rich and famous people deposited their millions. It was home to famous designer boutiques like Gucci, Luis Vuitton, Chanel, and others. Zurich was clean, and Swiss people were fashionable but seemed aloof and to themselves, a trait Hady appreciated.

"People in Zurich are reserved. They don't ask questions; they just accept you."

I realized Hady didn't mind this culture. It was the perfect place for him. He disliked inquisitive people. Any discussion about Alexandria and the family, he refused. It didn't take me long to sense and respect his wish. The past was still raw and painful. I resigned myself to wait until we met again.

At the airport, Hady had an icy look on his face. However, he hugged me with profound tenderness.

"I will visit you soon," I said.

He didn't reply. He waited for me until I crossed the security area, and we couldn't see each other. I choked up. My heart tightened with sadness. He needed me, but I was part of that past he wanted to forget.

∽

I looked for Jenny, my roommate, at the airport and on the airplane, but she was nowhere to be found. I thought she must have decided to stay with her parents. I looked forward to a letter from her. Before she left, she asked me to be the sister she never had. I agreed. Jenny needed to feel loved, and I crossed her path to help her straighten out her life. I just hoped her parents would do the same.

∽

As I received my invitation letter, Mama started the visa process without Papa's knowledge. She took her passport photo and mailed me a copy to show how serious she was. Mama looked different. During the last five years, she had lost weight and aged. I almost didn't recognize her. She wrote that it was diabetes. I promised to take her to the best doctors in Canada. I believed, with me and close to Hady, she would recover from her illness. When she wrote that her vision had weakened, I didn't understand that it was a manifestation of diabetes.

I missed her voice, her breath, her smell, her skin, and the peacefulness I enjoyed when I melted on her chest. Her heartbeat soothed me to the tune of love and comfort. I prepared myself to offer her the world. I lived with the dream to reunite again with Mama.

It was September 15, 1974 when I walked into the reception of the YMCA. I was emotionally drained and tired. The older woman on the night shift followed me to the elevator.

"Laila?" she asked.

"Yes," I replied.

"Welcome back."

"Thank you."

"The police looked for you," the woman said.

I dropped my suitcase on the ground. "Why?"

"Jenny committed suicide under the subway train," she told me.

I collapsed on a chair. "Why, and when? She went to Europe to see her parents, and why did the police want to see me?"

I was scared and shocked. The lady picked up my suitcase when she noticed my unstable hands. She gave me a glass of water and held my hand. I shook with fear.

"She came back five days ago. Her room was rented. She had no money for rent. She waited in the lobby for you. But I don't know what happened. The police came one day and asked about you. They said she had a photo of you in her hand when they collected her remains from the train tracks. . . ."

I muted her voice in my head. Her parents must have rejected her again. She came back to look for me, and I wasn't here for her. I buried my face in my hands and sobbed.

"She left something for you," the woman said softly. She walked to her desk and came back with a small blue booklet. "Jenny's poems. One of them she wrote for you."

I took it and left her office.

"You have a new roommate," the woman called after me.

I nodded and proceeded to call the elevator.

The lady called me back again. "I forgot to give you this," she said, and handed me a folded paper. "It came yesterday."

I thanked her and took the elevator to my room. I was too heartbroken to bother open it. I assumed it was a telegram about Rawyia's new address or phone number. I was more eager to read the poem Jenny wrote to me.

Guilt killed me. How could I forgive myself? I can't remember how long I sat on the chair with my luggage unpacked, wondering about Jenny's death. She had listened to my advice and counted on me. I had convinced her that all parents would be happy to connect with their children. She wanted so much to start a new life. She had even cut down on her marijuana usage. What prompted her to end her life this horrible way?

The sun had already melted into the horizon and the night spread a starless sky over the city. The wind wailed as I watched the rain pour outside my window, as if it shared my profound sorrow.

My left hand clenched, and I realized the crumpled telegram was still in my hand. I turned on the light and opened it.

"My dear sister, our mother is sick. She is in the hospital (Al Mawasah). Rawyia."

I read it again and again and again. I closed my eyes and opened them again. For a moment, I hoped it was all a dream and that I would soon wake up. When I saw my luggage next to me, I realized it wasn't a dream. Mama was sick in the hospital, and Jenny was gone. The wind echoed louder. I ran to the street, hoping the rain would put out the pain that burned inside me. I paced the streets, then collapsed on the first bench I saw.

Rawyia didn't ask me to come see my mother. But, when I

thought of Mama and how she must have wanted to see me, I couldn't have lived with myself if I didn't return to Egypt to be by her side. I wasn't sure if I could take another time off from work. I had to forget about education and the free life I worked hard to win. I feared the reaction of my father and Reda. Rawyia warned me often that, if I went back to Alexandria, they would force me to stay there. What if Reda went through with his threat and killed me?

At the YMCA, I was still not sure what to do. I placed a call to the hospital before I made any plans. The thought to tell Hady crossed my mind, but I to chose to spare him the worries because he had lost his passport and wouldn't be able to travel.

The phone took too long to ring. I lay down on the sofa in my wet clothes and closed my eyes. Memories of Mama raced in my mind—the peaceful look on her face filled me with comfort and hope. I remembered her smile that brightened my childhood's darkest days, her tender caresses that infused my body with warmth, her melodic voice that echoed love when she called me Louli, her happiness as she watched me enjoy the barbecued fish she had cooked on the side just for me. But it was the disappointed look on her face the last day I saw her before I left Alexandria that haunted me. She had come to my aunt's house, where I stayed, to bid me farewell. I thought she had come to take me back to Farook. She waited for me all afternoon in the salon, hoping I would come out of my room. I didn't, but I stood at the window and waited to wave goodbye to her when she left. I still remember when she turned back and looked up as if she expected to see me. She knew I loved her and that I suffered from having her go without the dose of her tender embrace. She waved goodbye and threw me a kiss in the air and said, "I love you."

The image of her as she dragged her feet and turned every few steps to wave goodbye still tormented me. Tears streamed down my face until I fell asleep and saw Mama in my dream in a big empty hall as she waltzed with my deceased aunt. I didn't know what the vision meant. But a thick fog shrouded my head and, no matter how hard I tried to lift it, it came back to envelop my mind.

The phone rang. I woke up, disturbed. It was a bad omen to see Mama as she danced with her dead sister. I remembered, when I was a young girl, that my Aunt Hamida interpreted a similar dream she had seen about her deceased father as he danced with her still-living mother. She told me that her mother passed away days after that dream. My stomach knotted and entangled my heart in a tightness that almost paralyzed my breath. I picked up the receiver.

"Hello," I said.

"Is this Laila?"

"Yes."

"The number you requested is on the line."

Then a new voice came on. "Alo, this is the hospital. Can I help you?"

"Yes, please put me through to Mme. Salma Bakr's room," I said.

"One second, please."

Rawyia answered the phone. "Alo, Laila? Is this you?"

"Yes, Rawyia. Please let me talk to Mama."

"Okay," she said.

"No, tell you what. I'll see you tomorrow," I told her.

I hung up. I didn't know what prompted me to change my mind. How could I ever miss the opportunity to hear her voice? Was it the dream? Was it the sound of her sobs I avoided, like she had done in the recorded tape she sent me? Was it my desire to spare her the emotional stress? Or was I protecting myself? Nevertheless, I planned a visit to Egypt for Mama's sake.

I took a shower and headed to work. I went straight to the manager.

"Good morning, Mr. Roy."

"Welcome back. How was your trip?"

"It was good," I told him.

I didn't know how to start. If I asked for another time off from work, I could end up without a job when I returned. However, the thought of Mama's illness gave me courage. I was ready to gamble.

"Mr. Roy, I need two more weeks off." I lowered my gaze to the floor. I sensed a surprised reaction from the way he pushed himself back in his chair. His voice was a mix of concern and disappointment.

"Why? And what for?" he demanded.

He waited for a reply but, before I did, he continued. "Where to? Switzerland again?"

"No," I whispered, my head still bowed.

"Speak up please, Laila, I can't hear you."

I opened my purse and pulled out Rawyia's telegram written in Arabic and handed it to him. He took a quick glance, then asked, "What does it say? I can't read this language."

I translated the content.

"I see. You want time off to go see your mother in Egypt?"

I nodded.

He stood up and walked toward me. Then he sat on the chair and asked, "How long will you be gone?"

I couldn't believe what I heard. I had known Mr. Roy to be compassionate. He granted me more than I was entitled to. He showed empathy beyond my expectations.

"I don't know how to thank you, Mr. Roy."

"No need for that," he said with a chuckle. "Just make sure to come back."

Mr. Roy was aware of my situation and about the circumstances that brought me to Canada. When I first started to work, he was patient and taught me everything I needed to know about my clerical position. He spent time with me after work hours and taught me how to handle my duties as a clerk. I didn't disappoint him.

I left the office, went straight to the bank, and withdrew some of my savings. I planned to stay in a hotel. I thought it better to have my own money while I stayed in Alexandria. I wasn't sure if I would receive any financial help. Mama was in the hospital. Rawyia, last I heard, had struggled to start a business after she lost her husband.

From the KLM Airline office in downtown Toronto, I bought a ticket on the next day's flight to Cairo.

CHAPTER XIX

BACK TO EGYPT

When I got back to the YMCA, I crashed on my bed, exhausted. I thought, if I slept, I could escape the constant heartache that dragged me into a depression since I heard of Jenny's death and my mother's illness. Early the next morning, I called a taxi and headed to the airport. The weather took a sudden turn, announcing the onset of the winter freeze. Snow flurries showered the streets, and there was a four-hour delay for the flight.

This was the first time I had returned to Egypt since I left Alexandria in 1970. Four years had passed, and so much had happened. Rawyia was home with her son, whom I was excited to meet. Hala graduated from college and eloped to marry her lover against my father's order. Samir joined the army. Reda was in town, and that was reason enough for me to stay in a hotel. Nevertheless, Mama was all I cared to see.

The flight made a stop in Montreal. A six-hour blizzard delayed the departure to Europe. I waited, my head about to explode, my heart pounding with anguish. I thought about ways to make Mama happy and to help her recover fast. I was sure my presence would fill her heart and mind with joy. I craved the comfort of her embrace and the warmth of her body against mine. I longed to cuddle up in her hospital bed. I vowed to take her back with me.

I was ready to face my father and brother. The love and longing I had for Mama gave me the courage and confidence to stand up to their aggression.

Then Rawyia invaded my reverie and made me smile. Just the thought of her was enough to suppress the anxiety in my heart. Our disagreements hadn't left a dent in the love we had for each other. Our souls remained as one. We behaved like twins who felt each other's pain and joy, even across the continents.

The anticipation exhausted me. I turned down the flight meal and fell asleep for the rest of the Atlantic passage.

In Holland, the weather couldn't have been colder. It halted the flight to Cairo and forced me to stay overnight. The airline accommodated the passengers at a nearby hotel and offered a dinner voucher. I ordered Edam cheese, fruits, and a French baguette, took a shower, and again fell asleep.

The next day the weather was still uncooperative, but better. In the evening, we resumed the flight to Egypt and arrived in Cairo at midnight.

It was Ramadan, the month when Muslims around the world practice one of the five pillars of Islam—fast from sunrise to sunset. When I left Egypt, I had abandoned all the traditional religious duties, my way to revolt against what my father had forced on us under the banner of Islam.

Against the sanctity of the holy month, I arrived in Cairo dressed in a black mini-skirt. During Ramadan, women must adhere to modest attire. My skirt wasn't modest. I enticed men to stare at my naked legs. In fact, I helped them commit the sin that would nullify their fasting.

Cairo Airport buzzed with travelers and employees. Egyptians don't sleep between sunset and sunrise. They stay up to take their last meal before dawn. For thirty days, their work schedules change to accommodate their fasting routine and allow them to practice their prayers on time. It's a month of devotion and spirituality.

To my surprise, I was happy to be back in Egypt. But that happiness was laced with fear and worries. I had several dreams where I was in Egypt, trapped at home, and unable to return to Canada. I worried those dreams would come true, but I was sure Rawyia would not let that happen.

I hadn't realized how much I missed Egypt until I landed. I thought maybe it was true, what Egyptians claimed, that one who drinks from the Nile will always come back. I didn't want to come back but, deep inside, I enjoyed everything around me, even the chaos and unruliness Egyptians were known for. I was flattered by men's attention and smiles but felt uncomfortable with the looks of dismay from women. Taxi drivers offered their services with a forceful attempt to carry my luggage. Everyone spoke Arabic—the language I missed and cherished.

Although it was the first time I had been alone in the middle of the night in Egypt—without Rawyia by my side—I felt safe. The security at the airport hailed an airport-approved taxi to my destination. The driver was courteous and polite.

"Would you accept payment in Canadian dollars?" I asked before I got into his car.

"Any currency from you will do," he said, opening the back-seat door. "The ride is on me." I saw him when he took his seat behind the wheel and disengage the meter.

Egyptians expressed kindness in different ways. He turned down the charges to show care and gratitude. I didn't take his offer seriously.

"Please turn on the meter."

"Young girl," he said in a warm voice, and pulled out a photo from his wallet. "I have three daughters as young as you. I will not hurt you."

His voice reflected sincerity. But I insisted he turn the meter on, and he did when he realized how uncomfortable I was.

"Where to?" he asked.

"The train station, please."

He glanced at his watch and said, "You must be heading to Alexandria. The last train for the day leaves in twenty minutes. I hope we make it on time. If we miss it, I will drive you to Alexandria and get there in two-and-a-half hours."

Even though I trusted the driver, I preferred to take the train. Cairo was alive. Stores were open for late-night grocery shopping, and restaurant workers prepared to serve the last meal before the start of fasting. Streets were decorated with traditional Ramadan lanterns. Call for dawn prayers echoed from the minarets. During the month of Ramadan, before people break their fast at sunset, Egypt turns into a ghost country. Even Christian Copts don't eat at restaurants out of respect to Muslims. Men socialized at cafes drinking tea with fresh mint served with sweets like Kenafa and Backlawa, playing backgammon, and smoking Shisha water pipes.

It was mid-Ramadan, and people crowded the streets, rushing to find bargains to celebrate the end of Ramadan with new clothes. Even banks were busy as people withdrew new paper money to give to young children—a tradition that's still practiced in Egypt today. Mosques everywhere buzzed with people who sought spirituality and closeness to God. The smell of the traditional Kahk—cookies made with flour and butter—permeated the air from every bakery. I had missed the elation of the Ramadan ambiance and was glad to once again spend that month with Mama, Rawyia, and my siblings.

I arrived ten minutes early at the train station. There were two men in military uniforms and a couple who stood on the tarmac. I sat on the nearest bench and remembered the last time I took the train from Alexandria to Cairo. I was under Rawyia's protection. This time I was alone.

I worried about facing Reda and my father. Dryness coated my throat. I needed to moisten my mouth with a drink. I glanced around, searching for a way to quench my thirst. I noticed the deliberate staring of the two officers. Their presence distracted me, especially when they walked gingerly closer and stood a few feet from me. I placed my small suitcase on my bare legs.

They smoked their cigarettes in utter silence. Their gaze hovered over me like the stare of two lions, each anticipating winning the prey. They stole my attention and, for a second, I wasn't able to think of Mama's illness and the family. I wasn't sure why they stood so close to me. Was it the mini-dress or the fact that I was on the tarmac alone in the middle of the night? I also noticed a couple standing close by, who eyed me every now and then with the admonishment of displeased parents. I had ignored the fact that girls in Egypt were reserved but more so during the month of Ramadan.

I dismissed their intrusion and stood up, pulled my shoulders back, and challenged the two officers' stares. However, the aura of authority their uniforms represented was overwhelming. I couldn't ignore them. I walked away, hoping they wouldn't ride in the first-class cabin with me.

The cafeteria was almost deserted; that made it easy to place a call to Alexandria before my departure. Not sure about the family situation, or Reda's whereabouts, I wanted Rawyia to collect me from the train station. She had written that she was back home with her baby. I hoped she would answer.

"Alo."

I recognized my father's deep voice. It was faint, as if surprised by the late call. That voice set in motion painful childhood memories—the yells, orders, punishment, and confinement. It was so loud, I wanted to hang up. But my father's mellow voice reverberated with a sigh as if he was not in the mood to talk. I hadn't spoken to him since I escaped from Egypt.

"Alo! Who is this?"

"It's me, Laila."

There was a deafening silence. My heart ached with disappointment. I hoped he had changed and forgotten the past. I had missed him and contemplated forgiveness. I had often thought of how he must have suffered when he lost us. Distance and time allowed me to see his character from a different perspective. Underneath the monstrosity of all he had done, I discovered a father who cared about his children. He wanted the best for us but treated us the way his parents and grandparents had treated their children—obey orders without questions.

"I know," he said.

Silence remained as we thought what to say next. My hopes evaporated. I grew up with this silent treatment he used to express displeasure. I figured he was still vexed with me for what I had done. I thought it would be good to find a place other than home to stay while I visited Mama. I assumed Reda was still angry as well. Before I panicked, he spoke.

"Where are you calling from?"

"I am in Cairo," I told him.

"What for?" he demanded.

My muscles tensed, and anger heated deep inside of me—as hot as lava. The pressure of bottled-up rage, which I suppressed for years, was ready to erupt. I wanted to scream, but my voice died. Fear took over, and I shook like I had before when I faced his violent eruptions. I couldn't believe the distance and our separation couldn't mellow down his controlling character.

There was a stony silence before I gathered enough courage and said, "I came to see Mama."

"Where are you?" His tone had softened, and his voice turned warm and loving.

"At the train station."

Still not comfortable with his intentions, I regretted, for a moment, telling him where I was. But when I thought of the three hundred kilometers between Cairo and Alexandria, I worried he would send Reda to fulfill the death threat to cleanse the family's honor. I grew up with his Jekyll-and-Hyde personality. It was all I knew.

"Stay where you are," he said with his familiar authoritative tone. "I will send you a driver."

I rejected his domination. The time had come to assert my independence.

"No," I said. "I will take the train."

There was a moment of silence before he released a long and slow sigh as if his brain needed to process what he had just heard.

"Do you have Egyptian money for the train ticket?" he asked.

"No, but I managed with Canadian dollars," I replied.

"Good, and be careful. Don't talk to anyone, and don't eat food on the train. We'll wait for you."

I hung up, shaking my head in amazement at how my father still thought I was the same girl he forced into an arranged marriage. Did he exhibit genuine care, or was he still the same person who controlled us? Fear and apprehension brewed inside my head. My solace would be to have Rawyia by my side. Unsure of what awaited me in Alexandria, I took my Canadian passport out of my purse and kissed it.

Shortly after, the train arrived. I chose a window seat in the middle of an empty cabin. A magazine vendor approached me. "Would you like a newspaper or magazine?"

At first, I hesitated, but decided a magazine would keep me busy during the three-hour ride. I flipped through the pile in his wicker bag and glanced at the cabin entrance often. When no one showed up, I picked up *Al Mossawar* and handed him a dollar bill. He expressed gratitude with a familiar gesture I still remembered: touching his lips and forehead with the dollar bill as a sign of appreciation of God's blessings. Then he jumped off the train before it picked up speed.

I resigned myself to the fact that the two officers rode in a different cabin. Although it was a bit disappointing, over all I was relieved. I needed to be alone, without distraction, to prepare myself for surprises that might complicate my mission in Alexandria. Besides, when I ran away from Egypt, I had vowed to stay as far away as possible from Egyptian men.

As I flipped through the magazine I saw, from the corner of my eye, the two officers open the connecting doors of the cabins and walk straight toward the seats to my left. I kept my focus on the open magazine and was able to monitor their actions. The one who sat by the window took off his cap, stood up, and placed it in the overhead mesh compartment. Once they settled down, they lit cigarettes and stayed quiet. I fiddled in my seat as I sensed their gaze all over me.

The engine chugged louder and rattled rhythmically as it picked up speed. I closed the magazine and my eyes to go back into my cocoon, where I thought of Mama and Rawyia. The faster the train went, the closer the moment of reunion approached. I smiled, and my heart raced with joy. Then the image of Papa and Reda invaded my daydreaming. I opened my eyes and frowned. Then, I noticed the two officers were still quiet, looking at me as if I was a puzzle. When our eyes met briefly, they uncrossed their legs.

I had forgotten that, in Egypt, train tickets were collected by a conductor as proof of payment. When the conductor stopped by for my train ticket, it took me a few minutes to look inside my purse.

"Take your time, Miss."

I rummaged through my toiletries and took out the cartouche of Gouloise I had bought for Rawyia at the Amsterdam Airport.

"If you cannot find it, it's okay. Ramadan *Kareem*. I know you have it. I will stop by later."

Even though I had no doubt he meant what he said, I was flustered. After all, Ramadan was the time when generosity, kindness, and spirituality reached their climax. The Muslim practices at that month intensified their benevolence. Still, I was embarrassed. Although I found the ticket, the conductor never came back.

The two officers watched me as I reached for the magazine and turned the pages, unable to concentrate. There was still a long way to Alexandria. I thought to move to a different seat but changed my mind and decided to ignore them. Yet, not comfortable with my surroundings, and for an unknown reason, I picked up a packet of cigarettes, opened it, and pulled one out. I pretended to look for a lighter or a match in my purse, even though I had none; I wasn't a smoker. Unexpectedly, the spark I searched for ignited the courage of the two officers. They stood and approached me. One held a golden lighter, the other a matchbox, ready to light my cigarette.

The looks of admiration and recognition were new to me. When I lived in Egypt, except for Ghassan, men didn't give me a second look. I didn't have the attributes Egyptian men appreciated in a woman. I was skinny with an olive complexion. The two officers' gallantry satisfied my ego, and I forgot for a moment why I was traveling to Alexandria. In fact, I enjoyed being the center of their attention.

When I looked up, I got a closer look at their faces and spotless khaki wool uniforms. I smiled. The officer with the golden lighter had a brass eagle and a star on his uniform's shoulder—a lieutenant colonel. He stood a few inches shorter than the other officer and was a little chubby around the waist. The desert sun had turned his olive complexion into a deep tan. The intense look in his eyes signaled an authority that demanded full obedience. He approached me, holding the lighter close to my face. I stood and chose the other officer, who stood one step behind with a matchbox in his hand.

He was at least five inches taller than me. He stood majestically straight, and proudly displayed his irresistible figure. The three brass stars on his uniform shoulder established his rank—captain. He stood behind at attention—a show of respect to his superior. But it was he who won my attention. Under his cap peeked eyes of hazel and honey with deep forest green at the edges. They shone like sunlight on polished marble and seemed to swirl together like a fern that crept over fertile soil. When he smiled, both colors sparked a glow that dazzled him with warmth. However, I noticed melancholy in his eyes when he handed me the matchbox. I took it with a smile to acknowledge his courtesy and to express my admiration.

We all went back to our seats. The three-star officer and I exchanged glances that triggered happiness, unlike the one I felt with Ghassan. It was powerful and scary. I reached for the magazine, thinking this would distract me. I remembered the promise I made to stay away from Egyptian men, and was sure nothing would develop from this attraction. I had come to Egypt to be with Mama and would go back to Canada once she regained her health. I placed the magazine back on the chair next to me and escaped to the train cafeteria.

There was no one to serve in the tea room. I crossed my arms and leaned against the window. The moon, almost in full circle, shined in the dark sky, and signaled the few days still left in Ramadan. The train passed by Kafr El-Zayat village, where a branch of the Nile ran across. In the distance, villagers rushed around in the street as they carried baked bread for their dawn meal. In a chorus, they sang the familiar Ramadan songs. In spite of their simple life, they seemed joyous and worry-free, and I daydreamed of a similar life where I would be as joyful as they were until I felt a tap on my shoulder.

I turned around, and there the officer who offered the matchbox stood at attention. He seemed unsure of my reaction, yet confident of his irresistible physical attributes—tall and fit like a Roman warrior. Above his Roman nose were those honey-green eyes framed by graceful eyebrows. I saw charm, honesty, gentleness, and sadness. There was something about him in a military uniform and the melancholy in his gaze that melted my heart. When he stared deep into my eyes, I couldn't help but blush. I had heard many songs that said, "He took my breath away." That line made sense when I saw him. A genuine plea crossed his face, and he changed from a handsome stranger to divine.

Surprise grabbed me by the tongue and gave me dry mouth,

and I'm sure he saw the shock on my face before I could hide it. I took a step back. However, the captivation of his smile danced on his lips, and the twinkle in his eyes disarmed me from my resistance and past promises I made to Ghassan.

"Can I join you?" he asked.

We were alone in the dark cafeteria, illuminated only by the intermittent moonbeam that splashed silver rays against the walls. At that moment, our souls bridged. Still, there was fear in my heart that waited to take over, perhaps to protect me, but I felt no danger in the officer's presence.

For a moment, my past and future were overshadowed by an unimaginable tidal wave of energy that pulled us closer. He shined my soul into brilliance, and the deep, warm tone in his voice crossed all barriers. It comforted me and took me to a place where the sound was the force that would transport me to a new world.

I bit my lip. I wanted to know more about him, but how could I start a conversation when I had just met him? My body flushed in warmth.

"Please do," I responded. "The trip is long, and I welcome the company."

He extended his hand and said, "Amer, Amer Shaker."

He squeezed my hand, sending another surge of warmth through my body.

"Laila," I said and wiggled my hand from his grip.

He faced me, leaning on the window. The light wind brushed against our faces. Stars shimmered around the moon, and silence pained me until he spoke.

"What brings you to Alexandra at this late hour?"

Startled by his intrusive question, and the way he held himself, the way he spoke, the look of unchallenged confidence in his eyes, I couldn't resist him. Magic was already at work. It wove threads of warm feelings between us. But I was scared to let my defenses down.

"I came to see my mother," I told him.

He nodded and turned his gaze to the road. I didn't volunteer more information. I watched him glance at the floor, then back to the street. I wanted him to ask more questions. I was comfortable to share more than I thought possible.

"If I am intruding, please tell me to stop."

I invitingly shook my head, and prompted him to smile and feel at ease to ask, "Where did you travel from?"

"Canada," I said. "I live in Canada."

"Vacation?"

"No, Mama is in the hospital."

At that moment, I came back to the reality of why I was in Egypt. My chin quivered. My eyes glistened with tears. I looked toward the sky and wished the moonlight would pacify me. Embarrassed with my show of emotions, I said, "I am sorry. I just haven't seen my mother for four years."

He stood silent, but I saw empathy in the way he looked at me. His whole show of concern seeped into my soul without words. I forced a smile and said, "Enough about me. Tell me about you. Do you live in Alexandria?"

He took two steps back. He managed to fake a grin that seemed to bury deep pain behind his strong façade.

"I have an apartment in downtown Cairo but, when I am off duty, I prefer to stay at my home in Alexandria."

I shook my head and said nothing, even though I wanted him to say more about himself before the train reached Alexandria. Then, as if he read the question that floated inside my head, he continued with mischief that lurked in his eyes.

"I live alone."

The disclosure perplexed me, setting my curiosity in motion. I discreetly glanced at his hands to check for bands. He didn't wear one. Still, I wasn't ready to conclude he was single.

"What do you mean alone? What about your parents?"

"I lost them both before I turned ten."

His explanation left me astounded instead of relieved. I couldn't find words to verbalize my reaction to his statement.

It was a mélange of different emotions—empathy, sadness, compassion, and a strange desire to take him in my arms for a warm hug.

"Do you want to know more?" he asked.

"Yes, please," I encouraged him.

"I won't bore you with the details of their death," he said, searching my eyes for approval.

"As you wish."

"My paternal uncle raised me," he said, then his attention drifted into the dark night, and he blinked as if he tried to catch the childhood images that raced in his mind. The sadness I found earlier in his eyes deepened and made him appear weak and vulnerable in his warrior uniform. I couldn't escape the intense feeling of admiration that took root in my heart, and it hurt me to see him struggle to control his emotions.

"I am sorry," I said and, before I could continue, he interrupted me as if he hadn't heard me.

"My uncle was abusive and took extreme measures to keep me from getting a college education. He forced me to work at a young age, but I persevered and challenged him until I got an engineering degree."

The more he talked, the deeper he reached into my emotions. I liked everything about him, even the smell of cigarettes on his breath. Somehow, I knew this connection had a beginning but no end.

"You must be wondering how I ended up in the military," he said.

I nodded and smiled.

"I was drafted and chose to remain," he explained.

"You like it that much?"

"No," he replied, "but it's not easy to find engineering jobs. How about you? Have you immigrated to Canada?"

"Yes."

"Alone?" he said asked, smiling like a child who waited for an answer to a forbidden question.

"Yes," I told him, grinning.

He released a deep sigh of relief, like a heavy rock had been lifted off his chest. Now that we had both established our no-attachment status, I invited him into the memory of my life journey without fear or restriction.

"I lived in Rouchdy. I will stay with my family," I said.

"I live in Mostafa Kamel."

The two districts are walking distance apart. I gathered he lived in an affluent area like Rouchdy.

"I was forced into an arranged marriage at fourteen," I went on. "I managed, after a long battle, to obtain a divorce and leave the country. I traveled to different countries before I settled in Canada."

Shock and amazement were written all over his face. My story was not something that happened in Egypt. Girls didn't just divorce and leave their homes, their family, and their country. This was a story never heard of before.

"When was the last time you saw your mother?" he wanted to know.

"Not since I ran away."

City lights popped up on the horizon as we approached Alexandria. I savored the cold, salty air of the Mediterranean—crisp and nostalgic. I opened my arms and refreshed my lungs with the breeze. I remembered how clean the wind was in Alexandria, compared to the polluted atmosphere in Cairo. I was glad to be back home.

"I see you miss Alexandria." He was watching me with a little smile on his face.

"Very much."

"How long are you staying?"

"Two weeks," I said.

"I hope you find your mother in good health."

"I hope so."

"Make sure to take the magazine," he said. "I wrote down my phone numbers on page ten."

This was what I'd wanted but couldn't get myself to ask. I wasn't sure if I would call him, but I was happy he wrote it down. Even though I liked him and was comfortable talking with him, I knew nothing positive would develop from our encounter. As an army officer, he couldn't leave the country, and I had already vowed to live as far as I could from Egypt or any Arab country. However, happiness had already nestled deep inside my heart, activating pleasant feelings and signaling fate was back again, knocking on my door.

"If you have no one to take you home, I would be happy if you would ride with me and Ahmed, my cousin, the one who offered you the golden lighter," he said..

I assumed this was a smart way to find out where I lived because he knew that it was impossible for me to ride with them. In Egypt, women didn't accept rides from strangers. Nevertheless, I was flattered. This was the first time a handsome Egyptian man had given me his phone number. Still, I wasn't sure if I would call him.

The train slowed down before it came to a full stop at *Sidy Gaber* station.

"Thank God for your safety back home," he said, and extended his hand

The wish was reciprocated when I gave him my hand.

"I hope to see you before you go back to Canada," he said.

"You never know." I smiled up at him.

The train approached the platform. The conductor opened the door, and Amer helped me with my luggage. I popped out my head and searched for the station from a distance to see who waited for me. The closer we got, the more nervous I felt. I wrung my hands and paced, my heart racing. *"Calm down,"* I thought.

The fear prompted me to ask Amer to stay close in case anything happened, but I changed my mind. He was a stranger, after all. If my father were at the platform, it would have angered him to see me with two men unknown to him. I hoped Rawyia would be at the station. She would protect me. I held the charm Mama had given me and prayed until the train came to a stop.

Amer and his cousin waited for me to leave first. They stood close by and, to my surprise, I felt safe. I looked for Rawyia and spotted her where she stood with Hala and my father. I carried my luggage and walked to where they stood.

CHAPTER XX

IN ALEXANDRIA AND MAMA'S DEATH

The platform seemed deserted. There was no one but Hala, Rawyia, and my father who waited. The crisp air had a cold bite to it. It was almost dawn, time for prayers, and *Suhoor*, the meal before fasting. Quran recitation echoed loud from all minarets, calling on people for prayers. The spiritual atmosphere couldn't quiet the fearful agitation of my heart. I had to face Papa with courage and act confident.

The first thing I noticed were Hala and Rawyia's eyes. They were red, and their noses also seemed red and swollen. They both carried white handkerchiefs. They blew their noses and wiped their eyes non-stop. I hugged Rawyia first, and then Hala, then back to Rawyia's embrace. She sobbed and didn't let go of me.

"I missed you, too, Rawyia," I said softly.

Rawyia sobbed louder, and Hala's tears streamed down her own cheeks. I pulled her to join Rawyia and me in the embrace. Then, I noticed that Papa's eyes glistened and reflected a sincere, remorseful stare. I felt sorry for him. The thought to ask him to join us in the embrace crossed my mind, but I wasn't sure of the sudden change in his character, or how to greet him. Affection was not an emotion we exchanged with him.

"Greet Papa; he misses you," Rawyia whispered.

Still unsure of my feelings, I ignored her and released myself from their hug.

"Why are your eyes red?" I asked.

"Hala and I have colds," she responded.

"I hope you didn't come too close to Mama at the hospital; you could give her your cold," I said, looking in their eyes for confirmation. Instead, the three exchanged a quick look, then Rawyia forced a smile. They were quiet. I expected Rawyia and Hala's excitement as they saw me, but then I remembered, as children, we were reserved around my father. We always spoke in whispers when he was home. We held each other's hands and walked a few steps ahead of him. He proceeded to the car, still maintaining his silence, followed by a young worker who wore a kaftan. He placed one suitcase on his shoulder and carried the small bag.

"Rawyia," I said, glancing behind to make sure my father wouldn't hear me, "is something wrong with Papa? He is reticent."

"Don't worry about him. He has been like that since Mama was in the hospital."

"What do you mean by 'was'? Is Mama back home?"

"I meant to say since she was sick," she said, kissing me on the cheek.

"I can't wait to see Mama," I said. "Hope no one told her about my visit. I want to see the surprised look on her face."

Rawyia squeezed my hand when we heard Papa pleading to God to have mercy and forgive him every time the words Allah Akbar, God is Great, echoed from the minarets. I assumed, as he looked at us, he had come to his senses and was repentant.

"No one told Mama," Rawyia murmured, and Hala sniffled louder.

We walked to the car, and the aroma of the dried Fava beans

we called *Foul* wafted from nearby restaurants. I watched the vendor and felt hungry as he prepared the Knafa. The shoppers' line was too long. *Foul* is a staple Egyptian dish, not just during Ramadan, but at everyday breakfast. The mix of fresh garlic, cumin, olive oil, and sesame paste over the Foul is an irresistible meal. But the shop that had the longest line was the yogurt place. People walked to their homes, holding several red ceramic containers filled to the brim with homemade yogurt. They chattered, laughed, and their faces lit with a spiritual smile except for Rawyia, Hala, and my father. They were like ghosts that floated through the crowd unaffected.

"Do you fast?" Rawyia asked with a smile.

"No, do you?"

We giggled just like we did as young girls, when we pretended to fast to avoid our father's wrath.

"No, but Hala does," she whispered.

Hala was quiet, as she had always been. She wasn't close to us at home.

Rawyia wore black pants and a pink sweater, and Hala a wool skirt and a green turtleneck top.

I pulled down my mini-dress, hoping to stretch it a few inches longer.

"Why did you wear a mini-dress? You knew you would see Papa," Rawyia whispered in my ears.

It was then I realized that Papa hadn't complained about my dress and that he had mellowed as Rawyia said. I looked around to get a glimpse of his facial expression. He was dazed, as if in a world different from the one we were all in.

It surprised me to see Rawyia change and have affection toward my father. She had forgotten everything Papa had done. She had always demonstrated maturity beyond her age, and now she rose up to a higher level only smart people attain—forgiveness. I wasn't open to forgiveness yet. On the other hand, she was a widow with a child, and in need of family support.

"Yes, he changed, but he still prefers to see us dressed according to the rules of Islam—covered from neck to toe."

We didn't discuss Mama's illness. I didn't want to hear something about Mama's illness that might upset me before I visited her. I wanted to surprise her, to help her regain her health while I was in Alexandria. I hoped to take her back with me.

We got to the car. Rawyia, Hala, and I took the back seat and my father sat alone in the driver seat. He didn't show any sign of displeasure. I could have sworn he looked relieved. He took a deep sigh before he turned the car on and drove away, looking at me in the rearview mirror as I sat in the middle. There was pain in his eyes. It melted my heart. I didn't know he cared that much about Mama. It pained me to see him sad.

As we drove, I noticed the road Papa had taken. It was opposite the way to the hospital. I remembered Al *Mawasah* Hospital was in *Shabby*. Papa passed it and was on his way home in *Rouchdy*.

"I want to see Mama before we go home," I protested.

Papa adjusted the rearview mirror, and I wasn't able to see his eyes. He ignored my request and drove. Rawyia and Hala gazed toward the street and pretended not to hear me. I pulled myself to the edge of the seat and tapped on Papa's back.

"Please take me to the hospital. I have come to Egypt for Mama."

"You can't see her now. It's too late," Rawyia said and held me tight to calm me down. But I wasn't convinced. Hospitals in Egypt, like many other institutions, didn't follow the rules. I expected my sisters to say something in my support. They didn't. Their faces were drenched in tears.

I hugged Hala. I knew how much Mama's sickness affected her. She was the one that stayed with Mama when Rawyia, Hady, and I left.

"Just take me to Mama. I am sure the hospital's staff will allow me to visit when I tell them that I have come all the way from Canada."

"Let her rest now, and we will take you there first thing in the morning," Papa pleaded. I had to succumb. It was 3:00 a.m., and we had already reached home.

"What time can I visit?" I asked.

"6:00 a.m.," Papa stammered.

I fiddled in my seat, agitated. I couldn't believe I was so close to Mama and my father decided when I could see her. His attitude took me back to the time I lived at home. I wasn't free to do what I wanted, and I couldn't leave the apartment except with Papa. Now, that same choking feeling resurfaced. To wait for three long hours before I could see Mama was unacceptable.

At the elevator, there was an eerie silence and a deliberate avoidance of eye contact with me. *Mama must be seriously ill*, I thought.

The apartment was cold, as Mama had taken the warmth with her. The chandeliers were lit, but the place was dark. An unfamiliar servant opened the door. She greeted me and disappeared.

Papa walked straight to his room and shut the door. I came face to face with Reda. He stood at the end of the hallway, hesitant and unsure how to approach me. My feet were heavy like sand and glued to the floor.

Rawyia whispered, "Don't worry. He won't harm you."

Rawyia's demeanor surprised me. She was calm and seemed to have forgotten what Reda had done. Although the vicious look had disappeared from his eyes, I was not ready to forgive him. His cruelty and abuse were still imprinted in my mind.

We proceeded to the kitchen. Hala, Rawyia, and I took seats around the table. Two servants stood close by, waiting for orders. One of them murmured, "May God bless you with patience."

"Get out and don't show me your face again," shouted Rawyia.

The other maid proceeded to make tea. The sound of the night was interrupted by a persistent morbid omen hoot of an owl. Rawyia, Hala, and the servant seemed disturbed.

"Shut that window," Rawyia ordered.

Again, I attributed Rawyia's outburst to Mama's illness. Hala closed her eyes and slumped her head on the table. Reda appeared at the kitchen door, and waited for one of us to invite him in. Rawyia looked at me for approval. I nodded.

"Come in, Reda."

He sat facing me. With his head bowed, he appeared like a kind and peaceful human being.

"You must be hungry," he said in a soft voice. "Would you like something to eat?"

His unusual warm approach prompted me to test his sincerity. "Would you take me to Mama now?"

Rawyia and Reda exchanged a quick glance. I sensed my request surprised them. Reda looked at Rawyia for an answer, and she faced me with eyes wide open.

"We can't. Papa said he will take you in the morning," she stuttered.

Rawyia and Reda helped set up the table while the maid served stuffed cabbage, lentil soup, and roasted veal. I was hungry but had no appetite. Hala lifted her head, excused herself and went to her room.

"Mama," Reda paused and searched for the right words, "she was hopelessly sick."

His statement struck me as foreboding, and it made me angry. Still, I convinced myself that he didn't mean what he said. All I wanted was to go see her. I wasn't open to discussion. I believed she would recover once she laid eyes on me.

Their reception was shrouded with a somber aura. I figured it was because Mama was in the hospital. This was the first time she had been admitted to a hospital. She never spent a night outside our home. When she got sick, it was enough to shower her with attention and love to make her feel better. Her absence was hard on everyone, including me. Mama took the warmth and joy with her to the hospital, and left the apartment cold, like a deserted cemetery.

Since I arrived, I hadn't seen a smile on anyone's face. It was disappointing. I expected Rawyia to demonstrate a happy welcome. But she claimed to have the flu. It wasn't just Rawyia. Everyone seemed aloof and teary eyed.

Ahmed, our step-cousin, wasn't in the apartment. No one volunteered an explanation for his absence, and I didn't ask. He was never someone I missed or wanted to be around. His abuse was fresh in my mind. Rawyia bickered constantly with him.

She had never accepted nor tolerated the authority Papa granted Reda to control us. Now, they acted differently, calm and respectful to one another. He even offered Rawyia a cigarette. I was flabbergasted at the behavior change, yet pleased they bonded as brother and sister. I had no doubt that Mama's illness helped them bury the past.

The needles on my wristwatch moved slowly, and I ran out of patience as I waited for the hospital's hours for visitors. I had to keep myself busy. I remembered I hadn't seen Rawyia's son, Adham.

"What time does Adham get up?" I asked.

A broad smile lit her face. Even Reda grinned. Adham seemed to be the source of cheerfulness amid the somber atmosphere in the apartment.

"Can I see him?"

Reda and Rawyia seemed to wait for a distraction to warm up the chillness in the kitchen. They both answered in one breath. "Yes, of course."

Rawyia took the lead, I followed, and Reda trailed us. We passed Papa's room. He sat in the dark with the door ajar. An amber light beamed from the hallway, fell on his droopy checks, his closed eyes, and emphasized his leg as it jerked. He reverted to such seclusion whenever he faced severe challenges raising us. But, this time, something profound disturbed him. He was slumped and mumbled prayers. He asked God for patience and strength to face the inevitable.

We tiptoed to our room and shut the door behind us. Rawyia had a dim light bright enough for me to see the bed I shared with her, the dresser that witnessed our moments of laughter and tears. On the brass hanger, I noticed some of Mama's clothes. I recognized the wool shawl she had always wrapped around her head through the cold winter days. I held it close to my face and smelled her scent. I kept it tight the same way she held me when I crawled into her bed to soothe me to sleep with her body warmth. I wrapped myself with her shawl to feel her close.

Rawyia and Reda watched me in utter silence. Their eyes glistened but reflected sadness.

"I miss Mama," I whispered.

Rawyia pointed to Adham, which shifted my attention to a happy moment.

Adham was sound asleep. His brows were covered with a shiny and dense fluff of golden hair. His eyelashes were so thick they clumped in bunches. He breathed with a rhythm that resonated as a fairy musical tone He was two years old.

"He must look like his father," I whispered in French.

Rawyia nodded with a smile. Reda had no expression. He looked like he was still in a world of his own.

We tiptoed back out. The maid had set up the table with tea, cheese, *foul* (dried Fava beans simmered overnight and served in the morning with olive oil, garlic, cumin, salt and pepper, fresh diced onions, and tomatoes). I still had no appetite, but I drank the tea. Reda and Rawyia stepped out again for a smoke. I shook my head in amazement and walked back to the kitchen.

"Don't go to the hospital, my lady," the maid pleaded. Not sure why she asked me not to go, I frowned and dismissed her. But she stood and repeated her plea. This is when Reda appeared and scorned her.

"Get out and keep your mouth shut," he ordered.

Rawyia softened her tone. She consoled the maid and asked

her to stay out. Rawyia was always kind to underprivileged people. She shared her allowance with the maids. In Lebanon, she went out of her way to feed the homeless in the street. It didn't surprise me to see her compassionate with the servant.

CHAPTER XXI

AMER

At 5:30, I asked Rawyia and Reda to take me to the hospital. They looked at each other, then faced me. Rawyia stood up and left the kitchen. "I have to stay with Adham. He will soon wake up," she said.

"Talk to Papa first," Reda suggested, then left me in the kitchen and stepped out for a smoke.

I found myself all alone with no choice but to walk into Papa's room and ask him to take me to the hospital. I dreaded that moment because, deep in my heart, I felt he was the reason behind Mama's illness. He never treated her with kindness, and she endured his mistreatment without objection. He thought of himself as the supreme power and did what he pleased with her and us. Mama had no opinion or input into our everyday lives, by order from our father, and she never complained.

On the contrary, she loved and respected him. She was brought up to accept her husband and his abuse because she believed God bestowed on men the power to control and discipline women, and that women had to obey. She bottled up her anger and paid the price with her health. Mama followed the rules of Islam, as she understood them, to win the afterlife's reward. Now she lay in a hospital bed, and he enjoyed a healthy life.

As I contemplated using a taxi instead of riding with him to the hospital, he appeared in the kitchen, still in his white shirt and dark blue pants. It was the first time I looked him in the eyes since my escape. Wrinkles carved grooves and trenches on his forehead, around his eyes and mouth, and changed the landscape of his once-smooth chocolate complexion. He stood with slumped shoulders, his hands in his pockets. He couldn't hide the deep sorrow in the way he looked at me, and the sincere love that radiated through the trapped tears in his eyes. It was the first time I felt a strong desire to hug him and tell him I was no longer angry with him, and that I understood how much he had endured as a father to provide the best for us. It was a brief moment of silent reconciliation.

"I am ready, Papa."

He froze for few seconds, then turned around and dragged his feet back to his room. I followed him.

"Are you ready to go?" I asked.

I had noticed that Hala and Rawyia stood mute behind the ajar door of our bedroom. At that moment, I didn't question their strange behavior or why they declined to accompany me to the hospital. I thought of how Mama would feel about my visit, and how much I yearned for her embrace, her tender smile, her melodic voice when she called me "Louli", her skin's scent she saturated with her favorite perfume, Je Reviews, and her eyes that twinkled love. I wanted to make up for all the tears that drenched her pillow night after night. I was determined to take her with me to Canada. Rawyia had told me that Mama's passport was almost ready, and Mama couldn't wait to go to Canada. I wouldn't allow anyone, not even my father, to jeopardize my plans.

"Come in and shut the door behind you," Papa mumbled.

"But it is almost 6:00, and I don't want to waste any time."

"Just sit down and listen to me," he said in a desperate tone.

He motioned with his hand for me to take a seat on his bed and face him. I complied.

He cleared his throat and then turned his gaze aside. I wiggled and cracked my knuckles to direct his focus back to me. He struggled with words to start. I couldn't guess why.

"I am listening, Papa," I said.

"I just wanted you to know, before you visit your mom." He talked with his head bowed. "I confess. I wasn't the best husband or the kind of man your mom deserved."

His confession brought back memories I hadn't forgotten. My heartbeats began to accelerate. I wasn't in the right state of mind to revive his cruelty. However, his confession was a relief. To admit that he had done her wrong was a change. I never thought I would hear that from him.

"When you, Rawyia, and Hady left, I couldn't take the shame and disgrace. I was consumed with humiliation and embarrassment. I left the country and settled in Kuwait. Loneliness helped me face my mistakes and understand why you have all shunned me out of your lives. I realized it was me and the way I had treated you and your mother. I regretted the mistreatment and decided to change."

I couldn't believe what I heard. He sounded merciful. I felt sorry for him. He had wasted so many years of his life without our love. Unfortunately, his confession came too late, but I remained quiet. I wanted him to end his speech.

"You believe me, don't you?"

I nodded.

"At my first visit back to Alexandria, I bought your mother what she had always wanted, and which I had denied her—a mink coat, black pearls, and the finest tea. You know how much she enjoyed her tea."

"Yes, I know."

"I was kind to her, and I even brewed the tea myself and prepared breakfast for her. I wanted her to forgive me, and she did. She told me so." Tears rolled down his cheeks.

"I believe you, Papa, but could we continue this conversation later on tonight?"

"You know your mother was fine and healthy. We had visitors, and she cooked a great meal. She even mentioned how she missed you as she cooked the seafood. She remembered how much you enjoyed the barbequed fish she prepared. I planned to let her visit you in Canada."

"You don't 'let her', Papa. She will come with me without your permission," I snapped.

"At dinner, she complained of stomach pain, but she continued to entertain the visitors. A graceful hostess like she always was. Suddenly, she turned pale and excused herself mid-dinner. I neglected her as I entertained our guests. We learned later that she had a severe bout of diarrhea and vomited. No one heard her."

"But, Papa, please, you can tell me all that later. I have to go," I said, and stood up to leave.

He grabbed my hand and pulled me to sit down. "Please wait until I finish."

I blew out a long sigh and sat down.

"Well, when the visitors left, I dispatched the family doctor to check her up. He couldn't make a diagnosis, so he dispatched two specialists. They, too, failed to determine what was wrong with your mother, and decided she would be better off in a hospital."

Home visits to family physicians were and still are prevalent in Egypt. I was glad Papa decided on hospital care instead. That was what Mama needed. But I still wasn't sure what the problem was. Papa had me worried. He danced around the reason for her hospitalization and, all through the conversation, he avoided eye contact with me.

"So what was the problem?" I asked.

He stood up, walked to the balcony, and stopped. He wanted to tell me something and I assumed Mama was gravely ill. Impatient, I got up to leave.

"Please stay," he pleaded.

Papa never used the word "please" with us. He ordered, and we obeyed. My heart sunk. I sat down.

"Neither the physicians at the hospital nor I could have done more to help your mother."

I was stunned and couldn't speak for a moment. My heart pounded, and a sudden ring in my ears muffled all sounds, even the echo of the words that came out of his mouth. I saw his lips move but could no longer hear him. In fact, I ceased to see him and cocooned within myself to guard the wishes, the hopes, the longing, and the dreams I saved to share with Mama.

Papa watched me with a desperate, sorrowful, and pitiful stare.

"Take me to Mama now."

"She is not there."

"What do you mean? You mean, Mama is d . . .?"

I couldn't utter the word that sealed her non-existence forever. Since I arrived, the thought of her death never crossed my mind. There had always been a speck of hope that breathed life into my longing for her embrace, her tender caresses, her angelic sweet smile, her soft voice when she called my name, and the plan to have her come live with me in Canada.

It had been twenty-four hours since I had learned of Mama's admission to the hospital. I saw no signs that indicated her death—no mourners and no recitation of the Quran blasted from the radio. None of my family dressed in black.

I grew up with rituals to follow when someone died. Family members and even friends dressed in black. Burial was within the next eight hours that followed a death. A special tent was set up to receive the mourners, and sugarless Arabic coffee was served. I saw none of that with Mama. I assumed she was morbidly ill, and I would still see, hug, and kiss her—tell her how much I cherished her and the sacrifice she made for my independence. I wanted to say to her that I had made it because of her help.

"Yes," he muttered, his voice choking," and we buried her yesterday at 3:00 p.m. before the *Asr* (prayer)."

Muslims didn't display their dead for farewell. The deceased must be buried before sunset. In the evening, mourners gather in the deceased's home and take turns reading from the holy Quran. This was all canceled.

I covered my ears, loaded my eyes with all the hatred I had carried through the years, and stung my father with a venomous stare.

He wept aloud. I collapsed on my knees. Everything inside me and about me shattered to pieces like broken glass. Darkness engulfed me and sucked me into an abyss.

Then I stood and circled over and over, slapping my face with both hands, and hoping to wake up from this nightmare. When I stopped, I saw my father, his face drowned in tears.

"I hate you," I screamed.

He extended his arms in a desperate move to absorb my pain with his embrace.

"Don't come near me," I yelled. "You killed Mama. You made her sick. Why is she in the ground, and not you?"

He came closer. I felt his breath on my face. His tears, loaded with remorse, streamed down his face. I had no empathy. I felt satisfied to see him taste the hurt he had put me through. Still, I gave him credit, at least, for his genuine concern and torment.

I don't remember how long we faced each other. The fire of anger roared inside me like a volcano ready to erupt. He reached for my hand one more time. But the fury that emanated from my eyes reflected irreconcilable blame. I backed away from him and out of the room.

Rawyia was at the door weeping. She was dressed in black, and I heard a faint sound of the Quran's recitation from the radio in her room. Then, at that moment, I realized that Mama was no longer a part of my world.

Tears blinded our vision. Rawyia and I embraced as we sobbed. Grief carved a hole in my heart and soul—a spot with the same shape as Mama. Nothing anyone could have done could console or pacify me. The agony was like a sharp needle that stabbed my heart with sorrow, regret and disappointment.

I never got to tell her I loved her one last time, or had a chance to hold her close and look into her peaceful face. She was my anchor and friend all through the time of my diaspora. She didn't die alone. She took my reason to live, my happiness, my hopes, my laughter, and my whole being with her. I had nothing left in me to help deal with my loss.

"I want to see Mama," I pleaded.

Papa came out of his room, and asked Rawyia to take me to our room.

"You will take me to the burial site, and open her grave, now!" I shouted.

I took off my high heels and ran to the front door. I wanted to lay down beside Mama and be with her forever. All my dreams died with her death. I didn't want to live without her.

Rawyia and Papa stood frozen, horrified by my demand. They could see I was determined to follow through with my ultimatum. Still, they didn't move. So, I took off, ran through the hallway, and out the front door. I skipped three and four stairways at a time. My eyes swam in tears, and my vision blurred. I couldn't see where I landed. I fell several times and called "Mama" until neighbors opened their doors and tried to calm me down. When I reached the last step, Hala, my younger sister, hollered, "Laila, wait for me."

I stopped. I needed her to take me to the burial place. I didn't know where Mama was buried, and I'd never before visited a cemetery. She handed me her handkerchief and my shoes.

"Laila, please wipe away your tears," she said, holding her own tears. "Our aunt told me that every teardrop we shed would fall on Mama like lava and burn her in her grave."

I wasn't sure if I should believe her, but I did. I didn't want my tears to make Mama suffer. It wasn't easy, but I managed to control their flow. Then I laid my hand on the pendant she had given me. I rubbed it hard between my fingers and hoped Mama's benevolent spirit would provide me with strength.

Before we hailed a taxi, Hala asked if we could walk one or two blocks to talk. I agreed.

"Did you know it's forbidden in the Quran to disturb the dead?"

"I won't disturb Mama. I just want to hug her one last time."

"We can't open the grave and unwrap Mama's coffin," Hala said firmly.

"What do you mean? I have to see her." I pleaded with her to understand.

"It's *Haram* (forbidden). Mama's body has been cleansed to prepare her for the afterlife. Her spirit is now in the hands of God. If we unearth her body, we would subject it to impurity, and Mama would not like it."

I held the handkerchief over my eyes. "Take me to her grave."

"Not today, and not before seven days."

Hala had witnessed the death of my aunt and was familiar with the rituals. I had no doubt about her reasons. Still, I wasn't ready to wait another day before I could visit Mama.

CHAPTER XXII

COPING WITH MAM'S DEATH

The walk took us to the next town of *Mostafa Kamel*. I hailed a taxi. As the cab stopped, an arm reached from behind me out of nowhere and opened the door. I turned. It was Amer, the officer I met on the train. I remembered he had mentioned he lived in *Mostafa Kamel*. He wore a white shirt and navy blue pants. He smelled of fresh soap.

"Good morning, Laila."

The surprise paralyzed me. I wasn't sure what to say and how to introduce him to Hala. We stepped out of the taxi. He glanced at my sister's black dress and, with a deep voice, he ordered the cab to leave. The timbre of his voice sent shivers down my spine. I never expected to meet him again. His intrusion pleased me.

"May your mother's soul rest in peace," he said to defuse the look of shock on Hala's face and mine.

"My neighbor knows your family. He told me last night about your mother. I am sorry, Laila."

A strange, yet pleasant sensation took over me when I heard him call my name.

Hala looked around nervously. She worried neighbors would see us with a stranger. This was not acceptable in Egyptian society.

"Could we sit in a café and talk?" he asked.

"Do you know him?" Hala asked.

"Yes, I met him on the train last night," I told her.

When I met Amer on the train, I didn't question why he crossed my path. But somehow I knew we would meet again. I had always believed that some circumstances in my life's journey happened for reasons, and Amer was one of those circumstances. He walked into my life when I needed him. In a way, now we suffered the same emptiness, where the absence of our mothers' affection settled in our hearts like a slash.

"We cannot sit with you in a public place," Hala insisted.

"I would love to invite you to tea at my home. It's two minutes away. I live with a male helper," Amer explained.

"Your apartment is safe," Hala blurted without hesitation.

I agreed to go. I needed some time away from home. At the time, the invitation sounded like a safe haven. I couldn't go back to where Mama's voice, laughter, smell, and spirit no longer existed. I knew I would suffer more to see her empty bed, the last towel she used, her shoes, the slippers she wore before she was admitted to the hospital, her favorite teapot still half-full of tea leaves, the leftovers of the last meal she cooked, the jars of spices in the pantry always with her fingerprints, her arrangement of the pots and pans and, most of all, her body scent that kept her presence alive in the apartment.

The three of us walked to his place. He rang the doorbell first before he used his key to enter the apartment. A middle-aged man stood in the foyer dressed in a clean white kaftan. He bowed as we stepped in.

The cooking aroma of Mousaka (eggplant baked with onion and minced meat) and barbequed lamb chops reminded me I hadn't eaten for a while. But I had no desire to eat. My appetite was buried with Mama.

Tall, slim green wood windows added depth and nostalgic charm to the apartment, and the high ceiling was decorated in the center with intricate medallions, a style of architecture adopted by the many foreigners who invaded Egypt. The white marble tiles that covered the floor gave an icy aura to the apartment. I shivered before I collapsed on the brown leather sofa and motioned Hala to join me. Amer excused himself for a few seconds and came back with a handkerchief.

It didn't take long for Hala to feel comfortable to talk. "Please tell my sister it is *Haram* to uncover dead people."

Amer fiddled with the small radio on his desk until he found the Quran station. He turned the volume down and said, "May God have mercy on your mother's and my parents' souls."

Tears began to gather in my eyes. Amer sat next to me. He wrapped my shoulders between his arms. I rested my head on his chest and unleashed my grief. He asked Hala to move to the fauteuil to give me room to lie down. I don't know how long I lay there but, when I woke up, I found Amer next to me.

"You slept for two hours," Hala protested. "We have to go back home."

"Soliman prepared lunch for us," Amer said.

"No, thank you, Amer, we must go," Hala insisted.

"Not me," I said.

"I can't go back without you. I will have to tell Papa where you are," Hala said, evidently appalled at the thought.

"Laila, here is the key to the apartment," Amer interrupted. "You can come back at any time and stay. I have a second home in Cairo."

Amer's generosity and trust surprised me. Amid all the agony I experienced, a thread of a long-term attachment weaved like magic. I was speechless, and so was he. A silent communication between us began as if we had known each other in the previous world. I took the key and clutched my hand tight around it. I was sure Amer had given it to me to keep the channel open between us.

I left with Hala to spare her trouble at home, and to make sure she kept the encounter a secret between us.

It was already dark when we walked back home. Although the details about Mama's last days tormented me, I asked Hala, "Talk to me about Mama."

"Papa cut the funeral short when you called from Cairo," she told me.

"Why? When did Mama pass away?"

"Yesterday morning," Hala exclaimed. "Papa worried that if you walked in during the funeral, you wouldn't endure the shock."

Tears rushed to my eyes.

"The strangest thing happened the night before," Hala continued. "Hours before Mama left us, I mentioned you were on your way. I wanted to cheer her up. She smiled, and her eyes welled with tears. 'I know, but Louli will be disappointed'."

My knees buckled. I could no longer hear Hala's voice. Mama's words shredded my heart. I listened to her voice, loud as the cars honking around us, and I saw her face through my blurred vision. I felt her strong presence. Joy filled my heart. Her soul hovered over me. I looked around, searching in space for her image.

"Hala, Mama is here with us," I whimpered.

"Yes, she is, for you to say goodbye," she choked. "My aunt said that Mama's spirit will roam around us for seven days after it left her body. Let's recite Al Fateha (the first verse in the Quran) for her soul."

Rawyia waited for us on the balcony. She took me in her arms when she opened the door. "Where have you been?"

"We'll tell you," Hala said. "First, let's give Laila something to eat."

"I want to know why and how Mama died so young," I demanded.

"She was healthy until she discovered Papa had an affair with a girl younger than any of us," Rawyia explained.

A flood of emotions drowned me into a of anger, sorrow and hatred. I had already blamed my father for Mama's diabetes, and for her separation from three of her children. But now, I heard he was responsible for her death. The shock of his betrayal crushed her to death. I will never forgive him.

For fifty-two years, she gave him love, respect, and devotion. He never appreciated her, and Mama never complained. She loved him unconditionally. My mother would have given him her eyes if he needed them. How dare he get himself a girlfriend? Where had his speeches of honesty, virtue, and honor gone?

"Apparently," Rawyia revealed with disdain, "the girl is the daughter of the lady he knew before he married Mama."

"I thought to wait a few days before we told her about Papa's affair," Hala said, shaking her head in disapproval.

Many times, I wanted to forgive Papa. I created excuses for the way he treated Mama and us to help me forget the past. But my sisters' statements ignited a fire of dormant anger inside me. I no longer feared my father. It was like the death of Mama gave birth to courage. I had to confront him.

Mama's spirit was still alive in the apartment. I could smell her scent in the air, and hear her voice resonate off the hallway walls. Her toothbrush was still in the glass cup where she had left it; her favorite face towel embroidered with pink roses was even folded on her rocking chair. It was impossible to stay in the apartment. I had to leave—but not before I faced my father.

I stood in front of their bedroom. The door was ajar, and the wood shutters were still closed. There was a morbid silence, as if the whole world had stopped with Mama's death. I knocked but heard nothing. Then I entered with heavy feet. This was Mama's room, and she was not inside to greet me, take me in her arms, kiss me all over my face, and tell me, as she done when we talked on the phone, "I missed you, Louli."

If Mama had sensed my visit, why couldn't she wait for me?

"Come in, Laila. If you wish to visit your mother's grave, I will take you."

Papa's voice startled me. I kicked the door open with my foot.

"Mama is not in a grave. She is alive inside me until I meet her. You go by yourself and stand with your feet over her grave," I shouted, as I forced my tears to stay inside my eyes. I didn't want tears to burn Mama's body. "I would advise you, instead, to ask her forgiveness, for abusing the love she had for you, for all the nights she wept for losing us, and for the disrespect and humiliation she suffered with you."

Papa stared with eyes ready to explode from shock. I wasn't afraid to unleash my anger; I couldn't feel sorry for him. On the contrary, I wanted to stand up for Mama and hurt him as much as he had hurt her.

"What would a younger wife offer you at your age?" I blurted out. "Sex? Is this what occupied your mind? Half of your children's lives were destroyed, and God knows what would happen to the other three. Did you plan for your young wife to share Mama's home? How about my brothers and sister, did you plan to throw them out? I don't want to ever see you again." I pointed my finger at him and then walked out.

To my surprise, Rawyia was compassionate and empathetic. She was not the rebellious sister that taught me to fight oppression and seek freedom from our father's dictatorship. She surprised me with her forgiveness, a new approach.

"Have mercy on him, La," she pleaded. "He's remorseful."

"Maybe I will one day, but only after years of psychoanalysis to rid myself of the hurt he caused."

Rawyia had no other place to go to with her son. She had to get along with Papa and everyone in the family. She was a widow with a toddler in need of shelter.

"I cannot stay in this apartment without Mama," I insisted.

"Where would you go? And when is your flight back?" Rawyia was concerned.

"In two weeks," I said. "Don't worry; I have a place."

"Please stay till tomorrow," she pleaded. "There are issues

you need to hear and understand about Mama and Papa as well."

"Papa's issues don't interest me."

"Mama asked me to explain them to you," she choked out. "You might reconsider leaving."

It was impossible to turn down Mama's request, even if it came through Rawyia. If I had taken the phone call while she was still in the hospital, she would have told me herself. The loss of the opportunity to hear Mama's voice for the last time dripped sorrow into my veins. Destiny intervened again and left me with a wound that would never mend.

Rawyia asked the maid to prepare something to eat and take it to our bedroom. Hala wanted to join us, but Rawyia dismissed her. I was surprised at her behavior, but she explained that we needed to connect like before, without Hala or anyone else.

"You know little about men's rights in a Muslim marriage," she said in her familiar bossy tone.

I turned my gaze away, shaking my head.

"Mama was sick for the past two years. She couldn't perform her duty as a wife."

My eyes bulged out of their sockets. Gall filled my throat and left a bitter taste. I tried to swallow, but my dry mouth wouldn't cooperate, and I couldn't restrain my anger.

"Which duties couldn't she perform?" I snapped, shaking her by the shoulders. "Mama gave her life, her health, her happiness, and she had nothing left to give."

"He wanted physical intimacy," she said, and lowered her gaze to the floor. "The Sharia grants Muslim men the right to keep four wives."

The Sharia is sacred for Muslims. It is the statutory law based on the teachings of the Quran and the traditions of the Prophet Mohammed. It was impossible to question, even though I was not convinced of the restriction it puts on women.

This did not sound like the same Rawyia who taught me

to reject the power bestowed on men by "God." She loved and supported Mama always. She was the one who suggested I take Mama to Canada. Still, Rawyia was in desperate need of my father's support for her and her child, but I was not.

"Would you have supported Mama if she took a younger man if Papa, for any reason, couldn't perform his duty as a husband?" I asked her.

Rawyia wrung her hands long enough to annoy me.

"Answer me."

"Mama wouldn't have done it," Rawyia said. "Besides, Sharia obliges the wife to accept the husband's three marriages—as long as he informs her before he signs the marriage contract. And Papa followed the Sharia law."

"So Papa wanted to take a wife younger than his youngest daughter for the sole purpose of fulfilling his physical needs, and you called that Sharia?"

"Yes," she mumbled.

"Would you have given consent to your late husband to take a new wife?" I demanded.

"Of course not," she asserted, "but some women would, and Mama was one. They stay in the marriage to keep the family together. Some lose interest in intimate encounters with their husbands. Some need financial support. Whatever their reasons, Sharia and social laws legitimize these marriages."

Rawyia sounded cold and disrespectful to Mama. Marriage is a commitment for sickness and health. This Sharia could have been suitable for its time and desert environment. Rawyia didn't accept it for herself, so why did she expect Mama to behave differently? I resented her excuses and disliked the changes I saw in her personality. I no longer cherished anything in the apartment, and nothing was left to remember except the smell of death that permeated the air. I took my suitcase and left, chased by a stunned look on everyone's faces.

CHAPTER XXIII

FALLING IN LOVE

My compass was out of synch; my feet took over, and I found myself at Amer's apartment.

At 10:00 p.m., the contralto voice of Om Kulthum, an Egyptian diva, echoed with the lyrics of *Aghadan Alqaq* (Will I See You Tomorrow), and reached my ears through an open door. Darkness filled the room except for a glimmer of light from the small radio on the night table. Brut infused with a musky male scent and the smell of cigarette smoke wafted through the air. A few seconds passed before my eyes adjusted, and I could see Amer lying on his bed, his head rested on one arm, and a cigarette between the fingers of his other hand. His eyelids flickered with the rhythm of the song.

I placed my suitcase on the floor and stood a few feet away. Serenity flowed like blood through my veins and encircled my heart. I remained motionless and wondered whether I should wake him or walk out. He had told me that he would go back to his second home in Cairo and stay there before he returned to barracks.

When he gave me the key to his apartment, he had invited me into his life. I knew, if I accepted his offer, I would fall into a destiny that waited to rewrite the remaining manuscript of my life, a future with Amer as the main character.

Amer had crossed my path at a time when I held my sorrow in a cup of pain. A spark of attraction ignited a new sentiment. The wall I had erected between Egyptian men and me crumbled. My tender soul had taken over. I once heard that love is most potent when mixed with anguish. While I drowned in grief, I found solace in Amer's support and attention. We never spoke words of love; we felt them. It was like fate had knocked on our door, and we responded with absolute submission. I decided to wake him.

Amer took me in his arms. We remained in that embrace for what seemed an eternity. The candle in my heart was ready to be kindled—the void in my soul needed to be filled.

"Will you come with me to Cairo?" he whispered.

"Yes."

Events rippled fast, like a stone thrown on a river's surface. It lifted me from the stable life I had built, and threw me into a euphoric abyss alien to me, and yet I was pleased and comforted.

I wanted to escape the reality of Mama no longer existing. My family was a constant reminder of my loss I couldn't face. Without Mama, I had no family. She was not just my mother but my sister, brother, and father. The rest of the family didn't exist anymore. She was the root that held us together, and no one could nurture the family after her. She remained alive in my heart. I never visited her grave. I refused to admit her death. Her memories, blue slippers, and mauve cardigan were all I took with me when I left Alexandria for the second time.

Amer's apartment was in a narrow alley in downtown Cairo, a short distance from the Egyptian Museum and AUC, the American University. His street, like many in Cairo, was dark and jam-packed with vendors and car mechanics. Patches of crumbled asphalt scattered between potholes and mud. The remnant of European architecture on buildings' facades pleaded for restoration. That alley bustled with people more than it could accommodate. It was crowded with nosy individuals who stared at us as we got out of the car. Full respect was given to Amer with a military salutation as he held my hand, passing through the rusty iron gate into his apartment building. The porter, with the luggage, followed us in utter silence.

The rusty iron rails of the stairway were covered with slabs of cracked marble, but still held their dignity. An aroma of Egyptian dishes wafted through the open windows where stray cats and dogs waited to catch leftovers dumped in the garbage pails outside each apartment. The air was stiff, laced a with rotten odor impossible to ignore. I covered my nose.

Once we reach the second floor, it felt like I stepped into a different world—spotless marble floors carpeted with Persian rugs, musk incense infusing the air with a pleasant fragrance, and closed wood shutters kept the apartment calm. Light, classic furniture gave the space a relaxed atmosphere. On my left was a salon and dining room. To my right, a long corridor connected the bedrooms and bathrooms to the rest of the apartment.

"Follow me," Amer said as he walked through the hallway. "This will be your bathroom." He walked to the first door on my right. "This is your bedroom."

I concluded, with relief, that we would sleep in separate rooms. Even though passion had already taken root inside of me, I was not ready to move to the next step. His apartment was a safe refuge where I needed to think out everything that happened since I arrived in Egypt.

"You will find towels in your bedroom," he said and left me. "I will make tea if you want to join me in the salon," he yelled back.

Exhausted, I sat on the chair, facing the mirror. I looked as I felt: sad eyes, droopy cheeks, and shoulders slumped. The flicker of hope I kept lit through my past ordeals had died. I wanted to jump in bed, cover my face with the pillow, and sleep. Nevertheless, I had to hang onto the rope of safety Amer offered. I took a shower, changed my clothes, and joined him for tea.

Amer served the tea in a china tea set. I was impressed, not with the way he served the tea, but with how he looked in his blue jeans and white shirt. He motioned me to sit next to him on the sofa. I did. I had developed trust in him but still felt a little uncomfortable in his apartment alone.

"I often invite my friends for dinner whenever I'm on leave," he started. "We order kebab and salad and eat together."

I nodded. Surely he didn't expect me to go along and join his friends.

"I can stay in the bedroom until they leave."

"No, please, I want to introduce you to them," he said with a wink. "I don't introduce women to my friends."

I didn't know what he meant. I was sure his friends would misjudge me. A woman who stayed with an unmarried man in his apartment is considered taboo in Egypt. However, an unspoken mutual trust had developed between us. It was like a current that pulled us into a sea of love. We surrendered to it. I didn't want to misconstrue his desire to introduce me to his friends. I took it as a gesture of proudness; I was overwhelmed.

"I prefer not to join you."

"As you wish," he said.

I excused myself and retired. Not long after, sleep took over, saving me from my anguish. Dawn hid behind the dark sky. Amer shook me to wake me up. I opened my eyes, disoriented. I sat up, perplexed.

"It's me, Amer," he whispered. "I heard you scream in your sleep."

I collapsed on his chest, and he enveloped me with tenderness. All my disturbed senses settled down. That moment, I wanted the world to stop. Our hearts beat the same passionate tune. We remained in each other's arms as one soul for the rest of the night. When we woke, I was entangled in a web of mixed and electrified sensations. He stole my willpower.

"I have to leave you for few hours," he said, struggling to pull himself away from our embrace. "I am on duty today," he continued. "It will take two hours just to confirm attendance."

I refused to let go.

"If I don't go now, they will deny me next weekend's leave," he pleaded.

I released him with difficulty and stayed in bed. A few minutes later, he appeared dressed in his khaki military uniform. I was again smitten with how handsome he looked in his attire.

"I have sent young Mostafa to buy croissants and cheese pâté," he said and kissed me on the forehead.

The minute he left, I was back to my sorrows and disappointments. Memories flooded my mind of Mama's endless suffering with my father. I thought of how much she loved him in spite of his harsh treatment and how she must have taken his infidelity. I was angry with God for giving men the right to keep four wives. How could that make it acceptable to any woman who loved her husband? According to the Quran, God put conditions on such marriages. Mama loved Papa and gave him children. She was healthy and faithful. He had no reason to look for a younger wife. Mama was fifty-two when she passed away.

I was angry with Rawyia as well. She had changed. She was no longer the same person that fought male dominance. In fact, she had fallen in love with a married man. When I disapproved of her relationship with Kader, she expressed a desire to accept his marriage proposal. She considered the status of a second wife.

I had always wanted to emulate Rawyia's behavior. I learned from her how to stand up for my rights, and I acquired the courage to be independent in Canada. I had planned to help her immigrate and share my life in the West. She disappointed me. It pained me to have the two women I cherished the most abandon me. Nevertheless, I called Rawyia to let her know where I was staying.

"Alo, La, where are you?" she asked.

"In Cairo, with the officer I met on the train."

The boldness of my answer took Rawyia by surprise. She was quiet. For the first time, she heard the new, assertive me.

"Have you planned to attend the seventh-day remembrance of Mama's death?"

"Mama is not dead," I snapped. "She is alive and will forever stay alive in my soul. Don't count on me to confirm her death. Don't worry about me. Engage your brain before becoming a second wife." I ended the conversation.

CHAPTER XXIV

AMER'S PERSONALITY

When I criticized Rawyia for her marriage to an Egyptian man, I never thought it would happen to me. The future I had planned and the promises I had made faded when I met Amer. It no longer mattered that he was Egyptian and an army officer who couldn't leave Egypt to live in a different country. I was smitten by his charm. I surrendered to my feelings. I didn't know why, when, and how I sank so deep in the sea of infatuation. It was like a magical miracle. I thought maybe Mama's spirit arranged the whole thing with Amer, to help ease the shock of her death. My life turned upside down like the entire universe had smiled, and time had forgotten us.

I was still in bed when Amer showed up after two hours. I heard his weighty combat boots as he approached and stopped at the open doorway. He wore his military cap. His smile melted me. I suppressed a wish to have him join me in bed. Desire gleamed in his eyes. I sat up and covered myself to my neck with the eiderdown.

"I need to shower," he said and winked.

"Me, too," I said, and blushed with embarrassment. "After

you, I meant."

"The bathtub is big enough for both of us." He offered his hand.

I shook my head. He excused himself and went to the bathroom. His facial expression spoke louder than words, full of the assurance that we belonged together despite our willpower. Something stronger than us already tied us together. We didn't need to say much to know that we would soon explore each other's sensuality and drown deep in emotion. I didn't need to be close to him to imagine what our future love interlude would be like.

Later, after the bath, we sat in the family room and drank Arabic coffee he brewed himself. He lit a cigarette. I surrendered to his open arms and rested my head on his chest. He picked up my cup of coffee and held it close to my mouth. I took a sip. He reached for his cup and drank while he smoked. We didn't say much. As a matter of fact, we didn't say a word. But we synchronized our heartbeats and witnessed in silence the birth of two stars illuminating the dark sky to celebrate the birth of our love.

"Have you been to a nightclub in Cairo?"

"Not with you," I said. "Before we met, my life in Egypt was a long night without love, hope, or desires."

"Let me take you to Al Moqatam's Hill to have dinner at a restaurant where we can enjoy this happy sky."

Before I replied, the telephone ring startled us. Amer's facial expression hardened and ignored the ringing until it stopped. Then it rang again. He sighed before he let go of me, lit a cigarette, picked up the phone, walked down the corridor to his room, and shut the door.

Thoughts played with my mind. I wondered who could be on the phone. Why didn't he want me to know? I concluded it was either work or a woman. Inevitably, someone as handsome as Amer must have had a woman in his life. However, there was nothing in his apartment that looked or smelled female.

Fifteen minutes passed before he returned. His face was flushed red, and deep furrows reflected his state of mind. He sat next to me and lit another cigarette before he guided me back into the same position on his chest. His heartbeats raced loud through the thin cotton of his shirt. I waited until he settled down before I resumed our conversation.

"Are you still in the mood for dinner?"

"Yes. But, before we go, I have something important to tell you."

I put my finger on his lips. I didn't want him to say anything to rob me of the magical moments I enjoyed. Still, I was curious to know, especially when I heard the determination in his voice.

"You will know sooner or later," he started. "So let me tell you now."

"Since you insist," I said. "Promise it won't upset me."

"I will make sure not to upset you," he said, kissing me on the forehead. "I have had a woman for the past ten years."

Silence took over. He waited for my reaction, but I couldn't comment. I thought I might lose the happiness I had found, and that he wanted to go back to his woman. Disappointment silenced my voice.

"A few months before you and I met," he explained in a warm tone, "Sanaa and I agreed to break up. I was relieved and thought she had her own life now. Surprisingly, on the phone just now, she asked to come over. When I refused, she insisted."

"You mean she is on her way here?" I snapped.

"Yes," he whispered, "I forgot to ask Sanaa to return the apartment key."

I stood up disturbed. "I must leave," I insisted.

"No," he blurted. "Sanaa will leave, not you."

Out of nowhere, a woman appeared in the foyer. She was short and chubby; her face was clean from makeup. She stood in utter silence as she eyed me from head to toe, giving Amer occasional angry glances.

"So this is the one you left me for?" she said, pointing at me with disgust.

Amer pushed her out of the apartment. He asked her for the key before he slammed the door shut.

"Last week," he said, "she forced herself into my apartment. I slapped her so hard and kicked her with my boots. She slid on that ceramic floor." He pointed at the hallway. "She landed on the glass door over there and broke her chin."

His unabashed cruelty shocked me. He reminded me of my brother Reda and my cousin Ahmed's aggressiveness. Amer was no different from other men; I left Egypt to escape their oppression and abuse. But, somehow, the seed of love had already been planted in my heart.

The tragedy of Mama's death left me confused. Amer came into my life at a time when I couldn't cope with the emotional rollercoaster. I needed to escape the trauma and the shock of my father's infidelity. Amer offered the comfort I needed. However, his cruelty was blatant; it scared me. When I asked him if he would one day treat me the way he treated Sanaa, he replied, "Of course not. You are different." I believed him. Even though, I wasn't sure what he meant by different.

Instead of regret for his despicable behavior, he demonstrated arrogance and disregard for my feelings. Still, I was attracted to him. However, deep inside, I wanted to control the emotions amassing inside my heart, and ready to erupt in a sea of love different from the love I felt for Ghassan.

"Get dressed, Laila," he said. "We are going out for dinner and to see a comedy show. Emam, the star, is a close friend of mine. Surely you know him."

"Yes, of course; he is my favorite comedian."

I had no desire now, nor was I in the mood for going out. I was still consumed with grief over Mama's death. However, I feared, if I declined, I would complicate the situation and face Amer's physical abuse. I was ready to move to a hotel but kept the idea to myself.

I put on a long black dress, gathered my hair into a chignon, and left my face untouched by makeup. When Amer came out of his room dressed in a camel suit and white shirt, against my will, I stood speechless with admiration. He had shaved and smelled of Aramis. We faced each other and, like we had read each other's minds, we succumbed to the unspoken explosion within us. A burst of love pulled us like magnets into a warm embrace. At that moment, I had a strong desire to merge into his soul without fear.

"I wish time would stop," he whispered in my ear as if he dwelled in my mind and owned it already.

The cuckoo clock in the foyer announced 9:00 p.m.; it was time to leave for our dinner and theater. We ignored it. I burned with lust, and the heat that radiated from his body intensified my passion. I wanted to taste his love. He didn't pressure me.

He drove his black Fiat. Our hands clasped; even when he shifted gears, he wouldn't let go of my hand. We didn't talk, but our souls were connected and communicated in silence. When I was with him, I forgot the world. He became my world. His charm and gallantry kept his offensive side at bay.

We ate barbequed pigeons—a delicacy appreciated by Egyptians. We finished the meal with Arabic coffee and then headed to the theater.

"My friend Emam is the lead actor," he explained.

I had heard of the famous comedian Emam. I had seen him on TV but never attended his plays. It was a treat when we sat in the front row—seats reserved for special guests. Emam acknowledged Amer and me with a smile. His pants were rolled up to his knees, and his shirt was missing a sleeve. He had a striped orange-and-brown tie, red socks and one shoe missing the sole. Hands in his pockets, he stood a few seconds and looked serious until he spotted a duster on the desk. He sauntered over to it with arrogance, cussing in whispers the fate that forced him to work at the attorney's office. He picked up the cloth and wiped the furniture with one hand still in his pocket. He didn't need to say much. His body language was funny; the audience roared with laughter, and we joined them. Amer's repeated kisses on my hand broke my concentration. However, I enjoyed the show. For two hours, happiness was our companion. I forgot my past and my future, relishing the endless sweet taste of love. That evening, the moon was bright and brilliant stars beamed radiance over us in celebration of our union. As I walked out of the theater next to him, I felt like a bride realizing her dream. I surrendered to love.

Soon after midnight, when we left the theater, we stayed in the car for a few minutes. Our lips met and ignited the longing we had for each other. He turned the engine on and sped to get out of the dark stretch of Al Haram Road. That was the last I remembered.

CHAPTER XXV

CAR ACCIDENT

When I woke up, my memory was a blank space, like a white wall bereft of photographs. The room was cold, the lights were dimmed, several tubes were hooked to both of my arms, and a needle stuck in my vein. A clear solution hung on a metal hanger and dripped into the catheter attached to the needle. A medicinal odor permeated the air.

A handsome man with a concerned expression stood by my bed. He called me Laila. His voice was familiar, but I couldn't remember who he was. A nurse with a smile stood next to him and offered me a glass of water. My forehead and chin burned with inflammation. There was chaos in my head. I didn't know where I was.

When the nurse left the room, I asked with a feeble voice. "What happened?" The man kissed me on the forehead, wrapped his arms around me and repeated, "Thank God, thank God, thank God."

"What happened?" I repeated.

"Not now, Laila," he pleaded. "I will tell you everything when you feel better."

The man was calm and seemed to know me well. I was pleased to relinquish full control to someone so handsome but was anxious to know more about him. He buzzed for the nurse. A few minutes passed before she walked in and attempted to turn the lights on. He whispered, "Keep the lights off."

The man gestured with his pointer finger to his lips to keep quiet.

"Go ahead and check her vitals," he ordered. "Then call her doctor."

After I drifted back into sleep, a hand shook me.

"Laila, wake up."

Aches pounded on my head like a hammer. I was sleepy. He asked me to stay awake. He propped my bed in an upright position and held me until I opened my eyes and got familiar with my surroundings. He stayed next to me on the hospital bed.

"Why am I here?"

"We were in a car accident," he told me.

I realized we were connected and that we must have been close. I relaxed and rested my head on his chest. I touched my chin and felt gauze and a Band-Aid on my forehead and chin.

"I want a mirror," I insisted.

"First, let me tell you what happened," he pleaded.

"Am I disfigured?"

"No, but you have a tiny cut on your left eyebrow and chin," he assured me. "I ordered a plastic surgeon to make sure no scars remained on your beautiful face."

I was at peace. Even though I worried about the injuries on my face and the loss of memory, I was comforted by his presence.

"Laila, I am Amer." He looked into my eyes. "I met you on the train as you traveled to Alexandria to see your mother, who was sick in the hospital. You live in Canada."

I was blank. However, I believed him. I could neither confirm nor deny my identity as he revealed, but something about his eyes awakened my memory. I was sure I had seen them before, and his voice had a familiar tone.

"What was your name again?" I asked.

"Amer."

I smiled. His name also sounded familiar. The past started to take shape and presence in my mind. It was like someone pointed a flashlight on my dormant memories; everything was crystal clear. My healing progressed, but I kept the slow process to myself. I waited for Amer to share with me the moment of full recovery.

When dawn light invaded the room through the wood shutters, a nurse announced that the doctor would be in in a few minutes. I felt groggy but anxious to resume my life as it was before the accident.

"Well, you're still beautiful and healthy," the doctor cheered.

Doctors have a way of restoring confidence, but his compliment didn't work. I knew I was anything but beautiful with deep cuts on my face.

"I expected you to stay in the coma longer. Nevertheless, you seem to be a healthy young woman. Or was it the love and attention you received from this young man? He never left your side for a second."

"How long have I been in a coma?" I asked.

"Twenty days," replied the doctor as he proceeded to remove the stitches. "You healed as expected, and you won't even see traces of the scars. As for the brain scan diagnosis, it shows no future problem with your memory. You can go home tomorrow, but not to Canada. We need to perform a few more tests to make sure you've recovered with no side effects."

When the doctor left, Amer squeezed himself next to me on the bed, and we stayed in each other's arms until the nurse walked in to check my vitals.

"How did the accident happen?" I asked.

"You don't remember?"

"No," I said, and looked at Amer, puzzled.

"It happened the night we went to the theater," he said,

looking worried, "as we drove back home along Al Haram Road. Don't you remember? It was pitch dark, and we crashed head-on with another car," he stressed with concern.

"I don't remember," I said.

He walked to the closet, rummaged through my clothes, and pulled out a yellow wool scarf.

"Do you remember this?"

"Yes, I remember," I said.

"You wore it around your neck."

"Yes, I remember."

"Well, it was this scarf that saved your life."

The conversation left me confused and shaken. I gathered something terrible had happened. I'd survived something more than just a cut on my forehead and chin and coma. Amer took me step by step to my pre-accident time. I remembered.

"Chunks of the windshield's glass shattered and pierced the scarf around your neck," he explained. "I am not sure who called the police but, when they arrived, they found you unconscious with blood all over your face. I was semi-conscious, and heard people whisper that I was dead. I took you in my arms and hopped in the police car. They turned on the siren and drove to a remote clinic in a village. The drive to a hospital in Cairo would have taken more than an hour. I worried I might lose you. I took you to the first clinic. It wasn't the best place for an emergency, but it was the only one close by that was open."

Amer was distraught as he continued. "The doctor at the clinic wasn't a plastic surgeon. He stitched the cuts to stop the bleeding. It was poorly done under candlelight," he choked. "I called my friend in the city. He picked us up from the clinic and took us to a private hospital in downtown Cairo. A plastic surgeon removed the stitches and re-stitched the cuts while you were still in a coma." He sighed with distress. "One of the top plastic surgeons sutured my wounds."

Amer ignored the doctor's advice to help me recollect events in slow motion and explained it all in one dose.

The horror of what happened intensified my worries about how my face would look. I touched my bandages. For a brief moment, I thought I experienced a dream. I couldn't cry or feel sadness. I was numb. As the nurse darted in and out of the room, I heard the doctor's assurance of my recovery. I smelled the nauseating odor of the hospital, sensed Amer's breath on my forehead, and wished it was all just a nightmare. I hoped I would soon wake up but I didn't.

Amid the confusion, I remembered I had a job in Canada, and that I was in Egypt to visit Mama, and that Mama had died. I also remembered Amer was an army officer. I was en route to full recovery. I asked Amer to arrange for a call to my manager at work. I had to let him know what had happened before he fired me.

I remembered Amer told me he could face AWOL punishment. I wasn't sure if he had obtained a leave permit or had extended his leave to stay with me. I wasn't concerned about my stitches as much the repercussions of his unplanned absence from his military duty. But he didn't look concerned, and I couldn't be any happier. There was no doubt in my mind that he shared my feelings.

During recuperation, Amer and I called Rawyia often. We updated her on my health. I asked her not to come to Cairo. She offered to send me money for the hospital, but Amer had already taken care of all expenses. He paid the hospital bill and bought me an open ticket to Canada to ensure my return. We behaved like we were meant to stay connected for years to come.

"How would you feel about living in Egypt?" he asked.

The thought had never crossed my mind. My future in Egypt was out of the question. I refused to entertain the idea, instead cherishing every minute I spent with Amer.

"How about you immigrating to Canada?" I said, even though I knew it was an impossible expectation and proposition.

"You mean, if I move to Canada, you would agree to marry me?"

His question shook the ground under my feet. A powerful intoxicating force weaved our fate and sealed our karma. It all began when he offered the matches on the train. I never imagined his approach would ignite a fire of passion that lasted beyond my two-week visit. I had lost my airplane return ticket to Canada, and perhaps my job.

Nevertheless, love ruled my world. There was nothing in my power I could have done to control my feelings. I wasn't sure if he was serious. Our hearts had connected, and I was happy with him. Still, marriage was a different story. What prompted him to make such a hasty decision? We had just met.

"Are you serious?" I said. "How could you, as a military officer?"

"I would resign." He spoke with a firm tone.

I believed him. However, I was confused. He had told me he never proposed to Sanaa, his previous girlfriend, but now, he wanted to marry me?

"Why me?"

"One meets his soul mate only once in a lifetime."

The more he talked, the deeper my feelings took root. Still, his abusive personality waved a red flag whenever my emotions dominated my heart and mind. I convinced myself that he was right when he explained that Sanaa had cheated on him and that she deserved what she got. It was easy to convince me I was different and that he would never disrespect or abuse me. I was flattered. Nothing could have changed what we felt for each other. It was as if fate had intercepted my life to steer me away from course again. I surrendered to love, but with trepidation.

"Let's not rush," I said. "We need time to get to know each other, even from a distance."

Amid the emotional uncertainty, I thought of Rawyia. She was the one I always trusted for advice. I had just lost Mama, and Amer had asked to marry me. He was the emotional shelter I needed after the loss of Mama. I struggled to ignore the hidden side of his abusive behavior. Still, I was unable to sever the strong feelings cemented in my heart. I needed Rawyia's logical talk to sort out my dilemma.

"Please be careful," Rawyia pleaded. "You just met this man."

"He asked to marry me," I said, hoping Rawyia would approve.

"Are you serious? The military forbids personnel to leave Egypt," Rawyia snapped. After all you went through to get to Canada, you want to come back to Egypt? Amer would not be any different from men you grew up with."

"He said he would resign."

"You believed him?" she scoffed. "You haven't changed. Still romantic and trusting people you don't know well. Go back to Canada. Don't allow any man to destroy your future."

Rawyia was right. However, I kept Amer's aggressive side to myself. I wanted to believe he wouldn't hurt me and thought I was different, as he said. I was infatuated. The fire of love roared in my heart and ignited my lust, desire, and longing to remain with him.

But the marriage proposal had inflated my ego. I was in my late twenties, eager to settle down and have a child of my own like Rawyia. I dreamed of a child that looked like Amer. However, I kept the dream to myself and postponed the answer to the proposal.

Against my doctor's advice, I decided to return to Canada. Amer arranged a farewell party and invited his closest friends. Some played the Oud, others drummed on Tabla and on the wood coffee table while they sang great love and farewell songs. They were happy for Amer and felt comfortable enough to ask when we would marry. I was pleased that Amer might have expressed to them his desire to marry me.

CHAPTER XXVI

IN PARIS

Around three a.m., Amer drove me to the airport. As an army officer, he obtained a permit to accompany me onto the plane. I was impressed. The farewell was harder than I anticipated. I didn't need to promise to come back. We both knew we would meet again soon. Before he left, he talked to the flight attendant.

"I heard you had a car accident. If you need anything, please press this button," she said.

I thanked her, closed my eyes, and recited verses from the Quran, which Mama had urged me to do whenever I traveled. The stewardess believed accidents could happen when we flew. Hence, prayer was not a bad idea.

"Please, try to stay awake," she urged. "We will reach Orly Airport in three hours. From there, the flight back to Canada will take ten hours, enough for a long nap."

I couldn't keep my eyes open. I drifted as soon as I finished my prayers. A few minutes later, the captain announced permission to unlatch seat belts. His voice startled me. I felt dizzy as I opened my eyes. I remained still in my seat until we arrived in Paris and disembarked. At the airplane door, the stewardess asked if I needed help. I assured her I was okay, even though my head hurt and my vision was blurred. I was too embarrassed to ask for help.

When I reached the first restaurant at the airport, I couldn't stand. I dropped on a chair and slumped against a table. I couldn't lift my head or open my eyes. The world around me spun. I was alone and scared. I forced myself to try to stand, but I couldn't. A man seated not far from my table approached, and asked in French, "Are you sick?"

"Yes, please, I need help."

A few minutes passed before an airport medical person arrived. He checked my vitals and asked me a few questions—where I came from and where I was headed. I informed him I had recently recovered from a car accident and had been in a coma for a month. I answered their questions with exhaustive effort, then passed out.

A beam of light met my eyes as I awoke from a sleep in a hotel room. I sat up and looked around. It took me a few seconds to remember what had happened. I saw an envelope addressed to me. I opened the letter and read, "Please contact the front desk." I still wore the black skirt and grey sweater I had on when I left Egypt. I searched for my luggage but couldn't find it. However, my head felt stable. I found a glass of water on the night table and drank it all before I called the reception desk.

"Alo, someone left a note for me to call."

"Yes, this is Laila, right?"

"Yes."

"Someone will come to your room and explain what happened."

"What about my flight to Canada?" I asked.

"Don't worry; we will accommodate you."

Soon after, someone knocked on my door. I thanked the girl at the front desk and hung up.

A middle-aged woman stood at the door when I opened it. She introduced herself as the Méridien Hotel manager.

"I am Monique," she said with a smile. "May I come in?"

"Please," I said.

"How do you feel now?" she asked.

"I am much better, ready to take the flight back to Canada."

"You passed out," she started. "Do you remember what happened?"

"Yes, I do. The car accident and the coma."

"Do you feel strong enough now to travel?"

"Of course," I assured her with enthusiasm. "I need to call my employer. I don't want to lose my job."

"Please, dial the front desk, give them the number, and they will connect you. It is daytime now in Canada."

She then handed me an airplane ticket for my return back to Canada.

"This is from Air France. A free open ticket. Your flight is tomorrow at 10:30 a.m.," she said.

I took the ticket and thanked her.

She stood up to leave and said, "Should you need anything, please contact the front desk. We wish you a safe trip back home."

"Thank you," I said, and closed the door behind her.

The eerie silence in the room gave me a shiver. I turned on the TV for company and sat at the edge of the bed. I still felt cold and lonely. I thought of what I had left in Egypt, and tears gathered in my eyes. Guilt tormented me. How could I leave Alexandria without a visit to Mama's burial site? I stood up and paced. What if Mama was angry with me? How could I make it up to her? Would she ever forgive me?

Moreover, how did I allow Amer to share my grief? Too many voices inside my head intensified my guilt. I called Rawyia.

"Are you back in Canada already?"

"No, I am in Paris."

"And?"

"I passed out before the flight back to Canada."

"Why? How do you feel now? Is this from your accident?" She was full of questions.

"Yes, I fly back tomorrow."

"You will be fine. Make sure to see your doctor in Canada."

I couldn't express anguish and cause more worry to Rawyia. I hung up. I escaped under the bed covers, but sleep was defiant. The voices of regret got louder inside my head. I asked Mama to come in my dream and tell me she had forgiven me. I turned off the lights and recited several verses from the Quran to bless her soul. Then, I saw the image of Mama as she stood by my bed, Amer next to her. She held a white handkerchief in her hand. She smiled and wiped my tears. When I opened my eyes, she wasn't anywhere in the room. Serenity enveloped me. I knew it was Mama's way to set me free from the guilt, and to bless my relationship with Amer. As I went back to sleep, I thought of Amer and hoped he would appear again. He didn't.

The next day, as the sun pushed dawn light through the thick golden drapery, I woke up fresh and intoxicated with love. Now, I had Mama's blessing. However, residing in Egypt was not a consideration. Amer would have to resign from the military first before I would accept his proposal of marriage. Although I had made up my mind to stay connected, I needed the distance to cement my feelings. I left Paris without calling him.

CHAPTER XXVII

BACK IN CANADA

In Canada, it was not as easy as I thought it would be to stay away from Amer. He was on my mind day and night. I thought of every minute I spent with him. I smelled him and heard his voice. I felt his touches and, most of all, his heartbeat still synchronized with mine. His photo was the last thing my eyes saw before I slept. I wrote to him at night and in the morning. I waited for his letters like my life depended on his responses. In each letter, we planned my next visit. We knew it had to happen. It was fate we couldn't escape, even if we tried.

Meanwhile, I resumed my life. I worked during the day, attended college at night, and connected with new friends.

We met on weekends and went skiing on holidays at the Hidden Valley Ski resort. They chose it for its proximity to Toronto and because it was an ideal spot for beginners. They wanted me to feel comfortable with skiing before a visit to the Glen Eden Resort, where they skied before I joined the group. They taught me how to cross-country ski. I was too scared to try downhill skiing. It was a different way of life from Alexandria. However, I enjoyed it and wanted to emulate them except when Tony, the Italian, and Roger, the Swiss, skinny dipped in the snow. I couldn't. My body was too sensitive from the Mediterranean warm weather. Besides, I was too shy to strip naked in front of them.

We connected like a family. Nevertheless, I kept my love for Amer to myself up until one evening. While I was dancing with Tony, he whispered, "Laila, I am not sure how to tell you this, but I would like to meet with you outside the group. This is the first time I have asked a girl to meet alone."

I froze, took one step back, and faced him, curious about his request. Tony was the handsome one in the group; all the girls tried to win his attention, and he was asking to see me away from the group? I had caught him several times looking at me with admiration. He also only danced with me. He talked about his family in Italy, and his dream to marry a girl who would agree to live in the village where he grew up. I sensed that the Mediterranean blood that ran in our veins, brought us close.

"We could talk now," I said.

"No, this is not the place to discuss a serious subject."

"Okay, how about Friday evening after work? We'll meet downtown at Toronto Eaton Center at 6:00 p.m."

We met at one of the mall's coffee shops. It was the first time I'd seen him in a suit since we met. He looked sharp, dressed in a camel jacket. It enhanced the honey color of his eyes. He even seemed taller. When we sat down, he bent his fingers, and then cracked his knuckles so hard I was concerned he might break them.

"Okay, I am ready," I said to shift his focus to me.

He smiled. Placing his hands on the table and leaning over, he looked me straight in the eyes and said, "I would like us to know each other outside the group. My intention is for a serious relationship if we both agree."

Any girl in my place would have accepted the offer. Tony was the hottest and most desirable bachelor in our group. His proposition flattered me. However, Amer owned and controlled not just my heart but my life. The time I spent with him, he behaved with gallantry, kindness, and satisfied my hunger for love. His cruelty to his ex-girlfriend was dormant in my mind.

My story with Amer remained a secret the entire time I was with the group. In spite of that, the Canadian and Swiss girls asked about the glow of happiness in my eyes and my apparent breathless excitement when I read Amer's letters.

"Introduce us to lover boy," they insisted.

I had told them how I ran away on my wedding night, and how I would never go back to Egypt. I wasn't comfortable talking about the love I shared with an Egyptian man, and how he couldn't leave Egypt.

Everything about me spoke love and joy as I read Amer's letters. I saved and prepared for my next visit to Egypt, my daydreams full of him as I listened to love songs, in particular, the Arabic ones. I tried hard to hide my personal life but failed. They suspected there was a man in my life, but I never confirmed it.

Tony sat across the table from me, searching my eyes for an explanation to my silence. I lowered my head and dug deep into my soul to find the right words to explain why I was about to turn him down. Tony saved me.

"Is there a man in your life?" he asked.

I nodded.

He cupped my hands in his and said, "It had crossed my mind that a woman like you must have someone in her life. Who is the lucky one?"

"The lucky one is an Egyptian whom I met on my first visit to Alexandria, before Mama passed away."

Tony and the group knew about Mama's death and the grievous trip back home, but not about Amer. The fate of the relationship with Amer was uncertain. Many obstacles stood between us: his military obligation, the continents that separated us, and the aggressive side to his personality. Besides,

I valued the freedom I had paid dearly to win. But I had no control over my feelings, and I felt love for Amer. No other man could change that, not even a man like Tony.

"So you plan to go back to Egypt?" he asked.

"Yes, but just for a visit."

A trip to Egypt was planned from the moment Amer and I said our goodbyes. Letters we exchanged continued to fuel my longing. He expected my visit, even though I didn't promise. It was a commitment between two souls.

CHAPTER XXVIII

RAWYIA'S STRUGGLE

Long days and sleepless nights dragged by, and news from Egypt following Mama's death carried unpleasant events. Rawyia's letters spoke of disturbing developments about her life at home. She had purchased a knitting machine to make children's clothes. Male buyers met with her at the family home. Reda and Ahmed asked her to move out if she continued to have male buyers. She called me once or twice a month to vent her frustration.

"It has become impossible to live at home. I worry about my baby." She choked on her words. "Adham is having nightmares. After Mama's death, Reda and Ahmed took full control of the family. Adham is afraid of them. I must move out for my son's sake."

"Where will you go?" I asked. "And where is Papa?"

"Papa moved out and settled with a girl younger than Hala."

"Why did he move out?"

"You know Reda and Ahmed wouldn't leave Papa's young wife alone," she told me. "They will abuse her sexually to force Papa to divorce her."

"Why?" I snapped.

"Papa planned to exclude our brothers from the inheritance and bestow the apartment building to his young wife."

"Papa couldn't wait the forty days mourning period?" I exploded and clucked my tongue.

"What have I told you about men? Don't ever forget that sex drives men's emotions and not the other way around, as it is with us women."

"Where do you plan to go?"

"Don't worry about me," she said.

A divorced woman in Egypt would have a hard time renting a place. Society would condemn her, since they had never seen her husband. They would see her as a Jezebel with the invisible Scarlet Letter stamped on her dress. Rawyia and her son would be pariahs in the community.

Aunt Hamida, the aunt that embraced us during our divorce ordeal in Alexandria, had passed away. Our aunt was the one family member that stood up to our father and would have offered Rawyia her home to raise Adham. Rawyia had no recourse.

"I don't know what to do or where to go," she murmured.

She wasn't the Rawyia I knew, the fighter. She sounded despondent. She talked with despair about how she wished to raise her son in a safer environment.

"All I want is to provide Adham with a happy life," she sniffled. "His father died while I was pregnant. I hoped my family would provide the fatherly love he missed."

"Why don't you and Adham emigrate to Canada?"

There was no better solution to offer her. I thought, if she joined me in Canada, it would be a dream come true. In Canada, she and Adham would have a safe life. Society would embrace them, and she would get all the help she needed to start a business. Besides, I was at a point in my life when motherhood started to consume my thoughts and emotions. I ached to have children, and thought Adham would fulfill this desire until I had my own.

"Have you forgotten that Adham was born on a boat and that, in Egypt, they refused to issue a birth certificate for him?"

From Rawyia's answer, I sensed she was open to solutions. I was also sure she would not go anywhere without Adham. He was the only person she ever loved more than she loved me. Adham needed a birth certificate to get a passport or to be added on Rawyia's passport. Fate had shut all doors to solutions and directed our lives to an unknown future. Again, I believed fate was mine to change.

During my last visit to Egypt, Rawyia had mentioned a married man she had met, and that she cared about him.

"Kader is a married man, but I care about him because he treats Adham like one of his own."

The statement didn't leave an echo in my mind at the time. The sad events of Mama's death occupied all my thoughts and emotions. Nevertheless, the fact that the man was married with children did surprise me. I was sure Rawyia had gotten over it and had never spoken about Kader again until we discussed Adham's birth certificate in one of our telephone conversations.

"What happened with the married man who treated Adham like one of his children?"

"You mean Kader?"

"Yes, Kader."

"What about him?" she asked.

"How about if he adopts Adham? That way, you could get his papers in order."

"I thought about it. However, there is no adoption in Egypt. You know it is against our religion," she said in utter disappointment.

"But not in Canada," I blurted. "I will adopt him."

There was silence. I knew Rawyia needed time to think. I planted the seed in her head and left her to decide what to do next—either nurture the idea or let it dry up and die.

CHAPTER XXIX

AMER'S MARRIAGE PROPOSAL

For the next three years, my trips to Egypt remained regular. I spent most of the visits with Rawyia. She had settled in Al Agamy, a city not far from Alexandria, and seemed happy. She hired two girls to work on the knitting machines while she took care of marketing and sales. When Adham turned four, she enrolled him in *Jardin d'enfants*, the kindergarten of a private French school. They were happy and content.

On one of my visits, Rawyia introduced me to Kader, the married man she had met when she lived with Aunt Hamida. Back then, she mentioned him with admiration, and wished he hadn't been married. They reconnected, and Adham called him Papa.

"Has he proposed yet?" I asked.

"Not yet, and I don't care if he doesn't," she shrugged her shoulders. "However, he asked for an *Orfy* marriage. The kind that has no rights in a court of law. I refused."

"Why are you still with him?"

"For Adham," she agonized. "I want him to have a father."

I knew then why she never discussed the adoption proposition. I couldn't shake the castle she had built for Adham, even though I knew it would crumble one day. She appeared comfortable and settled in her life.

She encouraged my relationship with Amer, even though she knew of his aggressive behavior. She wanted me close to her.

"All men abuse women in this country," she said.

"Don't generalize," I snapped. "There must be men out there who wouldn't abuse women."

"You're dreaming."

I knew she was right and, with every visit to Egypt, my apprehension grew. Male superiority and women's oppression hadn't changed. Rawyia was a living example, as was my younger sister, Hala. I learned Hala was in love and would like to settle down, but Reda and Ahmed opposed the marriage. I advised her to elope and get married. She did and was condemned, ostracized by the family. I couldn't leave my life in Canada to suffer injustice and oppression again.

The prejudice against women in Egypt set me on solid ground when Amer discussed marriage. I was determined not to move to Egypt for him or anyone else. I promised myself after every visit to end the relationship, but I couldn't. He was the blood that circulated in my veins. I couldn't control my feelings. Our passion grew deeper every time we met. I spent most of my vacation with him. We forgot time and the rest of the world when we met. We talked about ways to keep us together, but I made it clear that the only way was if he joined me in Canada. He assured me he was working on it. It wasn't easy to quit his military duty. Egypt was in a war of attrition to repossess the Sinai Peninsula from Israel, which Israel captured in 1967 during the six days *Al Naksah* (The Setback). Army officers and soldiers had an honorable obligation to remain on duty.

Amer and I suffered from the distance and time that separated us. He was tied up with his military duties, and I wouldn't compromise on where we would start our life together. He wasn't sure how long the standoff with Israel would last, or if he would ever be able to join me in Canada. Time wasn't on our side. My biological clock ticked louder. I approached my third decade anxious to settle down and have children. I had been in Canada for almost three years and had turned down several marriage proposals: An Egyptian professor, a Canadian architect, and Tony. I wouldn't be able to do that forever. I needed to get my priorities in order.

CHAPTER XXX

ADHAM'S SEXUAL ASSAULT TRAUMA

Besides my night courses in college, I settled into a secretarial job with a prestigious atomic energy company. I moved to an apartment in downtown Toronto and bought a small used car. I became the hot bachelorette among my friends. Almost all single men in the company invited me out.

It was this period in my life that experience taught me that men, in general, share an obsession with sex. Some that I met expressed a desire for physical intimacy from the first meeting; others were more reserved, but not for long. It was hard to open up or hear the sincerity of the ones who looked for a serious relationship. In the meantime, Amer and I remained as close and emotionally engaged as we had been. Nevertheless, I enjoyed the lavish dining and individual attention.

I kept the changes in my life to myself, and my trips to Egypt dwindled to one trip every other year. Rawyia and Adham were the main force behind my trips. Adham was the son I never had, and I grew attached to him. He called me "my Canadian Mama," and Rawyia approved. He was the joy of her life, and mine as well.

In one of her letters, she wrote that Kader had deserted them. His disappearance devastated Adham's psychological wellbeing. He asked for his dad, and she had no answer. She didn't know why Kader had deserted them.

In another letter, she wrote that Adham had skipped school and had woken up in the middle of the night, screaming. It was a recurring nightmare since Kader had left them. She hated herself for introducing him to her son.

Amid the chaos Rawyia experienced, I waited a few months before I reopened the subject of adoption. I believed I could help Adham overcome his anxiety. In Canada, he would be in a new environment and would have new school friends. I wanted him to lead a healthy, secure life. Rawyia turned me down, and I accepted her decision. She wasn't sure if she could emigrate to Canada to be with him.

Soon after the disappearance of Kader, I received a letter from Rawyia that tore my heart to pieces.

"My dearest sister,

I wish I listened to you and given you Adham. I wish I weren't selfish. I wish you had pushed me harder to adopt him. I wish I never came back to Egypt. I wish you were here to put down the fire burning in my heart. I want to take my son and run away from the world.

My dear sister, today I found Adham crouched in a fetal position under the stairs of our apartment building. He shook and moaned in pain, his pants soaked in blood. Some bastard raped him. I cannot write anymore."

Tears rained like lava on the word "raped" and consumed its letters. Anger paralyzed my mind and suffocated my heart. I took my fury out on the paper in my hand and tore it to pieces. I stared at the scattered letter on the carpet and imagined the horror of Adham's ordeal, how he must have been so confused and broken. Anger raged in my body, and I stomped on the ripped paper. And, the more I pounded, the louder Adham's cries echoed around me. He was four.

Rawyia and Adham had no support in Egypt. She couldn't incriminate the perpetrator in a court of law. She believed she could protect Adham's reputation in the neighborhood. In Egypt, parents of rape victims, whether boys or girls, fear the stigmatization of their children by their peers. They don't understand the impact of such an experience on their child's psychological wellbeing. No matter how much Rawyia loved her son, or how much she suffered, she didn't behave any different. She followed the culture she chose for herself and Adham. I couldn't undo the damage or help her. However, I called to convince her Adham needed therapy.

"Rawyia, did you take Adham to a doctor?" I asked.

"No," she snapped. "I am nursing my son's wound. I don't need help."

Her statement silenced me. I wanted to take Adham away, save him from this twisted culture, but I sensed this would be impossible. Rawyia was broken, and so was Adham. They needed to stay together. I postponed the subject of adoption.

CHAPTER XXXI

VISITING AMER IN EGYPT

The tragedy of Adham's rape, Mama's death, and Papa's marriage drowned me in pain, the kind of pain that squeezed my heart and suffocated my soul. The dormant volcano of mistrust of men had erupted in me. I had been a seedling struggling to grow, but pain turned me into a mature tree with deep roots, hard to knock down. From the womb of that pain, I was born into a new life.

For four years, I spent my vacations in Egypt. I continued to see Amer, and I still enjoyed his company, but marriage was no longer a possibility. The idea of sharing my life with a man born and raised in Egypt ceased to exist.

Following Mama's death, Papa took his young bride and left the country for work in the Gulf. Reda and Ahmed took control of the household. They forced Rawyia and Hala to move out. I learned months later from Rawyia that Ahmed, too, was also kicked out, and my younger brother Samir joined the army. Reda got married and settled in the apartment. These changes triggered a family feud for years between Reda, Samir, Rawyia, and Hala.

The family break-up brought me closer to Rawyia and

Adham. I visited them once a year. We exchanged letters and, every two weeks, we talked on the phone. It was expensive, but the joy of hearing their voices was worth every dollar I paid on my phone bill. I also filled one of my suitcases with presents and Rawyia's favorite Lindt chocolate with hazelnuts.

The last two visits to Egypt after Mama passed away, the arrangements remained unchanged. One weekend with Rawyia and Adham and the rest of the two weeks with Amer. However, following Adham's traumatic experience, I changed the plan. I spent one night with Amer before I went to Alexandria. It was during that trip that I discovered a different side to Amer. He wasn't the loving and passionate man I had known for the past two years. He exposed a selfish and out-of-control side to his personality.

Amer had ordered dinner—Kebab, rice, and salad, and had dismissed the servant for the evening. The apartment was clean, and several lit candles cast a romantic ambiance on our surroundings. He was attentive. When I shivered from the nippy December cold, he fetched a portable heater from his room, and turned it on to keep me warm. The jet lag had numbed me from head to toe; I felt sleepy. I wasn't my usual self. On previous visits, jet lag never bothered me. This time I was distant, and he felt it.

"Tomorrow morning, I leave for Alexandria," I announced.

His upper lip twitched, and his hands trembled. He shot me with eyes charged with aggression, which I hadn't seen before. My heart raced.

"Since when do you leave for Alexandria the next day after you arrive?" he demanded.

His voice had a combative tone that frightened me. I felt like a soldier under interrogation. For a moment, the warmth he'd provided in the room dissipated. I was cold, scared, and soaked in sweat at the same time. I remembered the bullying of Reda and Ahmed and the control of my father, and how Amer bragged about shoving Sanaa across the floor.

Negative vibes traveled between us. Silence tore the thread of communication. We read each other's minds with the same transparency as the magnetic attraction that pulled us together when we first met. I thought of Amer's anger and how to keep him calm as I planned my next move. After midnight, I took my time to clear the table after dinner, which was untouched. I glanced over to where Amer sat. He failed to hide his frustration. Now, both sides of his upper lip twitched. He lit one cigarette after another. He then tapped his fingers on the wood arm of his chair. The louder he drummed, the more uneasy I felt. He cocooned himself in silence, and I wondered, "What's next." I was frightened and nervous.

When Amer read the fear in my eyes, like a chameleon, he changed his demeanor, and appeared calm. The twitching ceased and, at the speed of light, the warmth in his eyes came alive again. At that moment, I realized that, behind his good looks and mesmerizing hazel eyes, an offensive side was ready to explode. I decided to leave.

"I would like to call a taxi," I said. "I want to leave now."

He put out his cigarette, and extended his hand, reaching for mine. I gave him my hand with trepidation. I no longer trusted him. It frightened me to see him change his personality so fast. I saw two different Amers—a sentimental one, and one that was about to lose control of his anger. I was ready to sever the relationship.

"Please wait for the morning," he said. "It is not safe to ride a taxi alone in the middle of the night."

I agreed and retired to the sofa. Amer sat on the chair opposite me. He stared at me with eyes full of anger. I felt trapped and scared. I closed my eyes to avoid confrontation. I thought of my late Aunt Hamida's description of abusive men. "Abusive men can be charming. They win the love and respect of people. They possess emotional intelligence, but in a negative way."

Amer fit that description. Even though he and I had developed warm feelings for one another, I had to use my head and sever this relationship before it was too late. I no longer trusted him.

At dawn the next morning, I called a taxi, and Amer left for his military duty. We refrained from any promises, but I knew he counted on my return. The flight back to Canada took off from Cairo International Airport.

CHAPTER XXXII

ME AND RAWYIA IN ALEXANDRIA

I had always missed Alexandria and the Mediterranean. The bond was and still is as strong as the umbilical cord that connects a mother to her baby.

When the taxi approached Alexandria, the driver drove along the Corniche. I opened the window to smell the sea and allow the cool breeze to play with my hair. I thought of the time Mama took us to the beach for swimming, and how she waited for us with patience till sunset. I could see her smile and hear her voice. The memory squeezed my heart. Her absence tormented me as we drove along those streets. I wanted to stop by the cemetery, but still couldn't visit her grave and confirm her death to myself. She was still alive in my mind and heart.

Rawyia occupied a small apartment in a two-story building sandwiched between two high-rises. I was surprised the driver located the place. It was well hidden from the main street. The apartment had one bedroom, a kitchen, and a living area. The family room and bedroom had windows that overlooked the cement walls of the high-rises. They had no access to the sun. Rawyia looked frail, and Adham pale, but he was happy to see me. He couldn't wait to open the presents I brought him—a battery-powered car, a train, chocolate, candy, three sweaters, four pairs of pants, and a pair of shoes. They kept him busy.

"Why live in the suburb so far from the city, and why chose a place so dark?" I asked Rawyia.

"I want to stay away from people to protect Adham."

Rawyia took me to the bedroom where she had her knitting machine. The two girls she had hired had already gone home for the day. Wool and cotton bobbins of different colors were scattered all over the floor.

"Where do you sleep?" I asked, as I looked around feeling sad.

"In the evening, I pile everything in one corner and clear the bed."

Rawyia was happy and giggling, but it was sad to see her and Adham live in a cramped and unhealthy apartment.

"Does Adham go to school?"

"Yes, of course," she said. "I walk my baby to school and drop in several times to make sure he's okay."

Rawyia untied a big plastic bag. "I knitted all this for you," she said. "Skirts with matching tops and socks. They will keep you warm in the harsh Canadian winter."

I couldn't believe she spent her hard-earned money and time on knitting for me. I couldn't hold my tears and hugged her.

"Oh, La, you're still emotional. I'm fine now," she assured me. "I'm free and safe with Adham and, as long as you come every year to visit, I can survive this life."

To Rawyia, freedom meant more than a life in a big house among family members. She and Adham seemed happy and content. The little she earned seemed enough. It pained me to watch her stay up late to finish customers' orders to make ends meet. All I could do was share my income and help her establish the knitting business.

She took my hand and said, "Come with me to the kitchen. I cooked your favorite chicken soup and pasta with fresh tomatoes, basil, and garlic." She giggled again.

Amid her difficult life, Rawyia was generous and thoughtful. She remembered how I preferred my pasta cooked. She liked it drenched in tomato sauce but made it the way Mama had prepared for me—fresh tomatoes, olive oil, and fresh garlic. A pot of chicken soup simmered on the stove. She took a spoonful and put it in my mouth.

"I didn't add lime," she said. "I remember you don't like lime in your soup."

It felt like the days we lived together in Cairo before we ran away from Egypt. However, this time, her son shared the time with us when he wasn't in school. We couldn't be happier.

"I know you miss the beach," she said. "We'll go tomorrow to Abou Keer, the seafront city. We'll ride a *Caretta*, remember, those small horse-drawn wagons, and have fresh fish from the sea barbequed right on the sand in front of our eyes."

Rawyia was joyous and excited. She wanted to give me a memorable time in Alexandria. Growing up, we never visited Alexandria's seashore cities like *Abou Keer* or *Sidi Abel Rahman*.

"I will even treat you to sea urchin fresh from the deep." Alexandrians preferred sea urchins they picked straight from the bottom of the waters. Vacationers caught them during the summer. They cracked them open with a knife, squeezed fresh lime and savored the delicacies all day long.

Rawyia made sure I had a fun-filled vacation. She took me to places I had never seen before.

The more I visited her and Adham, the deeper my commitment and responsibility toward them grew. I became the one person Rawyia trusted and reached out to when she needed help. She was also the person who guided me through my relationship with Amer.

"Look, La," she said, "while I cherish Alexandria, I would rather live somewhere other than Egypt."

"Are you saying you want to join me in Canada?"

"It's too late for me," she said. "But you've been offered a future in Canada. Don't give it up for Amer or any man in Egypt, even though I want you close to us."

Rawyia knew about Amer's physical abuse to his previous girlfriend. She wasn't surprised. She believed most, if not all, Egyptian men saw no harm in slapping and shoving women. "Muslim men gave themselves a divine right to beat up their wives."

The last day in Alexandria, Rawyia and I stayed up all night and chatted. She smoked like a chimney. We drank tea and snacked on feta cheese and left-over pasta. She wiped tears from her glasses and complained about time running so fast. When we heard the call for the Fajr dawn prayer, we fell asleep in each other's arms.

I had prepared my luggage the night before. In the early hours of the next day, Rawyia planted kisses on my forehead to wake me.

"La, wake up. The train to Cairo leaves in three hours," she said as she struggled to hold her tears. "We have little time before you leave."

Rawyia served me breakfast in bed—fried eggs with Basturma, seasoned air-dried cured beef, Kalamata olives, warm pita bread, and a pot of black tea. She sat across from me and lit a cigarette. I knew when she was sad, she wouldn't eat. She watched me, and I ate to make her happy.

At the train station, our farewell was as emotional as the previous ones. We stayed in each other's arms until the train announced the departure with repeated whistles. Rawyia stood on the tarmac and gave me last-minute advice.

"Use your head, not your heart, when you are in Amer's arms."

"I will," I grinned.

As the train's engine chugged along, we blew kisses until we couldn't see each other.

Three hours later, I arrived at the Cairo train station. Amer waited on the tarmac.

CHAPTER XXXIII

MIXED FEELINGS

Mama often said, "In life, we have no control over three things: The day we were born, the day we die, and who our hearts choose." So, when I saw Amer in his military uniform as he stood at the platform, searching for me with hazel eyes like two rare gems, and gleaming with longing, happiness lifted me off the ground. I didn't see his aggressive side. I liked what I saw. Our encounter was like a princess story, charming, elegant, and full of romance. I forgot the promises I had made and was smitten again by his charm.

Deep inside, I knew he was capable of physical abuse. Still, I listened to my heart's voice and muted the call of alarm that tolled in my mind. The intensity of attraction I felt when I saw him dampened all doubts about our relationship. I wanted to melt in his open arms, and I wished the clock would stop.

All my resistance melted when we embraced on the platform. We disregarded the culture that prohibits such actions in public. At that moment, it was only him and me in the world. We walked hand in hand to his car. The fragrance of Aramis and the joyous tune of my heartbeats intensified my perspiration. Our hands bathed in an elixir of desire.

"Three of my friends," he said and paused for few seconds, "Essam, Ahmed, and Mostafa, would like to meet you, and I hope you don't mind."

I was disappointed. I had a few hours before I flew back to Canada. I hoped we would be alone. I shook my head but said nothing.

"I want to introduce you," he said. "I have told them so much about you."

I faced him in disbelief. He kept his gaze on the road, smiling.

"I talked to my friends about how we met on the train. My friends know everything about us."

"Us? What do you mean?" I asked.

"You will know when we get home."

We stayed silent and, as he drove, we held hands. He squeezed my hand several times to interrupt my train of thought. There was strong telepathy between us.

※

Essam had a beautiful girlfriend with him, and the other two had no partners. When they saw me, they exchanged a quick nod of approval with Amer.

After the introductions, I felt comfortable, and understood why Amer considered them brothers. They gave me the same feelings as well. They joked, laughed, and threw comments about love and quick commitment. They ordered dinner, with Kofta, Kebab, stuffed pigeons, rice, and an assortment of pickles.

After dinner, they drank Arabic coffee and smoked cigarettes. Amer and I exchanged gazes full of desire. It was time to be alone. Amer's friends, however, wouldn't leave.

"C'mon Amer, we can't wait for the surprise," Essam winked.

"Amer drowned in love from head to toe," Ahmed snickered.

Amer anchored an adoring gaze on me. The passion in his eyes locked our hearts into a symphony of love, and emotions traveled between us faster than sound. All I wanted and thought of was to be in his arms. When he noticed the longing desire glisten in my eyes, he stood up and extended his hand. I surrendered. We ignored the envious stares of his friends and walked straight to his bedroom.

I felt safe with Amer like a joey in a kangaroo's pouch. Every bit of apprehension dissolved when our lips met in an elixir of infinite passion. The world around us stopped except for the beats of our hearts. We stood lost in an embrace until I couldn't tell which beats belonged to my heart. During that moment, our souls declared the marriage of our bodies and spirits. It was a silent commitment that we celebrated until the dawn call for prayers blasted from a mosque near his home.

The next morning, the aroma of the Arabic coffee interrupted my sleep. When I heard a commotion in the kitchen, I sat up and stretched. I found out later that he had prepared tea, and sent the porter to the local bakery for some cheese pâté and croissant. He then tiptoed back in the room and slipped in next to me under the cover. He wrapped his arms around me, and I buried my head in his chest, soothed by the crescendo of his heartbeats. He had mentioned that he had used up his days off. I figured he skipped work and gambled with martial punishment.

"Tea is ready," he whispered, printing love all over my face with his lips. "I also sent Mostafa, the porter, to buy cheese pâté and croissant."

"Please, go to work," I pleaded. "My flight isn't until 2:00 a.m."

"I will survive," he said.

The doorbell rang several times. We heard it but remained lost in our physical embrace, and our souls locked together like a magnet. When Amer tried to get up, he couldn't, and instead he pulled me tighter and kissed me on the forehead.

When we at last answered the doorbell and let the servant in, and had our breakfast, it was already noon. Amer received phone calls from his superiors, but he ignored them.

"One day I will resign from the military and marry you," he whispered.

I wanted to believe him, even though my heartbeat drummed a farewell requiem. I had an ominous feeling about our relationship. I couldn't explain it, but I felt it.

Time flew with the speed of a shooting star. At midnight, Amer drove me to the airport. We held hands in complete silence. He charged every squeeze with devotion and promises. At each stoplight, we ignored our surroundings, and our lips melted in a long kiss until cars blasted their sirens and flashed the high beams on our vehicle. Warmth radiated throughout my body and bathed our hands in perspiration.

At the airport, we parted with difficulty and made no promises for the future. We succumbed to our fate. What we had was a passion neither of us could control. However, the destiny of our love was a different story. Either he resigned from the military and joined me in Canada, or I abandoned my dreams and freedom and returned to Egypt. We couldn't commit or discuss both solutions. Nevertheless, I was sure that the next morning, we would breathe hope into our unsettled souls.

CHAPTER XXXIV

ADHAM'S DEATH

It had been almost a year since I was last in Egypt. A few months before my next visit, I received a phone call from Rawyia.

"La, Adham is in intensive care," she said, weeping.

It was midnight. I jumped out of bed and turned on the light to make sure I wasn't dreaming. My throat turned dry. I wanted a drink of water, but Rawyia's voice anchored me on my bed.

"La, are you awake?"

"Yes, Rawyia," I assured her. "Calm down and tell me what happened."

She cried more and louder. "A car hit Adham and slashed open his stomach," she wailed.

I couldn't talk, and my head spun. I dragged my feet to the kitchen and drank water. Rawyia continued to sob. We both knew nothing would make what happened easier. Rawyia was alone drowned in grief, and I was a thousand miles away.

"Rawyia, please calm down and tell me what happened."

I waited a few minutes and thought of what Rawyia had gone through since she returned to Egypt. I wondered if she would have been better off if she had stayed in Lebanon. Rawyia's ordeal was like a bad omen that warned me from life in Egypt with Amer.

"As he crossed the busy corniche boulevard," she sobbed. "I didn't know about the accident until a few hours later. I ran barefoot to the street, then took a taxi to the hospital."

Rawyia was breathless as she recounted how she found out. She moaned in pain. I felt her agony and desperation to have me by her side. I controlled myself to appear courageous for her.

"Tell me Adham will recover," I pleaded.

"They gave him a blood transfusion," she said. "The hospital staff refused to let me see him. The nurse told me that his chance of survival is almost nil. He lost a lot of blood."

I collapsed on the nearest chair.

"Pray for him, La," she choked out.

After she hung up, I realized I'd forgotten to ask if she had family support. She had severed the connection with the family after Mama passed away. Even though Rawyia and I talked on the phone often, she never expressed a desire to have me by her side.

"I don't want you to disrupt your life in Canada," she said. "You have a job now. Don't lose it because of me and my problems."

Rawyia knew that Adham's condition would affect me. She had always accused me of being emotional and had wanted me to use reason, not emotion, to deal with life's problems.

"Your presence will not change my son's health or his fate," she said. "I messed up my life. Let one of us continue the road to independence. We started together."

Still, Rawyia needed help. Samir, my younger brother, had stood by me during the ordeal of my divorce. He had always been critical of our father and brother's oppression. It was a dangerous mission for a fifteen-year-old, but he acted like a leader. Now, at twenty, and five years my junior, I trusted he would not hesitate to stand by Rawyia.

"Alo, Samir, this is Laila."

"I know," he said with a chuckle. "I haven't forgotten your voice. How are you? I miss you."

"I miss you, too," I said. "I called to let you know Adham has been in a car accident. He is in Shatby hospital."

"Going there now," he said, and hung up.

I was relieved that Rawyia would have Samir by her side. I knew he loved and cared about her.

Three months passed, during which I called Rawyia once or twice a week. The phone bill drained my savings but gave Rawyia the emotional support she needed. Although Adham made it, his recovery was slow, yet I was relieved he survived. However, Rawyia lost hope for his full recovery.

"Adham will never be the same," she said, her voice quivering. "He has developed an infection where they sutured the wound."

Not long after, Adham's health took a sudden dive into stubborn viral pneumonia that didn't respond to antibiotics. Within weeks, his body turned skeletal, and he was unable to fight the virus. I saw a frail young man in the photo Rawyia sent. His cheeks were sunk inward, and his lifeless eyes were buried between two protruding bones—his eyebrows and cheeks. The picture was blurred. I knew Rawyia's hands had trembled as she photographed him.

In the photo, Adham lay on the hospital bed. His thick chestnut hair covered his forehead and brushed his curled-up lashes when the nurse took another photo. His eyes were closed, and he appeared at peace as if he had succumbed to his destiny. Rawyia sat on a chair close by his bed. Her head rested near his face and held his hand.

My tears bathed the photos. For a moment, I wished she had never sent them. I wanted to remember Adham the way he had always looked—vibrant, healthy, and handsome.

"Rawyia, I won't come this summer," I said with trepidation.

"I understand," she said. "I don't want you to come, either. I regret sending you the photos."

"Please don't misunderstand me," I pleaded. "I love you both, but I don't want to see Adham in a hospital bed, and you next to him in agony."

"I agree," she said." Your presence won't change the situation."

⁓

I was in desperate need of affection—the kind of support Middle Eastern people give offers warmth and empathy, which none of my Canadian friends exhibited. They were kind, but they valued their time and used it wisely.

Tanya, my Italian friend, suggested I join the local community center. We searched in the *Toronto Star*, the local newspaper, and came across an advertisement that announced the grand opening of an Arabic club in a church not far from where I lived.

I visited the church on a Friday after work. I followed signs written in Arabic and English that led to the basement. The closer I got to the room, the louder Arabic music resonated through the walls. I recognized the different dialects: Egyptian, Lebanese, Jordanian, Syrian, and others whose origin I couldn't decipher. The melodic Egyptian song filled my heart with joy. I felt home.

I stood at the door, inspecting the room, the people, and each face. The aroma of common Arabic spices wafted on the air and tickled my appetite. I followed the smell with my eyes toward long tables covered with white paper along the wall on my right. At the corner, the small kitchen had an opening with a counter crowded with tea kettles and Arabic coffee. Kids played hide and seek by the round tables occupied by adults. Their voices and laughter brought joy to my soul. I smiled and waited a few minutes for someone to acknowledge my presence. No one did, so I proceeded to the first table.

"Hi," I said with a smile.

All sixteen eyes turned and faced me. One of the ladies stood up and took me in her arms.

"Ahlan wa Sahlam, welcome," she said, and searched around for a chair.

"Ahmed," she hollered, "fetch a chair."

Little Ahmed, who looked almost ten, dashed over and grabbed the first chair in sight. He dragged it to the table, then ran fast to escape the lady who ran behind him.

"Get the chair back, ya, Ahmed."

Ahmed handed the chair to the lady and called her Mama. A burst of loud laughter erupted from the people around us.

"My son is a little devil," she said.

She proceeded to return the chair, but the lady who chased Ahmed insisted it now belonged to me.

"You are a guest," she said. "I haven't seen you here before."

"Yes, it is my first day," I replied. "I am not sure how or what is needed to join your club."

"Oh," she said, hugging me again. "Don't worry about that. Have you had dinner yet? Even if you did, come and help yourself."

She took me by the hand. I surrendered. Her quick steps forced me to jog next to her walk, even though she was four times heavier than my sixty kilograms. When we reached the stretch of tables, she handed me a paper plate, and she took one herself.

"I am sure you miss Arabic food," she said, piling our plates with a bit of every dish served on the long table.

"This is too much," I protested.

"Eat what you can," she laughed, poking me with her elbow.

She demonstrated Middle Eastern generosity at its best. When we returned to the table, she left me and rejoined her group, giving me some privacy. The group continued their conversation about food, politics, and kids. I was comfortable until one of the men addressed me.

"So, what is your name?"

"Laila."

"Are you in Canada with your parents?"

I shook my head.

"You are here alone?"

I nodded.

The lady on my right hugged me and said, "You are not alone; consider us your parents."

Another lady across the table said, "Let her first eat dinner."

Their inquisition made me feel uncomfortable. Arab people wouldn't accept me if they knew I was a runaway and a divorcee. I decided to walk around before they delved deeper into my life. I picked up the two plates, still crowded with food, and dumped them into the nearest trash can. I wasn't hungry.

"How do you like the club?" one of the ladies asked.

"I'd like to join."

"Great," the woman on my right said, handing me a paper to fill out.

"Only fifteen dollars per month," the woman next to her said.

"I am Samia, the treasurer," she continued, and raised her eyebrows and smiled. "This is Mostafa, my husband. He helps me to keep the accounts straight. I hate numbers. But we like to volunteer."

She handed me a pen. I filled out the application and wrote a check for the amount. They all cheered, and Samia took the check and walked around the tables. She waved it to announce a new member. They clapped, and their welcome brought happiness to my heart.

Another lady from a different table handed me some flyers. I skimmed through them. They all announced Arabic activities—dance, concerts, private piano lessons, as well as Arabic language. One, in particular, caught my attention. Ratiba El Safty, the head of a group that played Egyptian classical music, was scheduled to perform during the summer in Toronto, Montreal, and Ottawa. They needed volunteers to accompany the musicians. I found my solace. I was fluent in French and could help the group in Montreal.

❧

The next morning, I called the phone number provided in the flyer and indicated my desire to volunteer. The group was due to arrive in three months. The commitment to join the club came at the right time to distract me from Egypt and Amer. The change of culture and the freedom women enjoyed in Canada made me realize life in Egypt wasn't attractive. With time, I had no problem staying away from Amer. Besides, his resignation from the military was more complicated than we expected. My annual visit back home ended that summer of 1978.

I wasn't aware of the courage it took me to lead an independent life until members of the musical group expressed admiration and respect. A journalist who toured with the group interviewed me and published the chat with my photo in the national newspaper *Al-Ahram*. After the chat was published, I received letters from young men in Egypt proposing to me. I was flattered and enjoyed the attention. However, I didn't give the proposals any consideration until one member of the Ratiba El Safti group asked, "Why aren't you married?"

The question surprised me. The lady didn't know the burden she put on me. Where would I start? What would she think of me? Would she still respect and admire me? So far, I hadn't explained to the group why I lived alone in Canada. I was in my late twenties but, still, back then, girls in Egypt didn't run away or live alone. I hesitated.

"You can trust me," she said, and squeezed my hands for encouragement.

"I was married," I mumbled.

"You mean you are a divorcee?"

I nodded.

"No need to be ashamed. You are young and could marry again."

Not sure what to say, I smiled. The lady was warm and almost as old as Mama. She expressed genuine concern and a desire to find me a husband. I found her pleasant and genuine.

"Do you want to get married?" she questioned.

"Eventually, I guess, when I find the right person."

"I have someone here in Toronto. I would like you to meet him. He is an Egyptian physician married to my cousin. He would like to introduce you to his friend."

"A blind date?"

"Yes," she told me.

I agreed to please her. I had no intention of marrying an Egyptian, period. Nevertheless, I thought a blind date would be a fun adventure.

"Just want to let you know," the woman continued, "the man was married before and has a child."

Her statement gave me peace. I was sure I would never marry an Egyptian, certainly not one divorced with a child. Still, I went along to make her happy. The group had one week left before they returned to Egypt. She arranged a meeting for the next day. The physician would pick me up from my apartment and drive me to his house, where I would meet his friend, my blind date.

CHAPTER XXXV

MEETING HAZEM

Rawyia gave me worrisome news every time we spoke. Adham had caught something terrible from the blood transfusion he received after the accident.

"Samir's girlfriend is a nurse," Rawyia started. "She suspects hepatitis C as the cause behind Adham's deteriorating health. I don't believe her."

"Did he get a blood test at the hospital?" I asked.

"Yes, he did, but no one gave me a straight answer. The doctor told me Adham would recover, but that his recovery would take time."

Physicians in Egypt don't reveal serious illness to family members. They believe the patient and family should stay hopeful to be able to fight the disease.

"If you could get the nurse on the phone, I will ask her," I said, as I thought that, if the nurse knew I lived in Canada where patients have the right to know everything about their health, she would reveal Adham's actual condition.

"I am sorry, Madame," the nurse said. "It's the hospital's policy. I cannot discuss patients' conditions with anyone, not even his mother."

"Is he going to make it?" I asked, but she handed the receiver to Rawyia.

"Stay calm and pray for Adham," I urged Rawyia.

"I wish you were with me," Rawyia mumbled.

"I am not sure if I want to come."

"You have changed, La," she said. "But I like the new you. Even though I never expected to witness these changes practiced on me."

"I love you, Rawyia," I said, and hung up.

Rawyia's understanding relieved me from guilt. Still, I stayed connected.

Amer didn't receive the same commitment. Phone calls between us dwindled to once a month and, every time we spoke, promises he made to quit the military and join me in Canada seemed more unattainable. The military turned down his repeated requests to retire from duty.

My heart ached from deprivation. The people I expected to quench my thirst for love—Mama, Ghassan, Rawyia, and now Amer— were gone. I had to stop following the mirage and resign myself to the fact that it wasn't meant for Amer and me to continue. Amer was my soulmate and remained as such. However, I was ready to explore my upcoming blind date.

It was May 1978. The Junior Hockey team practice game aired live on television. I had just come home from work and served myself a cup of vegetable soup I had prepared a day earlier. Before the game started, the phone rang.

"Hello, is this Laila?" a deep, warm voice asked.

"Yes," I responded.

"This is Doctor Nazih Nabil," he said, and paused. "The lady from Ratiba El Safty group gave me your number."

"Oh, yes, I know," I said with a chuckle. "You are the one who would like to introduce me to your friend."

"Yes," he said, and laughed out loud. "You saved me a long introduction. I wasn't sure how to approach an Egyptian woman with a blind date proposal as practiced in Canada."

I understood his apprehension. In Egypt, we don't have the concept of blind dates. Arab families, in general, called it *Gawaz Salonat*, an arranged marriage. This kind of arrangement helps to find a suitable husband for daughters who didn't receive marriage proposals. The *Khatba*, the woman assigned to find husbands for prospective girls, arranges meetings between two families who express interest in finding spouses. Before the girl meets a future husband, she is presented with his photo, and the man is given the girl's picture. When both approve of the physical traits, a meeting is arranged, followed by an engagement ceremony. This is the blind date concept practiced in Egypt.

"Have you heard the saying 'If you live in Rome, do what the Romans do'?" I said to break the formality in his tone.

"Hazem, my friend, will spend Saturday with us," he said. "He lives in Ottawa and spends the weekend with us when he visits his daughter. She lives in downtown Toronto with her mother."

The fact that Hazem had a child impacted me with negative emotions. I wasn't sure how to feel or react to this reality. Even though the lady from Ratiba's group informed me of his situation, I never wanted to spend my life with a man who had a child from a previous marriage; I wasn't experienced in stepmothering. Besides, my parents didn't divorce, and were never married before. With that thought in mind, my apprehension subsided.

"I am sorry," I told him, "but I don't want you or Hazem to misconstrue my visit as a commitment."

"My wife and I would love to meet you regardless of the blind date's outcome," he said, sounding satisfied with this.

"I agree. Where do you live?"

"If you don't mind, I will pick you up, and Hazem will drive you back to Toronto, where he will meet his daughter."

"Fine," I said, and gave him my address.

The arrangement of the blind date was fast. However, the

fact that Hazem lived hundreds of miles away and had a child made me feel less pressured. Instead, I was excited to make new friends. I needed a distraction to take my mind off of the unpleasant news that came from Egypt.

It was ten-thirty in the morning when the doorbell rang. I opened. A man in his late thirties and bald on the crown of his head stood at the door. He wore a half-sleeved white cotton shirt, khaki shorts, and white espadrilles. He smelled fresh and still had his Ray-Ban sunglasses on.

"Please come in," I welcomed him with a broad smile. "I will be with you in two minutes. Please help yourself to a can of ginger ale from the fridge. It's hot today."

"Thank you, I am Nazih." He introduced himself and proceeded straight to get the drink.

When I came back dressed in a light green sleeveless cotton dress with a deep décolleté, he stood up and walked straight toward me. I wasn't sure why he approached me, but I stayed calm. He was a physician and lived in Canada. He wouldn't hurt me. Still, I was aware that Egyptians, and Arabs in general, no matter how long they lived outside their countries, considered an independent woman who lived alone easy prey who would accept their sexual gestures.

I picked up my apartment key to leave.

"Let's go," I said and proceeded to the front door.

He stood and stared at me. My shoulder collided with his, but he remained immobile. Then he wrapped his arm around my waist and pulled me close to his face. I assumed he wanted to greet me the Middle Eastern style—a hug then a kiss on the cheeks is the customary welcome gesture practiced between family members, friends, and at social events between strangers. However, this custom is not practiced between men and women outside the family circle. I was sure Nazih was familiar with such a condition. I had to assume the worst when he trespassed over the cultural limitation. I pushed him away, horrified, and took two steps back.

"I am sorry," he said, and took a few steps back himself. "I didn't mean to..." He paused a few seconds and searched for the right word to use.

"You didn't mean what?" I demanded.

Nazih lowered his head, his hands trembled, and he remained mute like a child caught in an act of misconduct. He was shameful. For a moment, I thought of how Egyptian society treats boys as superior and above the law. But not in Canada. If I filed a sexual harassment report, he would be in deep trouble. He appeared remorseful. I decided to suppress the winds of anger before it extinguished the fire of my wit.

"Please forgive me," he begged. "Also, don't mention this to Hazem."

I nodded.

He walked out of the apartment and took the elevator alone. I collapsed on the sofa in complete shock. What had I done to make him think I would go along with his behavior? How dare he? Did he and Hazem want to test my integrity? How could I sit next to him in the car? What kind of people was I about to meet?

I thought about chasing after him to tell him to go back without me and to forget about the introduction to Hazem. I was still furious, not at him, but at all Egyptian men; I decided to teach them a lesson. I followed him down the stairs and took the passenger seat. I dared him to repeat his attempt.

"Please, forgive me," he said. His hands shook as he held onto to the steering wheel. The car swayed left, then right. "Promise you won't tell Hazem."

I didn't answer. I thought of how I could retaliate and teach Nazih a lesson. I thought Hazem must have known what kind of friend he had. Why hadn't he come to pick me up? Why didn't I take my car?

When we arrived, Nazih was still begging me to forgive him. I ignored him. There was a small blue Volvo parked outside. I assumed it was Hazem's car. I had always thought of people who drove this specific car as morons.

Nazih opened the door to his home with his key. He gestured me to enter first. The family room and the kitchen were in view from the foyer. A petite woman stood up and hurriedly tried to fix her messed up shoulder-length hair, and a short man, his back to us, appeared to be zipping up his pants. I stood flabbergasted. Next to me, Nazih stood in utter silence. The man and the woman turned around and faced us with a horrified look.

"This is Hazem and my wife Rosita," Nazih whispered.

I turned around to leave. Hazem ran after me. "It's not what you think. Please wait," he said. "We were undressing to jump in the pool. We didn't expect you so soon."

I didn't see swimsuits anywhere in the room. "You were getting ready for skinny-dipping?" I said.

Rosita had an embarrassed look plastered on her face, and I wanted to test her shame.

"Go ahead," I said, "don't let me stop you from undressing."

I was amused but curious to know how this threesome functioned. However, it seemed I was the only one who doubted Rosita and Hazem's sincerity. Nazih was nonchalant; he walked to the fridge, got himself a Molson, turned on the television, and stretched his legs on the coffee table. Rosita, still looking flustered, walked to the kitchen. She opened the fridge, then closed it, and stood motionless as she gazed outside the bay window above the sink. Hazem sat on the reclining chair and fiddled with a set of keys. I decided to stay. After all, I had no intention of connecting with Hazem.

Hazem's physical appearance didn't impress me. He was almost my height. I couldn't wear high heels if I ever went out with him. He flashed his beady green eyes and slipped on a false smile. His eyes were void of emotion. He lacked Amer's height, his warm voice, and the amalgamation of our souls when we looked at each other.

Rosita prepared lunch—all Egyptian dishes—dried Fava

beans, Tahini, Baba Ghanouj, Halwa, and pita bread. The conversation revolved around my interest in the Ratiba El Safty musical group.

Nazih didn't say much. I was uncomfortable.

Soon after lunch, I excused myself. Hazem offered to drive me back, and I accepted.

CHAPTER XXXVI

NEGATIVE FIRST IMPRESSION OF HAZEM

Hazem used his car key to open the door of the blue Volvo that I noticed parked in the driveway earlier. He exhibited a lack of courtesy when he entered the car first and then unlocked my door from the inside. His gesture earned him a zero for gallantry.

I got in the car and searched for my seat control.

"You looking for something?" he asked.

"Yes, I want to push my seat back."

"You don't need to," he bellowed over the noise of the engine. "People with longer legs than yours sat on that seat and never needed to push it back."

His brusque response hit me like a splash of icy water. My tongue froze. His attitude of control and lack of chivalry set me off. I dreaded the forty-five-minute ride to my home. However, I resigned myself to the situation and engaged him in conversation.

"When did you first come to Canada?" I asked to lighten the tension that escalated between us.

"1972," he said, turning to face me. "And you?"

"Same year," I said with a forced smile.

We remained for a few minutes immersed in our own thoughts. Neither of us wanted to elaborate on the coincidence. The mood Hazem had set in motion enveloped us in a web of aggravation.

"I should have taken a taxi," I said with a genuine tone of regret.

"I planned to drive to Toronto," he said. "My ex and my daughter live in the city. But I drove to Mississauga to meet you. I live in Ottawa. So, when I come every weekend to spend time with Rania, I stay in Toronto." Even the offer to drive me back to my apartment wasn't out of courtesy.

Hazem volunteered more information than I expected or wanted to know. Still, I had no doubt he spoke the truth.

"How old is Rania?"

"Seven," he told me.

"How long have you been separated from her mother?" I asked.

"We have been divorced for six years with no regrets."

It was nighttime, and we drove on the freeway. There was nothing to distract me. His statement of "no regrets" shocked me and added another negative impression about his character; I didn't want him to get into more detail about his past.

"How long have you known Nazih and his wife?"

"Why do you want to know?" The quick response and the shift of his body to the left was a visible sign of vexation. However, I continued.

"Just curious," I said. "You don't have to tell me."

I meant to put him on the defense. I was curious about Nazih's gutsy harassment when he picked me up and his wife's flagrant act.

"Nazih and I went to the same college in Egypt."

"How about Rosita?" I asked.

"What about her?"

"Did she attend the same college?"

He changed lanes several times and increased his driving

speed. When I saw the muscles of his jaw contract, I pressed more.

"Why didn't you pick me up from the apartment?"

The question pushed him to the limit.

"What you saw is not what you think," he snapped. "Nazih and Rosita have an 'open' marriage. I, too, plan to have an open marriage with my future wife."

I had never heard the term "open marriage" before, but I pretended to know, not wanting to appear ignorant. However, Hazem's reaction surprised me. I figured open marriage was something new and questionable.

"Am I under interrogation?" he blurted out.

He ground his teeth and a vein popped on his right temple. I figured future connection with Hazem was doubtful. His visible aggravation gave me the impression he found me intrusive, and he was apparently not a man who appreciated honesty. I compared him to Amer's self-confidence, truthfulness, and grace. Hazem failed. Still, I persuaded myself that no man would like to divulge the unpleasant side of his life to a woman he just met.

I glanced at my watch with a sigh. Hazem turned on the radio. A soft sound of the solo piano rendition of Fur Elise transported me to my childhood when I heard the Bagatelle as I performed ballet at school.

Hazem interrupted my reverie. "So, what brought you to Canada? And where is your family?"

I ignored his intrusive questions and kept my gaze fixed on the starless dark sky. I was immersed in a brief recollection of my life—marriage at fourteen, divorce at seventeen, left Egypt, traveled to Lebanon, worked in Italy, the complication with Amer and his military travel restrictions, and now in Canada, still unsettled. My biological clock was ticking fast. The urge to have a child of my own became a priority.

"I settled in Canada for my doctoral degree," he added.

"Aw, I am impressed," I said.

In reality, his education caught my attention. I was still influenced by the Egyptian culture that measured men's worth with their level of education. In Egypt, a man could be an abuser, foul-mouthed, alcoholic wife-beater, and still win respect if he was a college graduate, particularly with a Ph.D. However, society didn't forgive a woman who held the same credentials for any mistake. She must behave like Mother Teresa, irrespective of her educational background. Hazem's achievement failed to change my negative impression of his narcissistic character. I would have preferred he flaunted his degree later on, and only if I asked.

"Please take the next exit," I said, and ignored the stare of anticipation for a reaction to his doctoral degree announcement. "Take the first right and drop me off at the second apartment building."

"Would you offer me a glass of water?" he said with a chuckle, once we had stopped, and double-parked. "My throat is dry, and I have a long drive to my friend's home."

I couldn't turn him down. It wasn't part of my upbringing to refuse someone who asked for water. It was one of the many religious lessons I learned at home. I checked the time on my watch. I wasn't comfortable inviting a man, mainly an Arab, into my apartment. He would misconstrue the gesture and for sure misjudge my kindness. He was, after all, an Egyptian who was brought up in that culture. I remained silent and tried to figure out a way to turn down his request.

"I won't stay for long," he pleaded. "I will drink water and leave."

I nodded. He parked the car at the curb, and we walked into my apartment on the first floor. He plopped down on the sofa, and I disappeared into the kitchen to get him a glass of water.

"Would you like it with ice?" I asked.

"No," he replied in a whisper, and I felt his mouth almost touching my ear.

I turned around. Hazem wrapped his arm around my waist

and pulled me closer. I pushed him away and faced him with a stare full of disappointment. It was almost midnight, and I felt too embarrassed to scream and wake the neighbors. In spite of his small frame, he was muscular and seemed healthy. I was furious for allowing him to fool me. I blamed myself for disregarding the obnoxious signs he demonstrated from the time we met. What a despicable creature, I thought. He needed someone to deflate his ego and crush his arrogance. I decided to be the one.

"Please forgive me," he pleaded. "Can we start over?"

I could not believe his insolence. Nazih and Hazem had immigrated to a Western country and still couldn't liberate themselves from the superiority over women they practiced in Egypt. I was confident they had prior knowledge about the law against sexual harassment in Canada. Suddenly, I was not intimidated by his presence.

"Where would like to start over from?" I needled, staring at him with mistrust.

"I would like you to meet my daughter."

The request melted the resentment I harbored. I knew Egyptian men didn't introduce a strange woman to their family members until they upgraded her to the status of potential future wife. Was he testing my virtue? Did my immaculacy win his approval? How did he assume I would accept a meeting with his daughter? What an arrogant SOB.

"I am sorry," I said firmly, "but I have another arrangement for the weekend."

"I would like to get to know you better," he said. "In a few hours, I will pick up my daughter. We could go to the park and spend the day to get to know each other better."

"What would you like to know about me?"

"Everything," he said.

CHAPTER XXXVII

DATING HAZEM

Sunday, shortly after 1:00 a.m., the phone rang. I ignored it and buried my head under the pillow. When it stopped ringing, I disengaged the receiver. I knew it was a call from Egypt. No one ever called me at this hour except my family back home. But I was too tired and didn't want to interrupt my sleep. Then I remembered Adham was sick in the hospital and that I hadn't called Rawyia for several weeks. I placed the receiver back in place and, before I could dive into a deep sleep, the phone rang again.

"Alo, La, it's me," Rawyia spoke with a broken voice I recognized. She cried.

I was not ready for any bad news. I wanted her to spare me the news of her life's painful events. I shook from head to toe, and my heartbeat raced in anticipation for the worst.

"Please don't tell me something happened to Adham."

"I must tell you, La. I am all alone by Adham's grave. I just buried him a few hours ago, and he is not suffering anymore. He is with his father. You remember, Adham's father died before I delivered him."

My lips turned numb. The bitterness in her words drizzled

in my throat like sand and suffocated my voice. I reached for the glass of water on my night table and moistened the dryness in my mouth.

"La, he suffered for days. I couldn't see him in pain. I asked God to take Adham by his side. I know he is in a better place. Don't cry; just pray for his soul. I will live in the family mausoleum. The guardian family occupies one room, and I will sleep in another area. I already have a bed. I promised Adham I would stay close by until I join him soon. He expressed joy with a smile when I gave him my word. So don't be sad or even come over. Follow your dreams, and don't look back. I love you," she said, and hung up.

I don't remember how long I sat on my bed, sobbing. I couldn't understand why Rawyia's life turned sorrowful. Guilt ate at my conscience. But I feared, if I abandoned my life in Canada, I would destroy my future. I would not have accomplished anything if I had lived in Egypt. Rawyia was a living example. I took her advice, but committed to remain connected.

I tried to convince Rawyia to join me in Canada, but she chose to stay in the family mausoleum. She ceased to exist except for Adham's memory. She no longer worked. I supported her financial needs. She demanded that no one from our family know her whereabouts. I honored her request. In spite of Rawyia's affliction, she always volunteered her advice. We stayed in touch and exchanged news of our lives. She camouflaged her grief and projected a façade of resignation to her misery.

"How is your love life?" Rawyia asked sarcastically a few weeks after Adham's death. "Are you happy?"

She needed a distraction, and I engaged her. I took the opportunity to tell my story of Hazem. I wanted her opinion about my involvement with a divorced man who had a child.

"My love life changes often," I said. "You know me. I am still as romantic as I have always been. I've honored all your advice except for the one about romance."

She laughed. It was the first time I had heard her laughter since Adham passed away. It was a rare moment, and I sensed genuine happiness in her voice.

"I met a divorced man who has a child," I told her.

She was mute. Her silence made me nervous—a treatment I was familiar with when she disapproved of something I did.

"I just met him," I said. "No commitment."

"How long has he been divorced?" she asked.

"Six years," I replied.

"How old is his daughter?"

"Seven."

I didn't understand the reason behind her questions, but I was comfortable knowing Rawyia would assess my relationship using logic.

"So he divorced when his daughter was one year old."

All the time I was with Hazem, this calculation never crossed my mind. I didn't bother to ask, since we had not discussed a commitment of any kind.

"Yes, I suppose so," I admitted.

"Find out why they divorced," she said. "Don't believe him before you meet his wife. I have a feeling they divorced for a serious reason."

"Okay," I said. I was happy Rawyia was back with her bossy attitude.

"Stay away from him," she continued. "I don't owe you any further explanation. He has a child, and that's enough reason to sever this relationship. Find a man without baggage."

Rawyia might have a point. Still, I dismissed her suspicions. I was involved with Hazem. We met every time he came to Toronto to see his daughter. I kept this development from Rawyia.

"As always, I cherish your advice," I said to keep her in that engaging mood. "Stay in touch."

CHAPTER XXXVIII

STRUGGLING WITH EMOTIONS

On the first weekend of September 1978, Hazem changed the schedule of the visits to his daughter. He spent Saturday with me and picked Rania up on Sunday.

Hazem and I walked downtown and stopped at every store in the mall. One afternoon we visited a hat boutique, and I tried one on. I noticed Hazem's reflection as he stood behind me, staring in disbelief.

"What do you think?" I said, adjusting the hat's angle.

"Laila," he said, "stay still. Don't move and leave the hat on."

I complied.

He came closer with a grin, but he seemed lost in a world of his own. "Two years ago," he said, releasing every word with caution, "were you with a blonde friend at a soup restaurant on Young Street?"

"Was it you who said in Arabic 'I want to marry the brunette'?" I said, remembering it immediately.

Astonishment flooded through me. Our jaws dropped. We stayed mute, staring at each other, searching for a meaning to what we remembered. We stood oblivious to our surroundings, and tried to make sense of the revelation until the salesclerk interrupted, "Would you like to buy the hat?"

"She would," Hazem said.

I was glued in place and thought of whether what we had just confirmed was a prophecy for a future union between Hazem and myself. Was it a prelude to a chapter of my life still not inscribed? I shook to the core but was convinced our meeting wasn't a coincidence. It was fate in full action about to reshape my life.

Two years earlier, in 1976, a Dutch girl moved in with me. She earned her beauty from her Northern European parents–fair skin that turned bronze in the summer, crystal blue eyes and a golden mane that cascaded over her shoulders like a silk shawl.

We developed a close friendship. When Theya's boyfriend traveled, he left his red Camaro convertible with her. We cruised the crowded boulevard with the top down or promenaded the streets. We were opposite in appearance—me, brunette with a straw hat, and she, the striking blond who attracted attention. I thought Theya won the most admiring stares. She expressed the same thought. In her eyes, I was the one men favored with their smiles. Hence, she would go on the terrace of our apartment dressed in a bikini. She lay down under the sun for hours. She would then place her arm next to mine, hoping to achieve my olive complexion. We enjoyed each other's company.

During one of our visits to a soup restaurant, two young men on their way out brushed shoulders with us as we entered. One of them said in Arabic, "I want to marry the brunette one."

Even though I didn't turn around to see who spoke, the words left a nostalgic impression—he spoke in my mother tongue with an Egyptian accent. Such a compliment was always heard in the streets back home. Arab men, in particular Egyptians, don't shy away from expressing their admiration to women in public. It's a cultural practice that's hard to control.

Two years had passed before the memory of the compliment

I received on Young Street came alive at the hat boutique. The coincidence sent a shiver through my body. Hazem, too, had a look of disbelief, but his eyes reflected inner joy. It was like he had found something he had been looking for. I stayed silent.

He smiled a sigh of relief. I took off the hat.

"Please keep it on," he said, and helped to secure it on my head. "Allow me to buy it for you."

I kept it on and faced the mirror as I thought about that day back when I heard the Arabic statement. I knew fate was about to change my life one more time. I wasn't sure about my feelings. I was neither happy nor sad, but I was sure destiny was set in gear. It was a surreal moment. Hazem walked to the cashier and bought the hat.

"Let's have dinner," he said.

We sat in his Volvo. I took the hat off. Still holding onto our amazement, Hazem reached for my chin and turned my face toward his.

෴

At a steakhouse, Hazem asked the waiter for a quiet corner. He leaned forward and extended his arms on the table. It was like an invitation to surrender. I hesitated first, then my hands found their way into his. He squeezed them. I wasn't sure what he intended to send through his hands' squeeze. I felt nothing.

When the waiter stood at our table to take the order, Hazem placed the order for me.

"Two T-bone steaks with mashed potatoes and Caesar salad."

I chose to ignore his ill-manners. It was our first dinner date, and I wanted to make it memorable with pleasantries. Nevertheless, his deliberate dismissal of choice of meal left a sour impression.

Midway through dinner, Hazem said again, "I would like us to get to know each other better."

I wasn't sure what he meant, since we were already together. My warm emotions for Amer were still alive. I didn't have a passion button to switch on and off whenever the need arose. Matters of the heart are impossible to control or alter when young. My mind had already given up on a future with Amer, but my heart was a different story.

However, I was open for a long and lasting friendship, since I was consumed by the desire to have children. I shut down any thought that could hinder the fulfillment of this obsession. It was no longer a matter of falling in love with someone. I saw Hazem as a man who could offer a stable family if he proposed. He was educated and resided in Canada. He was an electronics engineer—a profession that would secure a decent life for my future kids and me. The one undesirable reality was the child he had with his first wife. I would have preferred someone without traces from a previous marriage. My passionate desire for motherhood would win over all barriers.

By December of the same year, Hazem revealed his love. It came sooner than I expected. We had known each other only a few weeks and met once a week.

"I am not sure how to start," Hazem said as he massaged his beard. "I hadn't felt this way with any woman before I met you."

"Which way?" I said in a disconnected tone, almost sarcastic, but with a smile.

"Love," he said. "I love you."

It was hard to pretend I was over my love for Amer. But, since Hazem was aware of that love and still committed himself, I was concerned, but not to the point of retreating, since it seemed that my dream of having children would be fulfilled sooner than I thought.

When I was with Hazem, I often called him Amer. He never complained, as if Amer didn't exist and was just a name. His behavior wasn't typical of Arab men—Arab men demonstrate jealousy and, in such cases, they wouldn't commit to a woman who addressed them by a past lover's name. Nevertheless, I believed he was wise and understanding until I called Rawyia for advice.

"I called him Amer many times, and he never got angry," I said.

"I warned you before. Something about this Hazem sounds abnormal," she said. "Did he propose yet?"

"No."

"If he proposes, and knows that Amer still owns your heart and mind, then he is bad news."

"I want to have children."

"If you marry just for that reason, you and your children will suffer."

I rejected her analysis. She had made her own mistake—she married a man as old as our father for a life of leisure, and not for love. She might have a logical point, but I wasn't ready to accept.

"I will make sure we don't suffer," I said.

"I don't know why you're so stubborn after all you have been through," she said with frustration. "Remember, you will also lose the independence you paid dearly to win—separation from Mama, alienation, no education, not to mention the disrespect you will face as a divorcee. Arab men don't value a woman with a shaky past like yours. If you need to have children, have them with a non-Arab man. They don't judge women by their past, especially if the circumstances were out of her control."

"How about you, Rawyia?" I said. "Have you found the ideal man you described?"

I hadn't forgotten that Rawyia had remarried to escape from Egypt. Her marriage wasn't a commitment of love. It was a marriage to fulfill a goal, and that was what I planned to.

"Laila, you're sentimental and will not survive a marriage just to have children," she said.

Rawyia made sense, but blindness happens when fate weaves the last thread of our future. We are the fate and the fateful, and what happens to us is nothing but our own fingerprints on the life we choose. When I left Egypt, I vowed to stay away from Egypt and not get involved with an Arab man. For years, I kept the promise, until I fell in love with Amer. Still, I chose independence over a future with him in Egypt. I had no intention to go off-track from the original commitment. Somehow, my wish to become a mother guided me away from my pledge.

I wondered if I had forgotten to sever the umbilical cord that tied me to Egypt. Back home, we had a saying, "He who drinks the waters of the Nile River will always come back." It seemed I had missed that water and the smell of the Mediterranean breeze. How else would I consider a friendship with an Egyptian man? Was I bound to my Egyptian blood, which I treasured as an heirloom that must be passed on to my children?

I wasn't aware of that inner struggle until Hazem crossed my path. Even though a dark cloud packed with his callous behavior, buffoon-like approach, and lack of moral principles hovered over me, I continued to see him.

CHAPTER XXXIX

HAZEM'S MARRIAGE PROPOSAL

The discovery mission started with my question about Hazem's mother, whom he had never mentioned. I remembered Mama saying, "A man's respect for his mother is the foundation to his appreciation of women." So, I decided to probe.

"You never asked about my mother," I said, "Mama." I started with a smile. "I adored her. She taught me the meaning of love and, because of her support and encouragement, I am here with you."

My brothers told me that not all men feel comfortable talking about their mothers. However, I expected him to jump into the subject, or show an interest about my family. Instead, he asked if I wanted to go for a walk along the Ottawa River. I agreed, thinking he would open up while we strolled.

"Tell me about your mother," I said, to lure him back into the subject.

"My mother had no time for me."

What did he mean? His mother had no emotional impact on him? I wanted to know more.

"I was the youngest," he said. "I had three older sisters and a brother."

It was hard to imagine anyone growing up not receiving his mother's attention. He stared at the astounded expression plastered I had on my face before he continued, "My mother also raised three step-children—two girls and a boy. My stepsister was like my surrogate mother."

So, his stepsister raised him instead of his mother? Why? Was that the bottom layer of more to come about his childhood? I was overwhelmed and hesitated to dig deeper.

"My stepbrother was cruel. I never liked him," he added.

Anger coated his voice. I suspected there was more he kept to himself.

"My stepsister and our maid took care of me. My mother was distant, and my father gave me the freedom to do what I wanted. He never once offered advice. He trusted me."

The repercussion of this kind of upbringing and its impact on his relationships with women wasn't familiar. I knew I faced a complicated man—a man who wasn't taught love by his mother. How could he provide this emotion if he never received it from the woman who gave him birth?

Curiosity consumed me, and the little information he provided won him my empathy. I thought he had suffered injustice growing up, and I attributed his lack of social and emotional maturity to the deprivation of his mother's love. I wanted to share with him my mother's compassionate devotion to her children. I wanted to be the first woman to introduce him to the love he hadn't received as a child. However, my curiosity didn't stop there. I wanted to know about his divorce.

"Why did you and your wife separate?"

"Better to ask why we married," he said, snickering.

Still dazed by his revelations, his reply sent me into an abyss where I no longer knew who he was, this man I had met on a blind date.

"I'm listening," I said.

"Well, my family thought I should marry. I just turned twenty-one. She was three years my junior and had big boobs, so I married her," he said, laughing out loud.

My head spun. I grew concerned about my connection with this shallow man. He obviously lacked maturity in spite of his high education. Was this how he based his choice of a wife and the mother of his children? Was the size of a woman's breasts so important to him? While I was lost in my reverie, I built a rejection statement to end the relationship.

"I have never spoken to anyone before about secrets of my childhood," he said.

So, he trusted me enough to confess his weakness and past mistakes. Still, I had many questions unanswered. Why would his parents urge him to marry? Why did he divorce when his daughter was a year old? Nevertheless, I decided to wait until later.

The sun had almost faded behind the horizon, and it was time to leave the park. But he wasn't ready, still wanting to unload the burden he had carried for years.

"I lived with her for six months," he said while we walked to the car. "My wife was pregnant when she left Egypt to start a job in Europe. She delivered Rania in Romania, then immigrated to Canada when our daughter was one year old. I got a scholarship for my doctoral degree at Toronto University. I joined them, but not for long. She asked for a divorce while I prepared for graduation. It was a mutual decision."

Still, he kept the reason for his divorce out of the discussion.

"Why did you divorce?" I asked when we sat in the car.

"Oh, she is crazy, not to mention inept. I called her Inspector Jacques Clouseau."

His insolent tone of voice disgusted me. She was the mother of his child. He had no scruples as he trashed her. How could I trust him?

"I see. You divorced because she was inadequate?"

"Yes, and also because she suspected my infidelity."

"You cheated on your wife?" I was aghast.

"I prefer not to talk about the past."

I was repulsed. I sensed irritation in his voice and uneasiness when he turned the engine on.

"Let's have dinner before I take you home," he said.

He stopped the car at the curb and tried to kiss me on the cheek. I pulled away.

"I am tired."

He followed me to my apartment. I left him outside and shut the door. I needed time alone to assess my feelings.

The next morning, I heard the doorbell. I didn't expect Hazem. He had said that he would spend Sunday with his daughter. I looked through the peephole and saw him.

Surprised, I opened the door, still in my pajamas. I was stunned that the sun hadn't greeted the earth yet. "Why are you here?"

"I canceled the visit with my daughter," he said.

He had on the same white shirt and jeans he wore the night before. His eyes were red and puffy. I wasn't sure what he expected. I didn't invite him in.

"I slept in the car," he said. "We need to talk."

With a hand gesture, I let him in and excused myself to put on something more appropriate. I slipped into a pair of jeans and a checkered chemise.

We left the apartment, took the car, and drove aimlessly until we reached a quiet street and parked.

"I haven't told you about my experience as a communication engineer during the 1967 war with the Jews," he started.

I was occupied with a more profound and relevant issue related to our relationship, and not a bit interested to know or remember anything about a war we had lost.

The sun was shy and hid behind thick grey clouds; birds tweeted their morning songs, and the crisp, gentle breeze tickled the maple tree we parked under. Orange leaves scattered on the windshield. Autumn settled in my heart, and spring had a long way to go before it infused me with promising thoughts about the future.

"Let's drive to the lake," I said.

I needed the peacefulness and clarity of the lake to help me listen without distraction. I wasn't sure how I would react to his experience or how the date would end.

It was the first time since I met Hazem that I saw his eyes glistened with genuine sorrow, and tears bathed his cheeks before he talked. He gazed into empty space and trembled. I was confused, and not sure how to react or comfort him. I reached for his hand. He pushed me away.

Like a chameleon, his demeanor changed from an uncouth man to someone sensitive and in desperate need of love. He was broken and vulnerable. I wasn't sure which side of his personality reflected the true man. Nevertheless, I was open to listening.

"When Egypt expelled the United Nations peacekeeping forces stationed in the Sinai Peninsula, the situation deteriorated between the Jews and us, and the war ended with heavy casualties. I was one of the officers who escaped certain death. Many of us in the military walked the desert for days under constant shelling. We hid in abandoned tanks with dead soldiers inside," he said and banged his hand on the steering wheel. I was startled by the force of his hand.

The furrows on his forehead deepened. He rocked in his seat, then said, "I don't know why my life was spared."

He obviously carried much anger and was ready to explode with a minor spark. I stayed quiet, digested every word he said, and imagined the horrific experience he had gone through. At that moment, I wasn't concerned about his sudden violent outbursts. Instead, I felt sorry for him.

The defeat of the Egyptian army during the Six-Day War was painful to me as well. I reached for the Kleenex box on the back seat and wiped my tears. Hazem's anguish and distress seemed raw and genuine. He surprised me. This was the shade of red that complimented the color wheel of his personalities.

"Please, change the subject," I said.

"I still have nightmares," he said. "We walked for days, not knowing where we were, and how we would get home. The moans of the wounded and dying soldiers still echo inside my head."

The detailed confession was hard to comprehend and absorb. I got out of the car and stood there, facing the lake. I let the fresh air diffuse the intense heat of anxiety and fear that burned inside of me.

He joined me and said with a broken voice, "Please forgive my anger."

Somehow, kindness blinded me of all doubts. His anguish quieted my apprehension and made me delve deep into my own past. My years in Alexandria were also turbulent. Although our sufferings differed, we both ran away from unstable childhoods. He wasn't close to his mother, his father let him do what he wanted without guidance, and the mother of his child deserted him. Was that enough reason to give the relationship a chance?

I was comfortable with the decision to continue with Hazem, even after I spoke with Rawyia.

"Hazem uses his war experience as a bait to attract gullible women like you," she said. "He has nothing else to offer an intelligent woman."

"Can't you trust my decision this time?" I snapped. "I am tired of your belittling."

"Hazem will never appreciate your love."

"One day, when you meet him, you will change your mind."

"I don't want to meet him" she said, "and I won't change my mind."

Rawyia's fear was legitimate, but not enough to convince me to stay away from Hazem. I gave him the attention he never experienced before, and he embraced me with a depraved appetite.

We continued to see each other for a few more weeks until

Christmas. On that holy day, we met after his visit with Rania. I expected a Christmas present, but he came empty-handed.

I prepared dinner—filet mignon, salad, and a bottle of Chianti. He poured himself a glass and started to eat. I struggled to dismiss doubts that screamed inside my head to reconsider the relationship. He interrupted my thoughts.

"You know it's the end of the year," he said, and sipped his wine with a grin. "Time to prepare the tax return."

I didn't want to talk about taxes at dinner, and on Christmas night, but wasn't surprised. His character had already fluctuated within the last few hours, from tactless to emotionally bruised.

"What's keeping you from preparing your taxes?"

"I would get a tax break if you decide to marry me before the end of the year."

Words died in my throat. I felt like I was lost in an intricate maze and couldn't find my way out. Every time I thought I had found the exit, I faced a dead end. How much did I need to know about him to reconsider my relationship with this unscrupulous man?

So it wasn't my physical attributes, my loving personality, my French education, my forgiving heart, my understanding about his messy and chaotic past, that prompted his desire to remarry. It was the financial gain he expected when he filed his taxes as a married man. Back then, I wasn't savvy about the tax return issue.

The mistake I have always made was believing life was promising. When I chose a road, I walked it to the end. But, this time, fate had different plans. The moment I got entangled with Hazem's past, my life turned upside down and I feared that, in no time, I would find myself living a new life.

Sometimes, wishes take us to a road lined with colorful flowers and shady trees. We choose to see the beauty of the illusion, and even smell its fragrance. But we soon discover it is a world of our creation to fulfill our dreams.

The journey I chose was carpeted with thorny flowers. Each represented an experience I lived. They looked colorful, bright and full of promising buds. Their fragrance infused me with a zest for the free life I wanted. However, their thorns left me scared with pain, disappointment, heartache, but most of all a determination to reach the goals I promised to myself, my sister and my mother.

The liberation voyage was the school where I learned lessons not found in academic education—self-reliance, stamina and appreciation to the minute gift life offers. Throughout the ups and downs I faced, I kept a kind heart and trust in people. I don't regret it, even though I failed to see the true color of the man I married. From that marriage, my wish to have children was realized, and their birth became the source of my true and lasting happiness.

www.ingramcontent.com/pod-product-compliance
Lightning Source LLC
Chambersburg PA
CBHW070537010526
44118CB00012B/1157